THE
INFERNAL
MACHINE
and
Other
Plays

THE INFERNAL
MACHINE AND
OTHER PLAYS BY
JEAN COCTEAU

A NEW DIRECTIONS BOOK

TABLE OF CONTENTS

THE
INFERNAL
MACHINE

translated by
ALBERT BERMEL

" . . . at that point where I can scarcely conceive (could my brain be an enchanted mirror?) a kind of beauty in which there is no misfortune."

"Like all my friends, I have tried more than once to enclose myself in a system and preach there at my ease. But a system is a sort of damnation . . . I have come back to seek shelter in impeccable naïveté. It is there that my philosophical conscience finds rest."

CHARLES BAUDELAIRE

"The gods exist; that's the devil of it."

JEAN COCTEAU

CHARACTERS

THE VOICE
THE YOUNG SOLDIER
THE SOLDIER
THE OFFICER
JOCASTA, *The Queen*
TIRESIAS, *The High Priest*
GHOST OF KING LAIUS
THE SPHINX, *The Goddess of Vengeance*
ANUBIS, *The Egyptian God of the Dead*
A THEBAN MOTHER
HER SON
HER DAUGHTER
OEDIPUS
THE DRUNK
THE MESSENGER FROM CORINTH
CREON, *Jocasta's Brother*
THE OLD SHEPHERD
ANTIGONE, *Daughter of Jocasta and Oedipus*

La Machine Infernale was first performed in French at the Théâtre Louis Jouvet in Paris on April 10, 1934, directed by Jouvet with costumes and décor by Christian Bérard.

The Infernal Machine was first played in this version at the Phoenix Theatre, New York, on February 3, 1958, under the direction of Herbert Berghof, with scenery by Ming Cho Lee, costumes by Alvin Colt, and lighting by Tharon Musser.

He shall slay his father. He shall marry his mother.

To counter this prophecy of Apollo, Jocasta, the Queen of Thebes, abandons her baby on a mountainside, with his feet pierced and tied. A shepherd discovers the boy and takes him to Polybus, King of Corinth. Polybus and his queen, Merope, have been lamenting their childless marriage. The baby, Oedipus, or *Pierced-feet*, spared by the bear and the wolf, comes like a gift from heaven. And they adopt him.

When he is grown to a young man, Oedipus questions the Oracle of Delphi. The god proclaims: *You shall murder your father and marry your mother.* At this, Oedipus makes up his mind to leave Polybus and Merope. But the fear of parricide and incest which drives him away brings him closer to his fate.

One evening, at the spot where the roads from Delphi and Daulia cross, one of the horses of a passing coach brushes against him; an argument flares up; a footman threatens him; he answers with his stick. The blow misses the servant and fells his master. The slain man is Laius, King of Thebes. This is the parricide.

The servants think they are being attacked and run for their lives, while Oedipus guesses nothing and goes on his way. He is young and restless; he soon forgets about this accident.

Shortly afterward, he hears about the Sphinx. This scourge, known as "The winged virgin" and "The bitch that sings," is slaughtering the young men of Thebes. It asks a riddle and kills those who cannot solve it. Queen Jocasta, the widow of Laius, is offering her hand and her crown to the man who conquers the Sphinx.

Like the young Siegfried to come, Oedipus hurries onward. Curiosity and ambition feed on him.

Then the encounter takes place. What is the nature of this encounter? Mystery. All that is known is: young Oedipus enters Thebes as a conqueror and marries the queen. That is the incest.

For the gods to be royally entertained their victim has to fall from very high. The years pass, prosperous years. Two daughters and two sons complicate the unnatural marriage. The people love their king. But a plague breaks out. The gods accuse a criminal, whose name they will not reveal, of polluting the city, and demand that he be hounded out. Reeling from one monstrous discovery to another, drunk with his own misfortune, Oedipus is finally caught. The trap closes on him. Everything is now clear. With her red scarf Jocasta hangs herself. With her gold brooch Oedipus tears out his eyes.

Watch now, spectator. Before you is a fully wound machine. Slowly its spring will unwind the entire span of a human life. It is one of the most perfect machines devised by the infernal gods for the mathematical annihilation of a mortal.

ACT ONE: THE GHOST

A patrol path around the ramparts of Thebes. High walls. A stormy night. Summer lightning. Raucous noise and band music heard, coming from the slum quarter.

YOUNG SOLDIER. They're laughing.

SOLDIER. They're trying.

YOUNG SOLDIER. They *dance* all night.

SOLDIER. They can't sleep, so they dance.

YOUNG SOLDIER. They get drunk and make love and spend the night in bistros, while I parade up and down here with you. Well, I'm sick of it! Understand? I'm sick of it!

SOLDIER. So desert.

YOUNG SOLDIER. No. I've made up my mind. I'm going to put my name down to challenge the Sphinx.

SOLDIER. The Sphinx? Why?

YOUNG SOLDIER. To have something to do. To put an end to this waiting around.

SOLDIER. You'd be frightened.

YOUNG SOLDIER. Me? Frightened?

SOLDIER. Yes, frightened. I've seen smarter and tougher ones than you, and they were frightened. But you think you can slaughter the Sphinx and win the big prize?

YOUNG SOLDIER. Why not? The only man who got away from the Sphinx alive — all right, I know he's crazy — but maybe it's true, what he says. Maybe it *does* ask a riddle. And maybe I'll *solve* that riddle. Maybe . . .

SOLDIER. You poor green bastard, you know that hundreds and hundreds of men, athletes and scholars, have been skinned alive by the Sphinx. And now you, a raw little recruit like you, wants to . . .

YOUNG SOLDIER. I'm going!

SOLDIER. Good for you. Be a hero!

YOUNG SOLDIER. I'm sick of the stones in this wall . . .

SOLDIER. That's right — explode!

YOUNG SOLDIER. . . . And that music . . .

SOLDIER. Get it out of your system!

YOUNG SOLDIER. And your ugly face! And . . .

He breaks down.

SOLDIER. Here, what's this? Not crying, are we? There, there . . . let's keep calm, now!

YOUNG SOLDIER. Go to hell!

The Soldier bangs his spear on the wall behind the Young Soldier, who stiffens.

SOLDIER. What's up?

YOUNG SOLDIER. Didn't you hear anything?

SOLDIER. No . . . Where?

YOUNG SOLDIER. It sounded to me as if . . . I mean, I thought . . .

SOLDIER. You're pale . . . What's wrong with you? Feel weak?

YOUNG SOLDIER. It's funny . . . I thought I heard a noise. I thought it was him.

SOLDIER. The Sphinx?

YOUNG SOLDIER. No, the ghost.

SOLDIER. He doesn't frighten us. Not our old ghost, Laius. He doesn't still make your guts quiver, does he? Perhaps the first time . . . But not afterward. He's not a bad ghost, he's a friend. Ah, the trouble is we're all jumpy in Thebes: you, me, the rich people, and the poor people; everybody except the few who always come out on top. We're tired of fighting an enemy we don't know, and we're tired of oracles and heroic victims and brave mothers. If we weren't on edge . . . all of us . . . instead of dancing and drinking over there, they'd be tucked up in bed. And instead of making fun of you, while we wait for your old friend the ghost to turn up — I'd be beating you at dice.

YOUNG SOLDIER. What do you think the Sphinx is like?

SOLDIER. Forget about the Sphinx.

YOUNG SOLDIER. Some people say it's no bigger than a rabbit, and just as timid, and that it's got a tiny head. But I say it has the head and breasts of a woman and sleeps with any man over eighteen.

SOLDIER. Don't think about it any more.

YOUNG SOLDIER. Perhaps it doesn't ask you anything. You meet it; you look at it; it winks at you; then you die of love.

SOLDIER. Go ahead! Fall in love with the Sphinx. Have a happy death. Know what I think? It's an old vampire, an everyday vampire, hiding out from the police.

YOUNG SOLDIER. With a woman's head?

SOLDIER. No, with a beard, a mustache, and a pot belly. It sucks your blood and then they bring you home with a wound in the same place as all the others: on the neck.

YOUNG SOLDIER. You think . . . ?

SOLDIER. Yes, I think . . . Watch it! The Captain.

They stand at attention. The Captain enters and folds his arms.

OFFICER. Stand at ease . . . easy! So this is where you see the ghosts?

SOLDIER. Sir —

OFFICER. Quiet! Speak when I ask you to. Which one of you dared to —

YOUNG SOLDIER. I did, sir.

OFFICER. Will you keep quiet? Who's doing the talking? Now, which one of you dared to send in a service report over my head, without following standard procedure? Well?

SOLDIER. Sir, it wasn't his fault. He thought . . .

OFFICER. Answer me — you or him?

YOUNG SOLDIER. Both of us, but it was me —

OFFICER. Silence! How does his excellency, the high priest, receive information from this post before *I* hear about it?

YOUNG SOLDIER. It's all my fault, sir. He didn't want to say a thing. But I felt I had to speak up, and as this wasn't a service matter, I told his uncle who works in the temple, and . . .

SOLDIER. My uncle! That's why I said it was my fault, sir.

OFFICER. That's enough. So this is not a service matter! It's a ghost matter, is that it?

YOUNG SOLDIER. That's right, sir.

OFFICER. A ghost who pops up while you're on patrol and says to you — well, what *did* he say?

YOUNG SOLDIER. He told us he was the ghost of King Laius, sir, and that he'd tried to appear several times since he was murdered. He begged us to find some way of warning Queen Jocasta and Tiresias.

OFFICER. And you didn't ask him why he wasn't appearing directly before the Queen or Tiresias?

SOLDIER. Oh, yes, sir. I asked him that. He said he wasn't free to reveal himself just anywhere. This is the most popular place, he said, for people to appear when they've been murdered. It's because of the sewers.

OFFICER. Sewers?

SOLDIER. Yes, sir, he was talking about the special stinks you get around here.

OFFICER. Ah! We're dealing with a ghost who has a sensitive nose. Tell me more about him. What did he look like? What sort of face did he have? How was he dressed? Were you frightened of him? Where *exactly* did you see him? What language did he speak? Did he ever stay for long? This isn't a service matter, of course, but I'd like to know what ghosts do with their time.

YOUNG SOLDIER. The first night we were pretty scared, sir. You see, he appeared very quickly, like a lamp coming on, right there in the middle of the wall.

SOLDIER. We both saw him the same time.

YOUNG SOLDIER. We couldn't make out his face or body properly. We could see his mouth when it was open, and he had a little white beard, and a red blotch near his right ear. He had trouble putting his words together — even saying them.

SOLDIER. That's because it took all his energy just to appear. Whenever he was speaking a little more clearly, he started to fade and we could see the wall right through him.

YOUNG SOLDIER. When you could see him, you couldn't hear him . . . and when you could hear him, you couldn't see him. He kept saying the same thing: "Queen Jocasta, . . . warn Queen Jocasta, warn her . . . please, I beg of you, warn the Queen, warn the Queen." Just like that.

SOLDIER. You could see he was afraid of fading out before he finished his message.

YOUNG SOLDIER. And then, remember *how* he faded out, the same way every time? The red blotch was the last thing to go.

SOLDIER. The whole thing only lasted about a minute.

YOUNG SOLDIER. We've seen him in the same place, five times, just before dawn.

SOLDIER. But last night was different. After what happened he thought we'd better let them know in the palace.

OFFICER. How d'you mean: "after what happened"?

SOLDIER. Well, sir, you know how being on patrol isn't exactly honey and roses.

YOUNG SOLDIER. We were sort of looking forward to the ghost last night.

SOLDIER. For entertainment. We had a bet on it. I said he wouldn't turn up.

YOUNG SOLDIER. I said he would.

SOLDIER. I said . . .

YOUNG SOLDIER. What's that moving?

SOLDIER. Where?

YOUNG SOLDIER. Straight ahead! Look — the wall's lighting up. Can't you see it?

SOLDIER. No!

YOUNG SOLDIER. It is, I tell you! The wall's changing! Look! Look!

SOLDIER. That's how it was, sir.

YOUNG SOLDIER. In the end we were glad when he did come.

SOLDIER. We'd been watching and staring till our eyes nearly jumped out of our faces. Then he appeared . . . uneasy . . . not fast like the other times. He said he had stolen into the Palace of the Gods and listened to a terrible secret. He said:

Acting it out.

"If they catch me, I shall die my last death, and that will be the end . . . the end. There isn't a moment to lose. Run! Warn the Queen! Find Tiresias! Please! I beg of you! They must be told!" And as he was pleading, the day was breaking.

YOUNG SOLDIER. But there he was . . .

SOLDIER. Fixed . . .

YOUNG SOLDIER. Frozen . . .

SOLDIER. Stuck . . .

YOUNG SOLDIER. Couldn't disappear!

SOLDIER. He tried — God how he tried! But he just couldn't. We thought he'd go mad. Then he asked us to swear at him, because he said that's the way to make a ghost disappear. But we couldn't — he's our friend. And the more he begged us, the more stupid we looked.

YOUNG SOLDIER. We tried, but we still looked stupid.

SOLDIER. It wasn't because we're not used to cursing the higher echelons.

OFFICER. Thank you, on behalf of the higher echelons.

SOLDIER. I didn't mean you, sir. I was referring to princes, crowned heads, the government and so on — the real high echelons. But the King was such a decent ghost, we didn't have the heart to use foul words. All we could think of was: "Go up in smoke, you poxy, whore-bent old crap-heap!"

YOUNG SOLDIER. Float off, you slime-filled, gut-stinking, son of a buzzard!

SOLDIER. Tame stuff like that. We might as well have handed him a bunch of flowers.

YOUNG SOLDIER. Then, as he hung between life and death, dreading the sound of the cocks and the sight of the sun, I thought of a good one. I said: "Go and stuff your crowing . . ."

SOLDIER. No! Don't say it. You'll embarrass the captain.

YOUNG SOLDIER. But it worked; the wall was only a wall again and the red blotch had faded away.

SOLDIER. We were tired out!

YOUNG SOLDIER. After that night, I made up my mind, if he wouldn't speak to his uncle, I would.

OFFICER. Your ghost isn't very punctual tonight.

YOUNG SOLDIER. He may never show up again.

OFFICER. Because I'm here?

YOUNG SOLDIER. No, sir, I mean, after what he told us last night . . .

OFFICER. If he's as proper as you make out, I'm sure he'll come back. Proper kings are punctual kings, aren't they?

SOLDIER. It's possible, sir, but it's also possible that even punctual kings, when they happen to be ghosts, can mistake a minute for a century. So if the ghost appears in a thousand years' time, instead of this evening, we'll be up there with him.

OFFICER. Of course he'll be here this evening. I'm keeping him away. As soon as I disappear — he'll appear.

Moving off.

Remember, no one except the patrol is allowed to use this path.

SOLDIER. Very good, sir.

OFFICER, *shouting.* And no one is allowed through without the password, man *or* ghost. Is that understood?

SOLDIER. Yes, sir.

OFFICER. Patrol! Carry on!

They stand at ease and break off. The Officer reappears unexpectedly.

Don't try anything. I'm keeping an eye on you.

He leaves.

YOUNG SOLDIER, *after a pause.* He thought we were trying to make a fool of him.

SOLDIER. No, he thought somebody else was making a fool of *us*. From now on, keep quiet about the ghost. We believe in him, but they don't.

YOUNG SOLDIER. Why?

SOLDIER. Listen, son. I get to know a lot of things through my uncle. You take the Queen, she's nice enough but people don't really like her. They think she's a bit —

He taps his head.

They say she's strange, and she has a foreign accent and she's under the thumb of Tiresias. She tells him her dreams; she asks him if she ought to get out of bed with her right foot or left foot first. And whatever he tells her to do turns out badly. He leads her by the nose, licks the boots of her brother, Creon, and plots with Creon against her.

Keep out of their way. They're rotten, all of them. I bet the captain thinks the ghost is like the Sphinx — a trick by the priests to make Jocasta believe whatever they want.

They pick up their torches, and start to move away.

YOUNG SOLDIER. All the same, when the King asks me to warn . . .

SOLDIER. A dead king isn't a king. And even if Laius *was* still alive, he wouldn't need you to run his errands.

They move off right, patrolling along the path, as Jocasta and Tiresias begin to mount the steps at the left.

JOCASTA, *she has the international accent of royalty.* Oh, not another flight of steps! I detest steps. Where are we? I can't see a thing.

TIRESIAS. Your Majesty, I didn't approve of this escapade, and . . .

JOCASTA. Zizi, this is not the time for a sermon.

TIRESIAS. You should have asked somebody else to bring you. You know I'm almost blind.

JOCASTA. What's the use of being a prophet? You can't even foresee the next step. I shall break a leg and it'll be your fault, Zizi, as usual.

TIRESIAS. The eyes in my head have dimmed, in favor of the inner eye of my mind, which has more important duties than to count steps.

JOCASTA. There, there, Zizi. You know I'm fond of you, but these steps infuriate me.

TIRESIAS. It was not my idea . . .

JOCASTA. We had to come, Zizi, we had to.

TIRESIAS. Your Majesty, please . . .

JOCASTA. Don't be obstinate. I had no idea there would be all these horrible steps. I know — I'll go up backward. Hold onto me. Don't be afraid; I'll guide you, and keep my head up. If I look down at the steps I shall fall. Here we go.

Slowly.

One, two, three . . .

They come into full view.

. . . four, five, six, seven . . .

Jocasta arrives on the platform and moves right. Tiresias, following her, treads on her scarf. She cries out.

Oh!

TIRESIAS. What is it?

JOCASTA. Your foot, Zizi. You're stepping on my scarf.

TIRESIAS. I beg your pardon.

JOCASTA. I'm not blaming you — it's the scarf. This scarf is against me. It's always trying to strangle me. One moment it catches in branches, another moment in the moving wheel of a carriage; then you step on it. I'm afraid of it, but I can't part with it. In the end, it will kill me.

TIRESIAS. How nervous you are!

JOCASTA. What's the use of your third eye? tell me that. Did you find the Sphinx? Did you pacify the people? There are guards posted outside my door, but how about the inanimate objects inside that are against me and want to kill me?

TIRESIAS. All this talk about objects . . .

JOCASTA. I can feel things, better than any of you. I feel them here.

She lays her hand on her stomach.

Has everything been done to find the murderers of Laius?

TIRESIAS. The Sphinx prevented further searching. You know that.

JOCASTA. I don't trust your silly methods. Exploring chickens' insides — ugh! — ridiculous! I know more than all of you, because I sense things. I can sense that Laius is suffering and wants to speak to us. I'm going to talk to this guard myself. This is my wish, and I'm your queen.

TIRESIAS. You don't understand me, my dear. I am an old, blind man. I only want to worship you and watch over you. And I still think you should be asleep in your room, instead of chasing after a shadow on these ramparts, on a night like this.

JOCASTA. I can't sleep, anyway. The Sphinx and the murder of Laius have unnerved me. You're quite right there. But I'm glad I don't sleep; when I do, even for a moment, I dream . . . always the same dream, and I am ill all the following day.

TIRESIAS. Shouldn't you tell me about it?

JOCASTA. No, I can't.

TIRESIAS. It's my business to interpret dreams . . .

JOCASTA. This one is too close to me, too personal.

TIRESIAS. The only way to free yourself of it is to tell me.

JOCASTA, *hesitantly*. I dream I am somewhere rather like this ledge. It's night, and I am holding a baby. Suddenly the baby becomes a sticky pulp which runs through my fingers. I scream and try to rid myself of it, but it clings to me. Then, when I think I'm free of it, it flies back and hurls itself against my face. And this thing . . . this pulp . . . is alive! With a kind of mouth that fixes on mine. And it creeps about me, feeling for my belly and my thighs . . . Oh!

TIRESIAS. My dear, my dear.

JOCASTA. I don't want to sleep again, Zizi. I never want to sleep.

Music becomes barely audible as she speaks.

Listen to that music. Where's it from? They can't sleep, either. They're lucky to have that music, Zizi. They too must have horrible dreams, and don't want to sleep. Who gave them permission to have music? Do I have music to keep me awake? I didn't know these places stayed open all night with music playing. Creon will have to forbid that music. It's scandalous. It must be stopped at once.

TIRESIAS, *taking her arm.* Please, let's go back. We authorized the music and dancing to keep up public morale. Without them there would be crime — even riots — in the slum quarter.

JOCASTA. Do *I* dance?

TIRESIAS. That is different. You are in mourning for Laius.

JOCASTA. So is everybody else! Yet they can dance and I can't. It isn't fair. I'll . . .

The Soldiers come back slowly.

TIRESIAS. Someone's coming.

JOCASTA. Oh, dear, I have all my jewels on.

TIRESIAS. Don't be afraid. It must be the patrol guards.

JOCASTA. Perhaps it's the soldier who sent me the message.

TIRESIAS. Wait. We'll see.

YOUNG SOLDIER. I thought so. Somebody over there.

SOLDIER. Where did they spring from?

Loudly.

Who goes there?

TIRESIAS. Look here, my good men . . .

YOUNG SOLDIER. What's the password?

TIRESIAS. You see, we should know the password. You've put us in an awkward situation.

JOCASTA. Password? What nonsense! Let me talk to him

TIRESIAS. These guards have their orders; they may not recognize you nor listen to me. This could be very dangerous.

JOCASTA. You make a drama out of everything.

SOLDIER. They're whispering. They're up to something.

TIRESIAS, *loudly.* You have nothing to fear. I am old and almost blind. Let me explain why this lady and I are here.

YOUNG SOLDIER. No explanations. Just give the password.

TIRESIAS. One moment, my good men; have you ever seen any gold coins?

SOLDIER. He's trying to bribe us. You stay here and I'll cover the path.

He goes back to cover the path, while the Young Soldier confronts Tiresias.

TIRESIAS. You're mistaken. I meant, have you ever seen the Queen's portrait on a cold coin?

YOUNG SOLDIER. Yes.

TIRESIAS, *points to Jocasta, who is counting the stars.* Now look at this lady. Don't you recognize her?

YOUNG SOLDIER. I don't see the connection. The Queen is quite young, but this lady . . .

Tiresias stops him.

JOCASTA. What's he saying?

TIRESIAS. He finds you rather young for the Queen.

JOCASTA. That's nice.

TIRESIAS. Where's your officer?

YOUNG SOLDIER. Never mind that. I've got my orders. Move on — and quick!

TIRESIAS. You'll hear more about this!

JOCASTA. Zizi, what's the matter now? What does he say?

The Officer comes along the path.

OFFICER. What's going on here?

YOUNG SOLDIER. These people don't know the password, sir.

OFFICER. Who *are* you?

He stops short.

Why, Your Excellency! My humblest apologies.

TIRESIAS. Thank you, Captain. I was afraid this young warrior would run us through.

OFFICER. You fools! Haven't you got eyes in your heads? I'll have you flogged! Twice! Three times!

To Tiresias.

I am so sorry, Your Excellency.

Young Soldier joins his comrade.

TIRESIAS. He was only doing his duty.

OFFICER. It's a surprise to find you here, Your Excellency. What may I do for you?

TIRESIAS. Her Majesty is here.

The three soldiers spring to attention.

OFFICER. My deepest respects, Your Majesty.

SOLDIER. What a mistake!

JOCASTA. No formalities! I want to know which sentry saw the ghost.

OFFICER. This young fool. If Your Majesty . . .

JOCASTA. You see, Zizi! I *was* right to come. Officer, tell that young man to come here.

OFFICER. Your Excellency, I don't think Her Majesty is aware of it, but this soldier will explain himself better through his officer.

JOCASTA. What is it now?

TIRESIAS. The officer has volunteered to act as an intermediary.

JOCASTA. The boy has a tongue of his own, hasn't he? Let him come over here.

TIRESIAS, *quietly*. You'd better not argue when the Queen wants her own way.

OFFICER. Very good, Your Excellency.

Roughly.

Now then, you! The Queen wants to have a word with you. Careful what you say.

In a low tone.

I'll make you pay for this!

JOCASTA. Come here!

OFFICER. Go on! Do as you're told. Nobody's going to bite you. Forgive him, Your Majesty. He still has a lot to learn.

JOCASTA. Ask that man to leave us alone with the soldier.

TIRESIAS. But . . .

OFFICER. But . . .

JOCASTA. If he stays for another minute I'll kick him.

TIRESIAS, *taking Officer's arm.* The Queen wants to be alone with the guard who saw whatever it was. Don't oppose her. She might easily make things bad for you, and I wouldn't be able to help.

OFFICER. Very good, Your Excellency. If I may say so, I don't think you should pay too much attention to this ghost story.

Bows obsequiously to the Queen after giving Tiresias a long salute.

Your Excellency! Your Majesty!

To Soldier.

You! The Queen wants to speak to your comrade alone.

JOCASTA. Who is that other soldier? Did he see the ghost too?

YOUNG SOLDIER. Yes, Your Majesty. We were on duty together.

JOCASTA. Let him stay then. I'll call him if I want him. Good night, Captain, you may go.

OFFICER, *loudly.* Your Majesty! Your Excellency!

In a low voice to the soldiers.

I'll see you later.

Exit.

TIRESIAS. You've hurt that officer badly.

JOCASTA. That's a change. It's usually the men who are hurt, not the officers. Now . . . how old are you, young man?

YOUNG SOLDIER. Nineteen.

JOCASTA. The same age. He'd be exactly the same age. How good-looking he is! Come a little nearer. What muscles, Zizi — look! And what darling knees! Fine knees are a sign of breeding. *He* would be very much like this. Isn't he handsome, Zizi? Look at this bicep — like iron.

TIRESIAS. I'm no authority, my dear. My sight is not good.

JOCASTA. Feel, then, feel! He has the thigh of a stallion. He's shy.

To Young Soldier.

Don't be afraid — he's quite blind . . . and old.

To Tiresias.

Heaven knows what he's thinking, poor boy . . . he's blushing. How adorable he is! And nineteen years old.

YOUNG SOLDIER. Yes, Your Majesty.

JOCASTA. Yes, Your Majesty! What a pity — he probably doesn't even know that he's good-looking. Now, did you really see the ghost?

YOUNG SOLDIER. Yes, Your Majesty.

JOCASTA. The ghost of King Laius?

YOUNG SOLDIER, *shakily.* Yes, the — er — King told us he was the King.

JOCASTA. You see, Zizi, with all your chickens and your stars, how much do you know? Listen to this child!

To Young Soldier.

And what did the King say?

TIRESIAS, *taking her aside.* Please be on your guard, my dear. Young people are reckless, ambitious, ready to believe anything. Can you be *certain* that this boy has seen the ghost, and, if he has, was it really your *husband's* ghost?

JOCASTA. You're an unbearable cynic. Always breaking the mood and shattering miracles with your logic. Let me question this boy on my own. You can lecture me later.

To Young Soldier.

How did the King speak?

YOUNG SOLDIER. Quickly, as if he had a lot to say. But he was all mixed up.

JOCASTA. That's Laius, poor dear. But why here on the ramparts? With all this stench?

YOUNG SOLDIER. That's just it, Your Majesty. He said he could only appear because of these marshes and stinks.

JOCASTA. How interesting! You never learned that from your chickens, Tiresias, did you? And what did he say?

TIRESIAS. You'll confuse him if you don't ask your questions in some order.

JOCASTA. You're quite right, Zizi. How did you see him? What did he look like?

YOUNG SOLDIER. Like a statue . . . a transparent statue in the wall. You could see his beard and his mouth — when he was speaking. And there was a red blotch on his temple.

JOCASTA. Blood!

YOUNG SOLDIER. We didn't think of that.

JOCASTA. It was a wound! How horrible!

The ghost of Laius appears.

What did he say? Did you understand anything?

YOUNG SOLDIER. It wasn't easy, Your Majesty. My friend noticed that it was a strain for him to materialize, and every time he came close to saying what he meant, he disappeared.

JOCASTA. My poor dear Laius!

GHOST. Jocasta! Jocasta! My wife, Jocasta!

They do not see him or hear him.

TIRESIAS. And did you catch anything that made sense to you?

GHOST. Jocasta!

SOLDIER. Yes, in a way, Your Excellency. He wanted to warn you, especially the Queen. But last time, he said he'd uncovered a dangerous secret to tell you, and he wouldn't be able to appear again if he was caught.

GHOST. Jocasta! Tiresias! Can't you see me? Can't you hear me?

JOCASTA. Didn't he say anything else? Anything in particular?

SOLDIER. It's likely that he didn't want to say anything particular to us, Your Majesty. He kept asking for you. That's why my comrade tried to get word to you.

JOCASTA. I'm glad you did, both of you. That's why I'm here. I knew it . . . I felt it. You see, Zizi, you and your suspicions! Tell me, young soldier, where did the ghost appear? I want to touch the very spot.

GHOST. Jocasta, look at me, listen to me! You soldiers — my friends — you always saw me before — why not now? It's agony! Jocasta!

SOLDIER, *touches the Ghost.*

That's where it was.

Banging on the wall.

Right there, in the wall.

YOUNG SOLDIER. Or in front of the wall. We couldn't quite make it out.

JOCASTA. Do you think he will appear again?

GHOST. Jocasta! Jocasta! Jocasta!

YOUNG SOLDIER. I don't think so, not after last night. There was a little trouble; Your Majesty may be too late.

JOCASTA. I am always too late, always the last one in Thebes to be told anything. All that time wasted, Zizi, with your chickens and your oracles. Now we shall know nothing — nothing at all! There will be terrifying disasters, and it will be your fault, Zizi, as usual.

TIRESIAS. Please remember that you are speaking in front of these men.

JOCASTA. And why not, when King Laius, the dead King Laius, has himself spoken in front of these men? He didn't speak to you, Zizi, nor to Creon. He didn't show himself in the temple. He showed himself on this patrol path, to these men . . . to this boy of nineteen, who is so good-looking and reminds me of —

TIRESIAS. I beg of you —

JOCASTA. Yes, it's true, I am excited. And no wonder! The tensions, the phantom, the music, the smell of decay . . . and there's a storm coming up; I can feel it, my shoulder is aching. Zizi, I'm suffocating!

GHOST. Jocasta! Jocasta!

JOCASTA. Didn't you hear anything? I think I heard my name.

TRESIAS. My poor lamb! It's dawn already; you're tired out and dreaming on your feet. Are you sure these young men didn't dream this ghost story while they were struggling to stay awake in this gloomy, swampy atmosphere?

GHOST. Jocasta — for pity's sake, listen to me! Look at me! My friends, you are good; don't let the Queen leave now! Tiresias! Tiresias!

TIRESIAS. Young man, would you move away for a moment? I want to speak to the Queen.

The soldiers step to one side.

SOLDIER. How about that? The Queen likes your knees.

YOUNG SOLDIER. Now, wait a minute.

SOLDIER. You're on the way up. Don't forget your friends!

There is the sound of cocks crowing.

TIRESIAS. The cocks are crowing. The ghost won't come now. We should go back to the palace.

JOCASTA. Didn't you see how handsome he is?

TIRESIAS. Don't open old wounds, my dove. If you had a son . . .

JOCASTA. If I had a son he would be handsome, he'd be brave, he'd solve the riddle, kill the Sphinx, and return as a conqueror.

TIRESIAS. You'd still be without a husband.

JOCASTA. All little boys say, "I want to be grown up so that I can marry my mother." It isn't so foolish, Tiresias. Is there a liaison sweeter, more cruel, and yet more proud, than that of a son and a young mother? When I touched that soldier a moment ago, who knows what he thought, poor boy; as for me, I almost swooned. *He* would be nineteen, now, Zizi, the same age. Do you think Laius appeared to him because of the resemblance?

A cock crows.

GHOST. Jocasta! Jocasta! Tiresias! Jocasta!

TIRESIAS. You men, is there any point in our waiting?

GHOST. For pity's sake!

SOLDIER. No, Your Excellency, I don't think so. The cocks are crowing. He won't appear now.

GHOST. Can't you soldiers see me? Can't you hear me?

JOCASTA. Very well, I'll come. But I'm glad I questioned the boy. You must find out his name and where he lives. Oh, I'd forgotten about these steps. The music makes me ill. Zizi, why don't we go back through the upper town, along the back streets? We can see the night life.

TIRESIAS. My dove, you're not serious?

JOCASTA. There you go again! You're infuriating. How on earth could anyone recognize me? I'm wearing my veils.

TIRESIAS. And your jewels, don't forget. Your brooch alone has pearls the size of eggs.

JOCASTA. Other people can laugh and dance and enjoy themselves. But not the Queen. I'm supposed to leave this brooch at home, where there isn't a servant I can trust. Tell the young soldier to help me down the steps. You can follow us.

TIRESIAS. But . . . the way he affects you . . .

JOCASTA. Yes, he does — he's young and strong. He can assist me, and I won't break my neck. Do as I say.

TIRESIAS. You! No, not you. You! That's it. Help the Queen down the steps.

SOLDIER. You've made the grade.

GHOST. Jocasta! Jocasta! Jocasta!

JOCASTA. He's flustered, poor darling! Somehow steps are against me; steps and brooches and scàrfs. I'm surrounded by things that are against me. They all want my death.

She cries out again.

Oh!

YOUNG SOLDIER. Has Her Majesty hurt herself?

TIRESIAS. No, you idiot! It's your foot!

Urgently.

Your foot on the end of her scarf. You almost strangled the Queen.

YOUNG SOLDIER. Forgive me, Your Maj —

JOCASTA. Don't be ridiculous, Zizi . . . the poor darling isn't a murderer just because he stepped on my scarf — the way you did! Don't let it upset you, my dear. His Excellency Tiresias is always quick to point out faults in others . . .

TIRESIAS. But, Your Majesty . . .

JOCASTA. Come. Thank you, my boy. Be sure to send your name and address to the temple. One, two, three, four. This is wonderful! Zizi, notice how well I'm going down. Eleven, twelve . . . Zizi, are you following? Only two more. Thank you. I can manage now. See if His Excellency needs any help.

Jocasta and Tiresias go off left. She looks back wistfully at the Young Soldier, and waves. Crowing is heard.

It's your fault! I shall never know what my poor Laius wanted. You and your third eye. . . .

Fades out.

GHOST. Jocasta! Tiresias! Have pity on me. . . .

SOLDIER. Look!

YOUNG SOLDIER. The ghost!

GHOST. At last! I've been calling you.

SOLDIER. You were there all the time?

GHOST. All the time you were talking to my wife and Tiresias. Why didn't you see me?

YOUNG SOLDIER. I'll run and bring them back.

SOLDIER. No use. When the carpenter arrives, the chair stops wobbling. When you walk into the shoemaker's, your sandal stops pinching. When you get to the doctor, the pain is gone. And if you bring them back now, he'll vanish.

GHOST. Alas, this man of the people has more understanding than a priest.

YOUNG SOLDIER. I *will* go.

GHOST. Too late! They are coming for me. I must give you the message. Tell the Queen . . . warn the Queen that a young man . . . is approaching Thebes, and that she must not . . . No, no . . .

Struggling, as though pulled by invisible guards.

The young man is her . . . the young man is our . . .

To the "guards".

I am going to tell . . . I know your plans and the penalty but I shall risk everything . . . she is still my wife . . . and I defy you to stop me from telling . . . from telling . . . no, help! Help! I had to tell her . . . to try to tell her . . . she was my wife . . . she was my wife . . . I had . . . I had . . . I . . . I . . .

He disappears into the wall. There is a taut silence as they stare after him.

YOUNG SOLDIER. He wanted us to warn his wife.

SOLDIER. Can't wait to run after her, can you?

YOUNG SOLDIER. It's not that.

SOLDIER. All he had to do was appear and speak to them. They were here, but they couldn't see him or hear him. Nor could we — until they left. That proves that kings become ordinary people like you and me after they die. Poor

Laius! Now he knows how hard it is in Thebes to be heard by the higher echelons.

YOUNG SOLDIER. But why did he choose us?

SOLDIER. Because we're ordinary people, that's why. Because we're here. Officers, queens, high priests — they always leave before it happens or come when it's all over.

YOUNG SOLDIER. What do you mean by "it"?

SOLDIER. I don't know. But I know what I mean.

YOUNG SOLDIER. Then we're not going to warn the Queen?

SOLDIER. You listen to me. Let princes deal with princes, ghosts with ghosts, and soldiers with soldiers.

There is a trumpet call.

CURTAIN

THE VOICE

Spectators, let us imagine that we can wind back the last few minutes and relive them elsewhere. While the ghost of Laius tries to warn Jocasta on the ramparts of Thebes, Oedipus encounters the Sphinx on a hill that overlooks the city. The same trumpet-calls, the same cock-crows, the same moon, the same stars.

ACT TWO: THE SPHINX

A deserted spot on a hillside overlooking Thebes, by moonlight. The road from Thebes (from left to right) passes across the front of the stage, and bends around a tall leaning stone. The base of the stone is held in place at the end of the platform and forms the entrance doorway on the left. Behind the remains of a little temple is a ruined wall. In the middle of the wall is an intact pedestal, which must have marked the entrance to the temple, and bears the remains of a chimera — a wing, paw, and haunch. Broken columns.

A girl in white, The Sphinx, is sitting among the ruins; a jackal's head rests in her lap, the rest of its body being hidden behind her. Distant trumpets.

SPHINX. Listen.

JACKAL. I can hear.

SPHINX. The final call. We're free.

Anubis gets up. The jackal's head belongs to him.

ANUBIS. It was the first call. There are two more before they close the city gates.

SPHINX. It was the final call; I'm sure it was.

ANUBIS. You're sure because you *want* the gates to be closed. We are not free. We have to wait. It was only the first call.

SPHINX. Perhaps I was wrong.

ANUBIS. You *are* wrong.

SPHINX. Anubis . . .

ANUBIS. Yes, Sphinx?

SPHINX. I don't want to kill any more.

ANUBIS. We have to be obedient. Mystery has its own mysteries, and there are gods above gods. We have ours; they have theirs. That is what's known as infinity.

SPHINX. You see, Anubis, *you* were wrong. There *is* no second call. Let's leave . . .

ANUBIS. If we don't kill anybody tonight, you'll be happy.

SPHINX. Yes, I will. Even though it's late. I'm nervous . . . someone may still come along.

ANUBIS. You're becoming more and more human.

SPHINX. That's my affair.

ANUBIS. Don't lose your temper.

SPHINX. Why do we always act without aim or understanding or explanation? Look at you, Anubis, why the Egyptian God of the Dead in Greece? And why with the head of a jackal? Because that's how superstitious people picture you?

ANUBIS. Amazing! You know, when you start asking questions, you really look like a woman.

SPHINX. You haven't answered me.

ANUBIS. Here's my answer: If we didn't appear to men looking the way they picture us, they wouldn't see us at all. That's logic. To us, Greece, Egypt, Death, the Past, and the Future are meaningless. And you know perfectly well *why* I have the jaws of a jackal. The divine rulers were very wise to give me a physique that isn't human; it saves me from losing my head, even this dog's head. I'm here to guard you, but if they'd given you a regular watchdog I know what you'd be up to: we'd be in Thebes right now, with me on a leash and you surrounded by a pack of young men.

SPHINX. You're foolish!

ANUBIS. You have assumed the body of a girl. That is why you feel sympathy for your victims, but remember that they are nothing more than zeroes wiped from a slate, even though each zero may be an open mouth crying for help.

SPHINX. That may be so. But here on earth it is so difficult to remember what we planned when we were gods. Here the dead really die — I kill them.

As the Sphinx is talking, looking down, Anubis pricks up his hears, sniffs, looks around and lopes off silently toward the ruins, where he disappears. A Theban Mother enters right front, with two children, A Boy walking ahead and A Girl whom the Mother is dragging along.

MOTHER. Look where you're going, not behind you. Leave your sister alone; go on.

Boy walks full tilt into the Sphinx.

Watch out! There! I told you. I'm sorry, my dear, he just won't look where he's going. Did he hurt you?

SPHINX. No, not at all.

MOTHER. I didn't expect to meet anybody here as late as this.

SPHINX. I haven't been in Thebes long. I'm going to one of my relatives in the country, but I seem to have lost my way.

MOTHER. Poor girl! Where did you say this relative lives?

SPHINX. Not far from the twelfth milestone.

MOTHER. Why I've just come from there myself, or very near it. We were at my brother's house. We sat around talking after dinner, you know how it goes, and here I am now still on the way and the children overtired and fidgety, and it's after curfew.

SPHINX. Good night.

MOTHER. Good night.

She makes as if to go.

Oh, by the way, don't hang about here. You and I, being women, may not have much to worry about, but I won't feel safe until I'm inside the city walls.

SPHINX. Are you afraid of bandits?

MOTHER. Bandits? No! What could they take from *me?* Where are you from? I can tell you're not from Thebes. I'm talking about the Sphinx.

SPHINX. You don't really believe that story, do you?

MOTHER. That story! You're young and, like all young people, you don't believe anything. No, you don't! Let me tell you something that happened in my own family. My brother — the one I just left —

She lowers her voice confidentially, and sits down.

— he married a tall, beautiful blonde from the north. One night he woke up and found his wife's body lying there right next to him *without a head or stomach.* What an unpleasant experience! She was a vampire. Of course, he was terrified at first, but then he took an egg and put it on the pillow where his wife's head should have been. That's how you stop a vampire getting back into its body. Then all of a sudden he heard a wailing. It was the head and entrails flying around the room like mad and begging him to take away the egg. My brother wouldn't. The head got angry; then it began to cry; then it kissed him. In the end, the fool gave in and took the egg away and let his wife back into her body. So there he is, married to a vampire. My

sons tease him about it. They say he invented the whole
story about the vampire, to cover up the fact his wife went
out at night — but with her head on somebody else's pillow — and her body. But I know better. My sister-in-law *is*
a vampire. If my brother says so, I believe him. It's the
same with the Sphinx. You don't believe in it, any more
than my sons do — you're all the same, you young people.

SPHINX. You have other sons?

MOTHER. I had four; now I have three. This rascal here
is seven. Then there's one sixteen and one seventeen . . .
and the way those two carry on about the Sphinx!

SPHINX. They argue?

MOTHER. My dear, they just can't live under the same
roof. The one who's sixteen is only interested in politics.
He says the Sphinx is a hoax. There might have been a
Sphinx at one time, according to him, but now it's dead
and the priests use it as a bogey to scare the people, and
the police use it as a cover-up for their inefficiency and cor-
ruption. Starvation — he says — rising prices, bandits in-
festing the countryside, no government to speak of, one
bankruptcy after another — Why? The Sphinx! The tem-
ples are crammed with holy offerings, he says, while mothers with families haven't a loaf of bread to call their own.
Wealthy tourists are leaving the city. Why? The Sphinx!
And he gets up on the table, shouting and waving and
stamping, denouncing the authorities, preaching revolution
and praising the anarchists — he'll have us all hanged.
Strictly between us, my dear, I know there is a Sphinx but
— you mark my words — they're taking advantage of it,
no doubt about that. What we need is a man, an iron fist,
a dictator.

SPHINX. It sounds as if you already have a dictator in the
family. What is his brother like?

MOTHER. Ah, now, he's a different case again. He de-
spises everything and everybody — his brother, me, even

the gods! He says the Sphinx would be interesting if it killed for the sake of killing — what a thing to say! — but it's hand in glove with the oracles. So he doesn't care about it, one way or the other.

SPHINX. And your fourth son? When did he ... ?

MOTHER. Lost him almost a year ago. He was just nineteen.

SPHINX. You poor woman! What did he die of?

MOTHER. The Sphinx.

SPHINX. Ah.

MOTHER. My young son says he was caught in a police trap, but I know better. The Sphinx killed him. If I live to be a hundred I'll remember that morning when they brought him home. I opened the door and there I could see the soles of his poor feet, and far, far off his poor little face. On his neck — just here — was a great wound, but the blood wasn't flowing any more. He was on a stretcher. I just said, "O-oh!" and fainted dead away. You never really recover from a blow like that. It's lucky for you you don't come from Thebes and have a brother. My third son — the one who jumps all over my table with his politics — he wants to avenge him. He hates priests, and after all, my poor son was one of the sacrifices. But what point is there ...

SPHINX. Sacrifices?

MOTHER. Certainly. When nobody could find the Sphinx, the priests insisted that it was calling for human sacrifices. They picked out the youngest, the weakest, the finest-looking.

SPHINX. How terrible for you!

MOTHER. I say again: what we need is a dictator, a man of action. Queen Jocasta is still young. From a distance you'd take her for twenty-nine or thirty. We need a ruler who'd marry her, kill the monster, punish the criminals, lock up Creon and Tiresias, straighten out our finances, cheer us all up and — well, somebody who would be on the side of the people and *rescue* us. . .

BOY. Mother.

MOTHER. Hush!

BOY. Mother, what does the Sphinx look like?

MOTHER. How should I know?

To Sphinx.

And now, my dear, with the little money we have left, they want to build a memorial to the victims of the Sphinx. Can that bring them back to us, I ask you?

BOY. Mother, what's the Sphinx like?

MOTHER. Poor child. And his sister's asleep. Let's go.

Boy examines the Sphinx's skirt.

Now, don't worry the lady.

SPHINX, *stroking his neck.* He's all right.

BOY. Mother, is this lady the Sphinx?

MOTHER. Don't be silly.

To Sphinx.

I hope you don't mind, dear. At that age they don't know what they're saying. Now then, come along, sleepyhead.

The Girl has fallen asleep in her arms. She takes the Boy by the hand and they move off.

BOY. Mother, is this lady the Sphinx? She is the Sphinx, isn't she, this lady?

MOTHER. That'll do now. Say good night to the lady.

BOY. Good night, Sphinx.

MOTHER. Good night, dear. Excuse me for talking so much. I was glad of a chance to catch my breath. Do be careful.

The second trumpet sounds.

There's the second call. After the third, we'll be locked out.

SPHINX. You'd better hurry. I have to be on my way, too. Thank you for warning me.

MOTHER. Take it from me, we need a strong man to free us from the scourge.

Exit.

BOY, *offstage.* Mother, if that lady isn't the Sphinx, who is?

SPHINX. Scourge!

ANUBIS, *reappearing from the ruins.* Don't let that woman disturb you.

SPHINX. I've been miserable for two days, Anubis, hoping this would end. Now I am going to make a wish, and if it comes true I shall never have to mount this pedestal again, never kill again. I wish for a young man to come and climb the hill . . . a fearless man. I shall fall in love with him, and he will answer the riddle, as if he were my equal. And when he gives the answer, I shall die.

ANUBIS. Only your human body will die.

SPHINX. Yes, the body that could make him happy. You see, Anubis, I was right. That *was* the last trumpet we heard.

ANUBIS. I tell you it was not.

He climbs on an overturned column.

It was the second. When I hear the third you can go. Oh!

SPHINX. What?

ANUBIS. Bad news.

SPHINX. Is someone coming?

ANUBIS. Yes.

SPHINX, *up beside him and peering offstage, right.* Anubis, I can't — I won't question him.

ANUBIS. You may look like a young mortal, but here's a mortal who looks like a young god.

SPHINX. What a stride, Anubis! And those shoulders! He's almost here.

ANUBIS, *hiding.* Remember: you're the Sphinx. I'll be watching, if you want me . . .

SPHINX. Anubis, listen . . .

ANUBIS. Sh!

Enter Oedipus upstage, walking fast, his eyes on the ground. He starts.

OEDIPUS. Oh, excuse me.

SPHINX. Did I startle you?

OEDIPUS. Not really. I was far away, and when I looked up . . .

SPHINX. An animal. You took me for an animal.

OEDIPUS. Almost.

SPHINX. Almost an animal? That would be the Sphinx.

OEDIPUS. I know.

SPHINX. Oh, you took me for the Sphinx. Thank you.

OEDIPUS. I was wrong. I can see that.

SPHINX. Nice of you to say so. But I suppose it wouldn't be a laughing matter for a young man to look up and find himself face to face with the Sphinx.

OEDIPUS. Or for a young woman.

SPHINX. It never attacks young women.

OEDIPUS. Young women don't usually go near the places where it's likely to be after dark.

SPHINX, *coquettishly.* Young man, you'd do well to mind your own business, and let me be on my way.

OEDIPUS. Which way is that?

SPHINX. I've never seen you before. Why should I tell you?

OEDIPUS. Perhaps I know.

SPHINX. You're very amusing.

OEDIPUS. You're inquisitive, like all modern young women. You want to know what the Sphinx looks like. Whether it has claws, a beak, wings. Whether it resembles the tiger or the vulture.

SPHINX. Oh, come now.

OEDIPUS. The Sphinx is the most mysterious criminal of our time. No one has seen it. Whoever finds it first is promised a fabulous reward. Cowards tremble. Young men die. But a young *woman,* like you, might easily venture into the forbidden region . . .

SPHINX. Interesting, but inaccurate. I'm returing to my relative's house in the country. I'd forgotten there was a Sphinx . . . and that the outskirts of Thebes weren't safe. I just happened to sit down for a rest on these rocks.

OEDIPUS. That's disappointing. All the people I've come across lately have been so dull. I was hoping to meet someone different. I'm sorry.

SPHINX. Good night.

OEDIPUS. Good night.

They pass. Oedipus turns.

I . . . .

SPHINX. Yes?

OEDIPUS. Forgive me, but I don't believe you. It's mysterious to find you here.

SPHINX. Is it?

OEDIPUS. An ordinary girl would have been too scared to probe about in a place like this.

SPHINX. You're getting funnier and funnier.

OEDIPUS. I know! You are my rival.

SPHINX. Your rival? Are you looking for the Sphinx?

OEDIPUS. I've been looking for a whole month. I was so excited when I found myself near Thebes, I was ready to challenge any white pillar of stone. And there you were, in your white dress, and . . . I mean, I thought you were after the same thing.

SPHINX. When you saw me come out of the shadow before, you didn't look like a man who was ready to contend with the Sphinx.

OEDIPUS. That's true. I was dreaming of fame. The monster would have taken me by surprise. Tomorrow I shall get my equipment in Thebes, and the hunt will be on.

SPHINX. It's fame you want?

OEDIPUS. I'm not sure. I know that I like stamping crowds, trumpets, banners, palm branches waving, the sun, the gold and purple, happiness, luck . . . life!

SPHINX. That's what you call life?

OEDIPUS. Don't you?

SPHINX. No, to me life is something quite different.

OEDIPUS. What?

SPHINX. Love. Loving someone, and being loved.

OEDIPUS. I shall love my people and they will love me.

SPHINX. You won't find love in the public square.

OEDIPUS. I don't expect to. The people of Thebes are looking for a man. If I kill the Sphinx, I will be that man. I will marry Queen Jocasta. She is a widow and . . .

SPHINX. And old enough to be your mother.

OEDIPUS. The important thing is: she's not my mother.

SPHINX. Do you believe that a queen and a whole people will give themselves to the first man to come along?

OEDIPUS. Of course, if he has conquered the Sphinx.

She laughs.

What are you laughing about? I'm not just "the first man to come along." I'm a prince; my father is the King of Corinth. I could have had anything I wanted at home. My parents were old and couldn't do enough for me. But it was all too slow. I like action, adventure. I was looking for any excuse to get away. One evening a drunk shouted, "You're not Merope's son; you're not Polybus' son . . . you don't belong here!" I pretended to be angry and thrashed him, but I knew that this was the chance I'd been waiting for. Next day I told my mother and father I owed it to *them* to ask the oracles the truth about myself. My poor parents! They wept and tried to prevent me, but I was determined to take advantage of whatever the oracles told me. Well, they told me I would kill my father and marry my mother.

SPHINX. What?

OEDIPUS. Yes, it scared me too — at first — but I soon realized that either the prophecy was nonsense, or the priests — who can send birds with messages from temple to temple — were plotting to trick me out of my inheritance. Anyway, the threat of parricide and incest gave me the perfect excuse to get away from home and go out into the world on my own.

SPHINX. I'm sorry I laughed at you. Please forgive me, Prince.

OEDIPUS. Certainly. Give me your hand. May I ask your name? Mine is Oedipus. I am nineteen.

SPHINX. What does the name of an unimportant girl of seventeen matter to you, Oedipus? You like illustrious names ...

OEDIPUS. You're laughing again.

SPHINX. And yet the best way for you to counter the oracle, I'd say, would be to marry a girl younger than yourself.

OEDIPUS. You sound like a mother in Thebes, talking to one of the few eligible young men left.

SPHINX. I didn't expect you to say a nasty thing like that.

OEDIPUS. Have I traveled over mountains and streams only to marry a woman who will soon grow into a kind of Sphinx? — or worse, a Sphinx with breasts and claws? No, thank you.

SPHINX. Oedipus ...

OEDIPUS. No, I'll take my chance. But here's my belt. It will identify you, if you want to see me after I kill the monster.

SPHINX. Have you ever killed before?

OEDIPUS. Yes, I have. A carriage with a man inside came by as I was walking along where the roads from Delphi and Daulia meet. One of the horses reared up and I knocked into a footman. The fool lifted his arm, and I swung my stick. He dodged and it struck the man in the carriage. The horses bolted, dragging him behind. I ran after them, but the servants fled and I was left with the blood-covered corpse of the old man and the tangled horses who were scrambling to free themselves and whining as they broke their legs. It was terrible!

SPHINX. Yes, it is terrible to kill.

OEDIPUS. It wasn't my fault, so I don't think about it any more. I have to keep my eyes fixed ahead and avoid sentiment. I have to follow my star.

SPHINX. Good-by then, Oedipus. My sex is distracting to heroes.

OEDIPUS. Not as distracting as you think.

SPHINX. And what if the Sphinx kills *you?*

OEDIPUS. Oh, no, it will ask me a riddle, and if I guess the right answer, it won't even touch me. It will just die.

SPHINX. And if you don't guess the answer?

OEDIPUS. I'm more intelligent and better educated than any of the rabble in Thebes.

SPHINX. That sounds promising.

OEDIPUS. This simple monster doesn't expect to be confronted by the pupil of the finest scholars in Corinth.

SPHINX. You've an answer for everything. It's a pity. I'm attracted to weak people, and I'd have liked to find some weakness in you.

OEDIPUS. Good-by.

SPHINX, *calling after him.* Oedipus!

OEDIPUS. Yes?

SPHINX, *fixing him with unblinking eyes.* Then for you — your heart, your mind, your soul — it's the Sphinx or nothing.

OEDIPUS. It's the Sphinx!

SPHINX. If there were somebody who could help you, somehow, would you be grateful to him — or her?

OEDIPUS. Of course, why?

SPHINX. Suppose I could tell you a tremendous secret.

OEDIPUS. You?

SPHINX. A secret that would bring you into contact with the enigma of enigmas, the human monster, the bitch that sings . . . the Sphinx.

OEDIPUS. You? . . . You? How could you — how? Or perhaps I guessed right. You were curious and you stumbled on the hideout. But no! I see now. This is another girl's trick — the baited hook.

SPHINX. Good-by.

OEDIPUS. Wait.

SPHINX. Good-by . . .

OEDIPUS. Please, I was very foolish. I'm sorry.

SPHINX. It's no use.

OEDIPUS. You want me to kneel down and beg your forgiveness? I said I'm sorry.

SPHINX. You're sorry you missed an opportunity.

OEDIPUS. Yes, I'm ashamed of myself. Tell me. I believe you now. But if this is a trick, I'll drag you by the hair and crush the blood out of your body.

SPHINX. Come here, then.

She leads him opposite the pedestal.

Close your eyes and count up to fifty. Do not cheat.

OEDIPUS. Be careful.

He closes his eyes.

SPHINX. It is your turn to be careful!

Oedipus turns to face the audience, lowers his head, and counts.

OEDIPUS. One ... two ... three ... four ... five ...

The Sphinx runs across and stands behind the pedestal. As Oedipus reaches the count of "fifty," a pair of wings sprout from the wing fragments of the pedestal, with the head and shoulders of the Sphinx between them. Her arms, in long spotted gloves, rest on the sides of the pedestal.

... forty-seven ... forty-eight ... forty-nine ... fifty!

Turns and draws in breath.

You!

SPHINX, *in a remote voice, joyous and terrible.* Yes, I ... I am the Sphinx.

OEDIPUS. I'm dreaming.

SPHINX. You are no dreamer, Oedipus. You know exactly what you want ... what you always wanted.

OEDIPUS. But why do you ... ?

SPHINX. Silence! Here I reign. Come forward. Nearer.

He struggles as though his arms are pinioned.

Hop, then.

He falls to his knees.

Crawl! It is good for heroes. That's right, forward! There's nobody watching you.

He advances on his knees, writhing in fury.

Stop! And now . . .

OEDIPUS. This is how you snare men and slay them.

SPHINX. And now, I shall give you a demonstration. I shall show you what would happen if you were some ordinary good-looking boy from Thebes and not Oedipus, who has the privilege of pleasing me.

OEDIPUS. I know how far I can trust your privileges.

SPHINX. Don't resist. Don't make it more difficult for me — I may hurt you.

OEDIPUS. I *will* resist!

He shuts his eyes and turns his head.

SPHINX. In vain you close your eyes or turn your head I do not charm through my voice or my sight

Chants.

I am more adroit than a blind man
Swifter than a gladiator's net
Finer than lightning
Greedier than insects
Slicker than the fingers of a pickpocket
Defter than the hangmen of the East
More buoyant and majestic than a fully rigged ship
Colder than a judge
More bloodthirsty than birds
More deceitful than the heart
More mysterious than the egg
More fatal than the stars
More fascinated than the snake licking its prey.

I secrete my thread; I pay it out,
Spin it back and wind it in;
I have only to will and these knots appear;
To think — and they tighten or slacken away
So fine is my threat that you cannot conceive it,
So volatile that you might imagine
Yourself the victim of some strange poison;
So rigid that if I make a mistake
One of your limbs will snap from your body;
So tense that the bow of a violin played
Between us would raise a celestial sound.
My thread is the curl of the sea and the rose,
Sinewed and supple and strong as the octopus,
Saved from the trappings of dimly known dreams,
And, above all, invisible, regal and still
Like the flow of blood through the veins of a statue.
My thread envelopes you, binds you, quiets you
In fine arabesques of drawn honey
Dropping into a pool of honey
Until you are wrapped in the hold of a reptile,
Numb as an arm you have slept on and deadened.

OEDIPUS, *weakly*. Let me go! Mercy!

SPHINX. And you would cry for mercy and you would not be the first. I have heard prouder men than you cry for their mothers; and seen more arrogant men in tears.

OEDIPUS. Merope ... Mother!

SPHINX. Then I would order you to come a little nearer: I would untighten your limbs.

He crawls forward further.

So! And I would question you. I would ask you, for example, which animal walks on four legs in the morning, two legs at noon, and three legs in the evening? And you would comb your mind till you could think of nothing but some tiny medal you won as a child. Or you would mumble a number, or count the stars between these broken columns. And then I would reveal the answer to the riddle. The animal is man. He crawls on all fours as an infant; he walks on two legs when he is grown up; and when he is old, he leans on a stick for a third leg.

OEDIPUS. Of course! How simple!

SPHINX. You would shout: "Of course — How simple!" . . . as everybody else does. Then . . . then, I would call my helper, Anubis. Anubis!

Anubis appears and stands on the right of the pedestal with his head turned to the side.

OEDIPUS. No! No! Please, Sphinx! Please don't. No!

SPHINX. I would make you go down to your knees. Down, down, further! That's right. You would bend your head . . . and Anubis would spring and open his wolf jaws . . .

OEDIPUS. A-a-ah!

SPHINX, *calmly*. I said, "Would." I said, "would bend," "would spring," "would open." Don't be terrified. It was all a performance, Oedipus, a mere performance. You are free.

OEDIPUS, *bewildered and incredulous*.

Free!

He moves his arm, his leg. He stands up, staggers, clasps his forehead.

I am free.

ANUBIS. Sphinx, he is not allowed to leave; he has not answered the riddle.

SPHINX. But —

ANUBIS. Ask him.

OEDIPUS. But —

ANUBIS. He must answer the riddle! Ask him!

Oedipus turns away and waits, motionless.

SPHINX, *with a last look of surprise at Anubis.* I'll ask him . . . I'll ask him. Which animal walks on four legs in the morning, two legs at noon, and three legs in the evening?

OEDIPUS. Why . . . Man. He crawls on four feet when he's small, walks on two feet when he's big, and when he's old, he uses a stick as a third leg.

The Sphinx sways.

I've won!

He runs off left. The Sphinx slips down behind the pedestal, disappears behind the wall, and reappears without wings.

SPHINX. Oedipus! Where is he? Where is he?

ANUBIS. He's charging down the hill toward Thebes to announce his victory.

SPHINX. Without so much as a glance at me, without caring . . . or even a "thank you."

ANUBIS. Did you expect anything else?

SPHINX. The fool! He understood nothing.

ANUBIS. Nothing at all.

SPHINX. After him, then, Anubis. Chase him! Bite him!

ANUBIS. I am not a dog and you are not a woman.

SPHINX. Forgive me. My hands are trembling and I'm like fire. I want to catch him, disfigure him, crush him, castrate him, flay him alive.

ANUBIS. That's more like you.

SPHINX. Help me, avenge me!

ANUBIS. You really hate this man?

SPHINX. I hate him.

ANUBIS. The worst that could happen to him would not be enough for you?

SPHINX. Not enough.

ANUBIS, *taking the side of her dress.* Look at the folds in this fabric. Press them together. Now, if you run a pin through them, then withdraw the pin and smooth out the material so that the folds are gone, do you think a simpleton would believe that those spaced-out holes were all made at the same time by the one pin?

SPHINX. Of course he wouldn't.

ANUBIS. Man's time is folded and hidden in eternity. But I, the God of the Dead, see the whole life of Oedipus unfolded, stretched out before me like a picture in one dimension. All the episodes, from his birth to his death, are pinpricks in the fabric of time.

SPHINX. What do you see, Anubis? I'm burning to know.

ANUBIS. The son of Laius and Jocasta is a scourge.

SPHINX. A scourge!

ANUBIS. A monster, a thing unclean.

SPHINX. Faster!

ANUBIS. The man he killed at the crossroads —

SPHINX. The man in the carriage —

ANUBIS. Was Laius, his father.

SPHINX. And . . .

ANUBIS. And he will marry Jocasta, his mother.

SPHINX. And I said to him: She is old enough to be your mother. And he replied: The important thing is, she is not my mother. Oh, Anubis, Anubis!

ANUBIS. His two sons will cut each other's throats. One of his two daughters will hang herself. And so will Jocasta.

SPHINX. The wedding of Oedipus and Jocasta — son and mother! How soon will he know?

ANUBIS. Soon enough.

SPHINX. If I could only be there.

ANUBIS. You will be.

SPHINX. Will I?

ANUBIS. It is time to remind you that you are not a young girl of Thebes. There is all eternity between you and this ephemeral body. You have assumed the role of the Sphinx. You are a goddess, the greatest of the great . . . Vengeance — Nemesis!

He prostrates himself.

SPHINX. Yes, Nemesis.

She turns, facing the ruins with her arms crossed, in a momentary trance. Abruptly she breaks away and runs upstage, staring after Oedipus.

I wonder how far off he is now. I want to see him run from trap to trap like a dazed rat.

ANUBIS. Is that the cry of the goddess, or the wail of a jealous woman?

SPHINX. The goddess. I shall be worthy of the role the gods have given me.

ANUBIS. At last!

SPHINX, *suddenly seeing Oedipus, she is no longer the goddess.* Why look! You lied to me, you dog.

ANUBIS. I lied?

SPHINX. Yes, liar! Liar! Look, Oedipus is coming back, he's running, flying. He does love me. He did understand.

ANUBIS. I told you how he will pay for his success.

SPHINX. See how he leaps from rock to rock, just as my heart ...

ANUBIS. Yes, he is so triumphant over your death that he forgot the most important thing.

SPHINX. Does he want to find me dead?

ANUBIS. Not you, my little fury — the Sphinx. He thinks he has killed the Sphinx, but he will have to prove it to others. Thebes will expect evidence, not just a fairy tale.

SPHINX. You're lying again. I'll tell him everything. I'll warn him. I'll save him. I'll lead him away from Thebes, and save him from Jocasta.

ANUBIS. Take care!

SPHINX. I will tell him.

ANUBIS. He's here. Let him speak first.

Enter Oedipus, downstage left, out of breath.

OEDIPUS, *saluting.* I am happy to see what good health the immortals enjoy after death.

SPHINX. Why have you come back?

OEDIPUS. For what belongs to me.

Anubis makes an angry movement. Oedipus steps back.

SPHINX. Anubis!

She points toward the ruins. He goes out of sight.

You shall have it. Wait here. I am a woman and I have lost, so grant me a last favor.

OEDIPUS. I've learned to mistrust your feminine tricks.

SPHINX. But then I was the Sphinx. You may take this mortal hide to Thebes, and the future will reward you ... as you deserve. I only want to shed this body, which, in the last few minutes, has become too narrow for me.

OEDIPUS. Very well.

She goes behind the ruins.

But hurry. The last trumpets will soon —

He is interrupted by the distant fanfare of trumpets.

You see, I speak and they sound. I must not be late.

SPHINX, *hidden.* Thebes won't keep a hero waiting outside her gates.

ANUBIS, *also hidden.* Hurry. You're spinning words and deliberately wasting time.

SPHINX, *still hidden.* Anubis, did you ever have to retrieve any other goddess from the earth?

OEDIPUS. Sphinx, you're wasting time.

SPHINX. That's fortunate for you, Oedipus. I just remembered that if you appear in Thebes with the body of a girl, instead of a monster, the people won't acclaim you — they'll stone you.

OEDIPUS. That's true. Amazing . . . women think of everything.

SPHINX. They call me the virgin with claws; the singing bitch. They'll want to see my fangs. Anubis, our faces are no more than masks. I want to take your jackal's head.

OEDIPUS. Perfect.

ANUBIS. Do what you like; anything to bring you back to yourself.

SPHINX. I won't be long.

OEDIPUS, *with a laugh.* One, two, three, four . . .

He begins to count, as before . . .

ANUBIS. Sphinx, now what are you waiting for?

SPHINX. I'm so ugly, Anubis. I'm a real scourge now. I'll frighten him.

ANUBIS. He won't even see you.

SPHINX. Why, is he blind?

ANUBIS. Many men are born blind and don't realize it till the day truth tears their eyes open.

OEDIPUS. Fifty!

ANUBIS, *to the Sphinx.* Go on . . . go on!

SPHINX. Here I am. Farewell, body of the Sphinx.

She comes out wearing the jackal's head, staggers, and collapses.

OEDIPUS. It was about time.

He picks up the body and poses with it downstage right, holding it across his outstretched arms.

Now, how shall I carry it? No, too conceited — like the actor I saw in Corinth.

He tries holding it under one arm. Two giant figures, representing the gods Anubis and Nemesis, appear behind the ruins in rainbow-shimmering veils.

No, that looks like a hunter sneaking home after killing his dog.

ANUBIS, *the form on the right.* If we gave him at least the title of a demigod, it might disinfect you of human contact.

NEMESIS, *the form on the left.* He is so young . . .

OEDIPUS. I know — Hercules! He threw the lion over his left shoulder.

He does so.

That's it. Like Hercules. Like a demigod.

ANUBIS. He is fan-tas-tic!

OEDIPUS. I have killed the filthy monster.

Takes two steps forward.

NEMESIS. Anubis, the earth stifles me.

OEDIPUS. I have saved the city.

Two more steps forward.

ANUBIS. Come, let us ascend.

OEDIPUS. I will marry Queen Jocasta.

Two more steps.

NEMESIS. Poor, poor Oedipus!

OEDIPUS. I will be king!

Exit.

The veils flutter around the two figures. There is a crowing of cocks. The stage lightens as dawn breaks.

CURTAIN

THE VOICE

From dawn onward the coronation and wedding festivities have continued. The crowd has just cheered the Queen and the conqueror of the Sphinx for the last time.

Everyone goes home. Nothing is heard now in the palace square but the sound of a fountain. Oedipus and Jocasta are at last tête-à-tête in their bridal chamber. They are asleep on their feet, and although destiny drops a few polite hints, they are too tired to see the trap that is closing on them forever.

ACT THREE: THE WEDDING NIGHT

A platform represents Jocasta's bedroom, red as a butcher's shop set down among Municipal buildings. A wide bed covered with white furs. At the foot of the bed, an animal's skin. To the left of the bed, a cradle.

The Young Soldier is just visible on the extreme right, sleeping by a fountain in the courtyard "below" the bedroom window.

Oedipus and Jocasta are wearing their coronation robes. They have had an exhausting day and move slowly, wearily.

JOCASTA. Oedipus, my darling, it's been a long day, yet you are so vigorous. I hope this room doesn't stifle you, like a cage or a prison.

OEDIPUS. No, my dearest, it's a haven after all those processions and rituals, and that crowd, shouting for us under the windows . . .

JOCASTA. Not for us — for you!

OEDIPUS. You are me, and I am you.

JOCASTA. You'll have to face it, my young hero. They hate me. They hate my clothes, my accent, the black on my eyelashes, the red on my lips, my hunger for life.

OEDIPUS. No, they hate Creon. What a cold, hard man he is! I shall make them love you again.

JOCASTA. You came just in time. I couldn't go on any more.

OEDIPUS. How could your room ever be a prison to me? Your room ... and our bed?

JOCASTA. Would you like me to have the cradle removed? After the baby died I could not sleep without having it near me ... I was so lonely ... But now ...

OEDIPUS, *mumbling*. But now ...

JOCASTA. What did you say?

OEDIPUS. I said ... I said ... that it's the — the dog ... he ... the dog at the fountain ... the fountain dog ...

He nods.

JOCASTA. Oedipus! Oedipus!

OEDIPUS, *waking with a start*. What is it?

JOCASTA. You were falling asleep.

OEDIPUS. I was? No!

JOCASTA. Yes, you were, dear. You were saying something about the dog ... the fountain dog.

She giggles vaguely.

OEDIPUS. Nonsense.

JOCASTA. I was asking whether I should have the cradle taken out ... if it disturbs you.

OEDIPUS. This muslin ghost doesn't frighten me. No, it will be the cradle in which my luck will grow, with our love, until we can use it for our first son. And later ...

JOCASTA. My poor darling, you're falling asleep again, and yet we stay here ... standing here ... standing on this wall ...

OEDIPUS. On this wall?

JOCASTA. This rampart wall.

Startled.

A wall? Eh! I . . . what's happening?

OEDIPUS, *laughing.* This time, you're the one who's dreaming.

JOCASTA. Was I asleep? Did I say anything?

OEDIPUS. Only something about a rampart wall. We're a fine pair on our wedding night. Jocasta, if I happen to fall asleep again — are you listening? — please wake me up, and I'll do the same for you. We can't waste this night of nights.

JOCASTA. My darling, we have all our life.

OEDIPUS. We're alone now. Let's take off these heavy clothes. We're not expecting anyone, and . . .

JOCASTA. Don't be angry, dearest, but while my women are seeing to my hair, you have to receive a visitor.

OEDIPUS. A visitor? At this hour?

JOCASTA. Yes, it's pure formality.

OEDIPUS. In this room?

JOCASTA. In this room.

OEDIPUS. Who is this visitor?

JOCASTA. Now, don't be annoyed. It's Tiresias.

OEDIPUS. Tiresias? No . . . no . . . no!

JOCASTA. Listen —

OEDIPUS. Tiresias, standing in for your family and giving out . . .

He laughs.

. . . last-minute advice.

JOCASTA. My silly darling, it's an old Theban custom for the high priest to bless every royal marriage. And besides, Tiresias is our old uncle, our watchdog. I am very fond of him, Oedipus, and so was Laius. He's nearly blind . . . there's no sense in offending him and setting him against our love.

OEDIPUS. Yes, but . . . in the middle of the night!

JOCASTA. For our sake . . . for the future! Have him in for just five minutes and hear what he has to say.

She kisses him.

Please?

OEDIPUS. I warn you — I won't let him sit down.

JOCASTA. I love you!

Long kiss.

I won't be long. I'll let him know he can come in. Be patient. Think of me.

Exit. Oedipus strikes regal attitudes in front of the mirror. Tiresias comes in left. Oedipus sees his reflection and wheels around.

OEDIPUS. Well? I am listening.

TIRESIAS. Who gave you the impression, Your Highness, that I was going to preach?

OEDIPUS. Nobody, Tiresias, nobody. But we're tired. Suppose I pretend that you've already delivered your advice. I bow, you give me your blessing, and we'll have observed the tradition.

TIRESIAS. This procedure is certainly called for by tradition in the case of a normal royal marriage. It's customary and, I admit, irritating. But you'll agree, my lord, that your coronation and marriage could hardly be said to fit into the "normal" category.

OEDIPUS. What an elegant way of saying that I have fallen on Thebes like a tile off a roof.

TIRESIAS. Your Highness!

OEDIPUS. Whatever fits into categories, Tiresias, smells of death. To escape from categories, we must strike out in a new direction — that's what distinguishes masterpieces and heroes. Only originality surprises — and rules.

TIRESIAS. I agree. And I know that when you have listened to me you will appreciate that I too am trying to strike out in a new direction.

OEDIPUS. To the point, Tiresias, to the point.

TIRESIAS. Very well. Frankly, Your Highness, I have to warn you that your auguries are most unfavorable.

OEDIPUS. I was waiting for that! This is not the first time that the oracles have been against me, and I have outwitted them.

TIRESIAS. Then you believe they can be outwitted?

OEDIPUS. I am living proof of it. I have killed the Sphinx, freed the city, and I am claiming what you promised. Tell me this: why have the gods thrust me forward till I have reached this room in this palace if my marriage displeases them?

TIRESIAS. You are trying to settle the problem of free will in one sentence. I'm afraid that you are drunk with power.

OEDIPUS. The power that is being taken from you!

TIRESIAS. May I remind you that you are speaking to the high priest?

OEDIPUS. Must I remind you, high priest, that you are speaking to your King?

TIRESIAS. To the husband of my Queen, Your Highness.

OEDIPUS. Jocasta has already put all her power into my hands. Tell that to your master.

TIRESIAS. My only masters are the gods.

OEDIPUS. In that case, tell it to whoever is waiting for you.

TIRESIAS. You are a stubborn boy. You make no effort to understand me.

OEDIPUS. I understand you perfectly! You take me for an adventurer and I'm in your way. You hope that I found the Sphinx already dead. That I bought it from the man who really killed it, like a hunter buying a hare from a poacher. Well, even if I did, who will the conqueror of the Sphinx turn out to be? A common soldier, possibly; the very type of person who has been a threat to you every minute of every day; who has kept Creon awake at nights. A lowly soldier whom the crowd will raise in triumph, and who will claim what you promised . . .

Shouting.

. . . do you understand that? What you promised!

TIRESIAS. He wouldn't dare to.

OEDIPUS. Aha! I made you say it! So much for your promises.

TIRESIAS. The Queen means more to me than my own daughter. I have to watch over her. She is weak, romantic, easily misled . . .

OEDIPUS. You are insulting her.

TIRESIAS. I love her.

OEDIPUS. She needs no love, other than mine.

TIRESIAS. Do you really love her, Oedipus?

OEDIPUS. With all my soul.

TIRESIAS. Do you love to take her in your arms?

OEDIPUS. Most of all I love to be taken in her arms.

TIRESIAS. Thank you for making the distinction. You're young . . . very young. Jocasta is old enough to be your mother. Yes, I know what you are going to say . . .

OEDIPUS. I am going to say that I have always dreamed of that kind of love . . . a love — almost maternal.

TIRESIAS. Don't confuse love with love of glory. Would you love Jocasta if she were not queen?

OEDIPUS. The same, stupid question. Would Jocasta love *me* if I were old and ugly, if I were not a stranger who appeared suddenly at a crucial time? Of course love is contagious when you touch purple and gold! Jocasta's high position is part of her. Within her body are fold upon fold of purple, far more regal than the cloak across her shoulders. Yes, I love her, Tiresias. Our love reaches back into eternity. And I have at last found my rightful place at her side. She is my wife, my queen. I have her and I am keeping her.

TIRESIAS. Do not ignore the signs I have seen, Oedipus, nor the extent of my wisdom. I have good reason for being apprehensive of this marriage.

OEDIPUS. Somewhat late, isn't it?

TIRESIAS. How much do you know about women?

OEDIPUS. Nothing at all. And I'm going to surprise you even further, and give you something to laugh at — I'm a virgin.

TIRESIAS. I *am* astonished.

OEDIPUS. So the high priest — no less — is astonished to find that a boy from the country has the pride to keep himself pure for a unique occasion. You would have preferred some debauched prince, eh? A puppet who could be manipulated by Creon and the priests?

TIRESIAS. Stop mouthing these accusations, like an angry child!

OEDIPUS. Do I have to command you again — ?

TIRESIAS. Command? You are insane with pride!

OEDIPUS. Don't provoke me any further. My patience is at an end.

TIRESIAS. You are arrogant . . . arrogant and crude!

OEDIPUS, *shouting.* I warned you!!

He takes Tiresias by the throat.

TIRESIAS. Let go of me!

OEDIPUS. You're afraid of me. I can read your real motives, here, in your blind eyes.

TIRESIAS. Ruffian! Murderer!

OEDIPUS. Yes, I'd be a fool not to murder you. If I only dared to, I . . .

Suddenly with wonder.

Why — why, look! In those blind eyes!

TIRESIAS. Let go of me!

OEDIPUS. The future! *My* future . . . a crystal ball!

TIRESIAS. Do not attempt to see what should not be seen.

OEDIPUS. I *can* see . . . I can see . . . my marriage . . . contentment, wealth, two sons, daughters . . . and Jocasta, beautiful as ever, in love with me, a mother in a palace of happiness. You lied to me. You lied.

Peering closer.

Now it's becoming blurred. What's happened? . . . I can't see — it's you; you're doing it. I want to see more, I must.

TIRESIAS. You are cursed!

OEDIPUS, *recoiling, releasing Tiresias, and clutching at his eyes.* A-a-ah! You have blinded me, thrown pepper in my eyes. Help, Jocasta, help!

TIRESIAS. I swear I didn't.

OEDIPUS, *writhing on the ground.* You're lying. Water, quickly! My eyes are on fire!

TIRESIAS. You tried to force a message from my ailing eyes, a message I haven't yet deciphered myself.

OEDIPUS. Water, water, quickly! I am blind!

TIRESIAS, *laying his hands on Oedipus' face.* Now, now, be still . . . . I forgive you. Your sight will return, I promise. You reached out for what the gods are keeping in darkness, and they are making you suffer for your presumption. Are you still in pain?

OEDIPUS. Not as much. Ah! It was fire, a thousand pins, a cat's claw tearing at my eyes. Thank you . . .

TIRESIAS. Can you see?

OEDIPUS. Not too well, but I can *see!* I was sure I'd been blinded for good and that it was one of your tricks. Whatever it was, I deserved it.

TIRESIAS. We believe in miracles when they suit us. When they don't suit us we become cynical and call them sorcery.

OEDIPUS. Forgive me. I am hotheaded and revengeful. I love Jocasta. I was impatient for her, and this — this moving image of the future in your eyes, bewildered me.

TIRESIAS. But can you see yet?

OEDIPUS. Thank you, yes.

TIRESIAS. I have to ask; I'm almost blind.

OEDIPUS. I am ashamed of my behavior. You are a blind man and a priest.

TIRESIAS. I was speaking for your good and Jocasta's.

OEDIPUS. Tiresias, I owe you something in return, a secret I swore never to tell.

TIRESIAS. A secret?

OEDIPUS. When I saw you and Creon whispering during the coronation — don't deny it — I decided not to reveal my identity; now I have changed my mind. I am no vagabond, Tiresias. I am the only child of King Polybus and Queen Merope of Corinth. This marriage bed will not be debased. I am a king, and the son of a king.

TIRESIAS. Your Majesty.

He bows.

A word from you would have dispelled our uneasiness. My little dove will be so glad . . .

OEDIPUS. No, wait. I want you to say nothing tonight. Jocasta still loves the stranger in me. Tomorrow will be time enough to end the illusion. By then she will be submissive and ready to learn that Oedipus is not a prince from the sky, but simply a prince. Good night, Tiresias. Jocasta will be back soon. I am tired, and we want to be by ourselves.

He waves him out imperiously.

TIRESIAS. Very good, Your Majesty.

He stops at the door, left.

Oh, I almost forgot.

OEDIPUS, *haughtily.* Yes?

TIRESIAS. This evening after the temple closing, a girl came into the oratory and, without introducing herself, handed me this belt and said: "Give this to Oedipus and repeat this message to him word for word: 'Here's my belt. It will identify you, if you want to see me, after I kill the monster.' " With that, she broke into laughter and was gone.

OEDIPUS, *snatching the belt.* So this is your last card; a plan to turn Jocasta's mind and heart away from me. You have already worked it out. A fine story it makes: a previous promise of marriage ... a girl bent on revenge ... a scandalous scene in the temple ... and the belt as a pledge of love ...

TIRESIAS. I am merely bringing a message.

OEDIPUS. Unwise and unsuccessful. Now hurry away with the bad news to Prince Creon. I'm not frightened — it isn't that easy. On the contrary, I frighten you, Tiresias, admit it. Although you are an old man and I am a boy, Tiresias, I frighten you!

He kneels on the animal skin. Tiresias stands like a statue. The thunder rolls.

TIRESIAS. Yes, I am frightened.

He retreats backward. His voice rings out.

Oedipus, Oedipus, hear me! You are seeking classic glory. But there is another kind of glory. Infamy ... the last refuge of the arrogant who defy the stars.

Exit.

Oedipus is still staring at the belt. Enter Jocasta in a nightdress. He stuffs the belt under the animal skin.

JOCASTA. Well, what did the old ogre have to say? He probably suggested you are too young for me ...

OEDIPUS. Jocasta, you are beautiful.

JOCASTA. Or that I'm too old for you.

OEDIPUS. No, he suggested that I was in love with your pearls and diadem.

JOCASTA. Always spoiling everything.

OEDIPUS. He didn't frighten me; I frightened him. He admitted it.

JOCASTA. To accuse *you* of being in love with my pearls and diadem.

OEDIPUS. That's how I always want to see you, *without* your jewels — white, young, and beautiful.

JOCASTA. Young! Oedipus, you mustn't lie to me.

OEDIPUS. To me the face of a young girl is as empty as a blank page. It doesn't compare with the magnificent, sacred beauty of your face — matured and mellowed by fate, yet as tender as — Jocasta, you're weeping. What's the matter? What did I say?

JOCASTA. Am I so old, then . . . so very old?

OEDIPUS. My darling, you're the one who keeps saying . . .

JOCASTA. Women say these things hoping to be contradicted, hoping they're not true.

OEDIPUS. How stupid of me. Don't cry, my darling. Kiss me! I only meant . . .

JOCASTA. It doesn't matter. I'm being silly.

She dries her eyes.

OEDIPUS. It was my fault.

JOCASTA. No, it wasn't. There now, the black is running into my eyes.

Oedipus fusses over her.

It's better now.

OEDIPUS. You're almost smiling again.

There is a distant rumble of thunder.

Listen to that.

JOCASTA. Yes, the weather, it makes me nervous.

OEDIPUS. Look at the sky. It's clear and filled with stars.

JOCASTA. Yes, but whenever the fountain murmurs silently and my shoulder begins to ache, it means a storm and summer lightning.

She leans against the window. Flashes of summer lightning.

Oedipus, come here quickly.

OEDIPUS. What is it?

JOCASTA. The sentry. Lean forward a little! To the right. He's asleep. Isn't he handsome, that boy, lying there with his mouth open?

OEDIPUS. I'll throw some water in it.

JOCASTA. Oedipus!

OEDIPUS. I'll teach him to sleep when he's guarding his Queen.

JOCASTA. Let him sleep peacefully. The Sphinx is dead and you're alive. Let the whole city sleep peacefully!

OEDIPUS. He's lucky.

JOCASTA. Oedipus, it's not that I want to make you jealous, but this boy . . .

OEDIPUS. What about him?

JOCASTA. That historic night when you met the Sphinx, I went to the ramparts with Tiresias. A soldier had reported seeing the ghost of Laius. And that's the same young soldier.

OEDIPUS. And, of course, there was no sign of the ghost of Laius?

JOCASTA. None at all, unfortunately. Poor boy. I touched his arms, and I said to Zizi: "You touch him! Go on — touch him!" I was all confused because he reminded me of you. And, it's true, he is like you, Oedipus.

OEDIPUS. How could he have reminded you of me? You hadn't met me then.

JOCASTA. Yes . . . it must have been because my son would be about his age. Yes, I am confused. You know, you're very handsome. I love you!

Pause.

Oedipus!

OEDIPUS. Yes?

JOCASTA. I think you were right not to tell the story of your victory to Creon, Tiresias, or anybody else —

She puts her arms around his neck.

Except me . . . You should tell me.

OEDIPUS, *freeing himself.* You promised not to mention it again.

JOCASTA. That was yesterday. Today, I have the right to share your experiences.

OEDIPUS. Certainly.

JOCASTA. Do you remember how you kept saying: "No no, Jocasta, I'll tell you later, when we are alone"? And now, here we are.

OEDIPUS. You always get what you want. Very well, then, be still. I'll tell you.

JOCASTA. Oh, Oedipus, I'll be perfectly still.

She lies down, closes her eyes, and remains still. Oedipus begins hesitantly to lie and invent. The storm persists outside.

OEDIPUS. Now then. I was getting close to Thebes, following the goat track round the hill to the south of the city. I was thinking about the future and about you. I imagined you less beautiful than you are, but still very beautiful . . . painted and perfumed and sitting on a throne, surrounded by ladies-in-waiting. Suppose I do kill the Sphinx, I was thinking to myself, would I, Oedipus, dare to ask for the promised reward? Would I dare to approach the Queen? And I walked on, dreaming about it. Till suddenly I heard something. My heart was beating wildly. It was a kind of singing; the voice was inhuman. Could it be the Sphinx? In my bag was a knife, I slipped it inside my tunic. Then I crawled forward. You know those ruins of a little temple on the hill, the other side of the hill?

Silence.

Jocasta! Are you asleep?

JOCASTA, *waking with a start.* Eh? What? Oedipus!

OEDIPUS. You fell asleep.

JOCASTA. I didn't.

OEDIPUS. You did! You ask me for a story and then you fall asleep.

JOCASTA. I heard everything. You were talking about a goat track.

OEDIPUS. I was a long way past that.

JOCASTA. Don't be cross with me, dear.

OEDIPUS. I? Cross with you?

JOCASTA. Yes, you are, and you're right. I'm ashamed of myself. That's what happens as we get older.

OEDIPUS. I'll begin the story again, but first, we must sleep a little to shake off this drowsiness. The first one awake wakes the other. Promise?

JOCASTA. I promise. Queens know how to snatch a little sleep between appointments. Give me your hand. Tiresias was right: I am too old.

OEDIPUS. Perhaps so, here in Thebes, where girls are ready for marriage at thirteen. But what about me — I'm just as sleepy — am I too old?

JOCASTA. It's different with you. It's the sandman, as children say. But there's no excuse for me. I finally get you to tell me the most wonderful story in the world, and as soon as you begin, I drift off like an old mother in front of the fire. Was I talking in my sleep?

OEDIPUS. No. I thought you were listening; you were so quiet. Why? Have you any secrets you're afraid of giving away?

JOCASTA. No; I was only afraid of those silly things we sometimes say in our sleep.

OEDIPUS. You were still, like a picture. Good night, till soon, my queen.

JOCASTA. Till very soon, my king, my love.

They sleep side by side, hand in hand. Murmuring of the fountain. Distant, intermittent thunder. A flash of very bright dream lightning. The animal skin is pushed up by the head of Anubis. On the end of his arm is Oedipus' belt. Oedipus tosses uneasily.

ANUBIS, *slowly, mockingly.* I'm more intelligent and better educated than any of the rabble in Thebes. This simple monster doesn't expect to be confronted by the pupil of the finest scholars in Corinth. If this is a trick, I'll drag you by the hair and crush the blood out of your body.

His voice rises like the howl of a dog.

Crush the blood out of your body . . . out of you . . . oo . . . oo . . .

JOCASTA, *mumbling in her sleep.* No, no, not that pulp, not that sticky pulp . . .

OEDIPUS, *in a heavy, distant voice.* I'll count up to fifty: One, two, three, four, eight, ten, eleven, fourteen, fifteen, fifteen, fifteen, three, four . . . .

ANUBIS. And Anubis would spring and open his wolf jaws!

He disappears through the trap door, replacing the animal skin above him.

OEDIPUS. Help! Here! Come here! Anybody! Help me!

JOCASTA. What is it, my darling? Oedipus, I was fast sleep.

She shakes him.

Wake up!

OEDIPUS. No! Oh, no! Please! Mercy!

JOCASTA. It's all right, my darling. It was a dream.

OEDIPUS. No, no!

He wakes.

Oh! Where was I? Jocasta? It's you. What a terrible nightmare!

JOCASTA. There! It's all over. You're in our room . . . in my arms.

OEDIPUS. Didn't you see anything? . . . The animal skin. What did I say?

JOCASTA. You were shouting: "No, no! Mercy!" Who was torturing you?

OEDIPUS. I don't remember.

JOCASTA. You're soaked with perspiration. It's my fault; I let you fall asleep with all those heavy clothes on, those gold ornaments and clasps and those sandals that cut into your feet.

She tries to raise him: He falls back.

Come now. What a big child! I can't leave you lying here soaked to the skin. Don't make yourself so heavy. Help me!

She takes off his tunic and rubs him down.

OEDIPUS, *vaguely.* Yes, mother.

JOCASTA. Yes, mother! What a child! Taking me for your mother!

OEDIPUS. Forgive me, Jocasta. I'm still half-asleep. I was far away, with my mother, and she's always worried that I may be too cold or too warm. You're not angry?

JOCASTA. As soon as I've seen to you, you can go right to sleep again. You *are* a well-brought-up young man, you know. You must have had a very fine mother. I'm not jealous. I have good reason to love her, too, for bringing you up for me — for us.

OEDIPUS. You're very sweet.

JOCASTA. Now for your sandals. Your left leg . . . and your right.

Taking off his sandals, she utters a cry of horror.

OEDIPUS. Did you hurt yourself?

JOCASTA. No . . . no!
She recoils, staring at his feet like a mad woman.

OEDIPUS. Oh, my scars. I didn't realize they were so ugly. My poor darling, did they frighten you?

JOCASTA. How did that happen? . . . Those holes.

OEDIPUS. My nurse was carrying me through the woods, when a wild boar came out of the undergrowth. She was terrified and let me fall out of her arms. As the animal was attacking me with its tusks, a woodcutter killed it. I should have warned you.

JOCASTA. It's nothing.

OEDIPUS. We're exhausted and half-asleep; that's why everything frightens us. You've just come out of a bad dream, and . . . Jocasta, you're white as a ghost.

JOCASTA. Those scars, Oedipus, they remind me of something I am always trying to forget.

OEDIPUS. What?

JOCASTA. Oedipus . . .

OEDIPUS. *What?*

JOCASTA. My — linen maid. When she and I were eighteen, we were both expecting a child. She worshiped her husband and wanted to bear him a son. But the oracles foretold so terrifying a future for the child that, after giving birth to a boy, she hadn't the courage to let it live.

OEDIPUS. What do you mean?

JOCASTA. Imagine the will power it takes for a woman to destroy the life that has come from her own body, the child she wants to bring up as her ideal on earth.

OEDIPUS. And what did she do?

JOCASTA. She pierced the baby's feet, tied them together, and secretly carried it up to the mountainside where it was left at the mercy of the wolves and bears. .

She hides her face.

OEDIPUS. And her husband?

JOCASTA. Everybody believed the child had died a natural death and that the mother had buried it with her own hands.

OEDIPUS. Is she still alive?

JOCASTA. No.

OEDIPUS. So much the better for her. Otherwise, I'd have put her to death.

JOCASTA. The oracles were clear. Against them, an ordinary woman feels weak and lost.

OEDIPUS. To kill, to destroy the flesh of one's own flesh ... to break the line deliberately ....

JOCASTA. Oedipus, let's speak about something else.

OEDIPUS. Yes, we had better speak about something else. I couldn't love you, if you tried to defend her.

JOCASTA. But Oedipus, try and feel as that girl must have felt ... helpless, intimidated by the priests ...

OEDIPUS. She was a linen maid! That's her sole excuse. Would *you* have done it?

JOCASTA, *with a gesture.* No, of course I wouldn't.

OEDIPUS. It doesn't take the determination of a Hercules to defy the oracles. I could boast about my miraculous deeds, but all I did to counter the prophecy was to turn away from my family, my inheritance, and my city. And the further I came from my city — and the nearer I came to yours — the more I felt I was coming home.

JOCASTA. Oedipus, please kiss me.

OEDIPUS. Yes, my love.

JOCASTA, *tenderly.* You're a child.

OEDIPUS. I'm not a child.

JOCASTA. Oedipus, let me just close the grille gate. I don't like it left open at night.

OEDIPUS. Let me.

JOCASTA. You stay here. While I'm up, I'll take a look in the mirror. After all this excitement, heaven knows what I must look like. Don't watch me. Turn the other way.

OEDIPUS. I'm turning now.

He lies across the bed, with his head on the cradle.

Now I'm closing my eyes. I no longer exist.

JOCASTA, *going over to the window.* That young soldier is still asleep. He is half-naked. It's not warm, tonight, either. Poor boy!

She goes to the mirror, then stops, listening. A drunk appears on the square, talking very loudly.

DRUNK. Politics! Politics! Don't talk to me about politics! It's a dirty business . . . enough to drive a man to drink. What's this? A corpse? . . . oh, no! Excuse me! It's a soldier. I salute the army! I salute the sleeping army!

Jocasta tries to see what is happening.

Politics! It's a disgrace . . . a disgrace!

JOCASTA. Oedipus!

OEDIPUS, *half-asleep.* Uh?

JOCASTA. There's a drunk out here and the sentry's asleep. I'm afraid of drunks. Send him away and wake the soldier up. Oedipus, please.

She shakes him.

OEDIPUS. I secrete my thread; I pay it out, spin it back and wind it in . . .

JOCASTA. What is he saying? He's so sound asleep. I could die and he would never know.

DRUNK. Politics!

He laughs coarsely and sings.

Jocasta lays Oedipus' head back on the cradle and goes to the center of the room, listening.

> Your Majesty the Queen,
> What does this marriage mean?
> Your husband is too young for you,
> Too young and far too green.

JOCASTA, *softly.* How they hate me!

She tiptoes to the window and back again, and watches Oedipus, glancing toward the window now and then. The Drunk's voice is punctuated by the fountain's hum and the crowing of cocks. She rocks the cradle lightly.

DRUNK, *singing again.*

> Your Majesty the Queen,
> What does this marriage mean? . . .

If I was a politician, I'd say to the Queen: Your Majesty, this young upstart is not the man for you. What you need is a solid, sober citizen like myself.

YOUNG SOLDIER. Hey! Move on!

DRUNK. I salute the awakened army!

YOUNG SOLDIER. Move on! And quick!

DRUNK. Ask me nicely.

YOUNG SOLDIER. Want me to lock you up?

DRUNK. Politics all the time! What a business!

He sings.

> Your Majesty the Queen . .

YOUNG SOLDIER. Be good. It's late. Please.

DRUNK. Certainly, certainly. You asked me nicely.

Jocasta cannot see herself in the mirror because of the dawn and moonlight conflicting. She takes the mirror legs and frame, leaving the mirror itself attached to the scenery, and brings them forward to confront the audience so that she is staring at them through the empty frame.

The Drunk sings again, now far off.

Your husband is too young for you,
Too young and far too green.

Oedipus is snoring gently, rhythmically. Jocasta faces the empty frame, massaging her cheeks up and up again. The sentry walks to and fro, the cock crows, and a distant trumpet wails.

CURTAIN

THE VOICE

Seventeen years go by swiftly. The great plague of Thebes looks like the first setback in Oedipus' astonishing run of luck. For the gods have designed their infernal machine so that misfortune shall be disguised as good fortune. After false happiness the King shall know true unhappiness, the true consecration. And this King of Spades, who has been manipulated by the cruel gods, will be made, in the end, into a man.

ACT FOUR: THE KING

*The red drapes of the bedroom are removed into the
flies, leaving the platform surrounded by walls, which grow
until there is a kind of courtyard and well. The outside of
Jocasta's room is seen as a balcony overlooking the yard
and accessible to it through an open doorway in the center,
below. Lighting suggests the plague.*

*Oedipus, looking older and wearing a small beard, is
standing near the doorway. Tiresias and Creon are to the
right and left. Center, right, a boy, the messenger from
Corinth, is kneeling.*

OEDIPUS. What have I done now, Tiresias, that will provoke a scandal?

TIRESIAS. As usual, Your Majesty, you are exaggerating.
I said, and I say again, that a man should receive the news
of his father's death with less joy.

OEDIPUS. Indeed?

To Messenger.

Don't be afraid, tell me, boy, what did Polybus die of?
And how did Merope take it?

MESSENGER. King Polybus died of old age, Your Majesty.
And Queen Merope is almost too old to understand what
happened.

OEDIPUS, *cupping his hand to his mouth.* Jocasta, Jocasta!

Jocasta parts the curtains and comes on the balcony, wearing her red scarf.

JOCASTA. What is it?

OEDIPUS. How pale you are. Are you ill?

JOCASTA. It's the plague, the heat, the hospital visits. I was resting on my bed.

OEDIPUS. This messenger brings wonderful news from Corinth, worth disturbing you for.

JOCASTA. Good news?

OEDIPUS. My father is dead.

JOCASTA. Oedipus!

OEDIPUS. Tiresias condemns me for being pleased about it. But the oracle told me that I would kill my father and marry my mother. Poor Merope! She is very old, and my father, Polybus, died a good natural death.

JOCASTA. I never thought the death of a father was something to be happy about.

OEDIPUS. I loathe conventional tears and sentiment. I was very young when I left my father and mother. I have no particular affection for them now.

MESSENGER. Your Majesty, if I may explain . . .

OEDIPUS. Something else . . .?

MESSENGER. On his deathbed, the King of Corinth asked me to tell you that you were only his adopted son.

OEDIPUS. What?

MESSENGER. One of Polybus' shepherds found you on an open hillside, at the mercy of the wild animals. He carried you to the Queen, who longed for a child. The shepherd was my father. That is why I was chosen to bring you this message.

TIRESIAS. This young man must be exhausted after his journey. He had to come through the disease and smells of the city. Perhaps it would be better if he had a meal and some rest before we question him.

OEDIPUS. You want to prolong the torment. You think my universe is about to crumble. But you don't know me, Tiresias. Don't laugh yet.

TIRESIAS. I am trying to warn you against your unfortunate habit of asking questions, wanting to know and understand everything.

OEDIPUS. I'm not afraid to find out who my parents were . . . whether I'm the son of the Muses or of some vagrant. I will know.

JOCASTA. Oedipus, you're excited. Tiresias is right. You believe everything you're told, and then —

OEDIPUS. I stand up to the severest blows, and then all of you plot to prevent me from discovering where I come from.

JOCASTA. There's no plot, my love. But I know you . . .

OEDIPUS. Nobody knows me, neither you nor I nor anybody else.

He turns to the Messenger.

Now, tell me more. Don't be afraid.

MESSENGER. That's all I know, Your Majesty, except that my father found you half-dead and hanging by your wounded feet from a branch.

OEDIPUS. So that's where these fine scars came from.

JOCASTA. Oedipus, Oedipus, please come up here.

OEDIPUS. So that was my cradle. And the story of the wild boar was false, like all the others. Well, it's still possible that I'm the son of a god and a nymph of the woods, and that I was reared by wolves. Don't laugh yet, Tiresias.

TIRESIAS. You are unjust.

OEDIPUS. At any rate, I didn't kill Polybus . . . but, now I come to think of it, I did kill a man once.

JOCASTA. You?

OEDIPUS. Yes, I. Oh, don't worry. It was an accident, pure bad luck. But nothing to do with parricide, I assure you. During a fight, I killed a man in a carriage.

JOCASTA. Where?

OEDIPUS. At the crossroads of Delphi and Daulia.

JOCASTA. At the crossroads of Delphi and Daulia!

She disappears as though drowning.

OEDIPUS. You could make a wonderful catastrophe out of that, Tiresias, if you assumed that the old man was my father. But incest is a little more difficult, don't you agree, Jocasta? Jocasta?

He looks around.

That's perfect! After seventeen years of happiness, an unblemished reign, two sons and two daughters, this noble lady has only to learn that I'm an unknown — which is why she loved me in the first place — and she turns away from me. Well, let her sulk! I can face my destiny alone.

CREON. Your wife is ill, Oedipus. The plague has demoralized us all. The gods are punishing the city; they demand a victim. There is a monster among us. They insist that we find him and drive him out. Day after day the police have been searching and the streets are obstructed by dead bodies. And your wife is ill. You don't see how much you are asking of her. She is an aging woman, while you are a man in your prime. And every mother in Thebes is worried about the plague. Instead of turning on Jocasta, you might have tried to understand her.

OEDIPUS. I know what you'll be planning next, Creon, my devoted brother-in-law. With the aid of the priests, and your police force, you'll persuade the people of Thebes that the monster in hiding is none other than myself.

CREON. Don't be absurd.

OEDIPUS. You're capable of worse than that, my friend. But Jocasta . . .

Calling.

Jocasta, Jocasta, where are you?

TIRESIAS. Let her rest, Oedipus, let her rest.

OEDIPUS. Yes, perhaps I should. We must get back to the facts.

MESSENGER. Your Majesty, I've told you all I know —

OEDIPUS. My feet were pierced and tied together . . . I was left on the mountain. And I wondered why Jocasta . . .

Quietly.

It is hard to give up illusions. I am nothing as illustrious as the descendant of a wood god, but merely the son of a linen maid, one of the people, a local product.

CREON. What are you talking about?

OEDIPUS. Poor, poor Jocasta! I once told her what I thought of that linen maid, without knowing it was my mother. Oh, she must be terrified, desperate. Wait for me. I must question her, I must bring the truth to light, and end this cruel game.

He leaves by the center door. Creon ushers the Messenger out, right.

CREON. We must restrain him, for his own sake.

TIRESIAS. Creon, there is nothing you can do. A storm is coming from the depths of time and its thunderbolt is aimed at this man. Let the thunderbolt follow its course. You must wait; you must not move or interfere.

Oedipus appears on the balcony, holding on to the wall with one hand.

OEDIPUS. You've killed her for me! She is hanging . . hanging by her scarf . . . dead! She is dead!

Oedipus goes out of sight. Creon starts forward.

TIRESIAS, *to Creon.* Stay! As a priest I command you. It's inhuman, but we must stay here and hold silent. The circle is closing.

CREON. I'm her brother. I have the right to . . .

TIRESIAS. You must not interfere.

OEDIPUS, *at center door.* You've killed her for me. She was romantic, weak, ill. You made me say I was a murderer. Whom did I murder? Through a blunder, a pure blunder, an old man on the road — a stranger.

TIRESIAS. Oedipus, your blunder killed the husband of Jocasta, King Laius.

OEDIPUS. The two of you. Now I see the shape of your plot . . . and it's worse than I thought. You insinuated to Jocasta that I had murdered Laius . . . that I had killed the King so that I could marry her.

TIRESIAS. Oedipus, you did kill King Laius, Jocasta's husband. I have known it for a long time. But I have never spoken about it to you, or her, or Creon, or anyone else.

OEDIPUS. Laius! That's the answer. I am the son of Laius and a linen maid.

He shouts.

The son of Laius and your linen maid, Jocasta!

TIRESIAS. Creon, if you want to act, speak now. Quickly!

CREON. Oedipus, because of you my sister is dead. I did not speak before because I wanted to save her life. I know the secret of your birth.

OEDIPUS. The secret?

CREON. The most hidden secrets eventually give themselves up. A man sworn to secrecy confides in his wife; she mentions something to a friend, and so it spreads. Shepherd, come in.

An old Shepherd comes in, trembling.

OEDIPUS. Who is this man?

CREON. The man who carried you, bleeding and tied, up on the mountain, on your mother's orders. Let him speak.

SHEPHERD. If I speak I bring death on myself. Why couldn't I have died earlier, so that I never had to live through this moment!

OEDIPUS. Whose son am I? Strike, strike fast!

SHEPHERD. Alas!

OEDIPUS. I am close to something that should not be heard.

SHEPHERD. And I to something that should not be spoken.

OEDIPUS. You must speak. I will know.

SHEPHERD. You are the son of Jocasta, your wife, and of Laius, your father, killed by you at the crossing of three roads. Incest and parricide. May the gods forgive you!

OEDIPUS. I have slain my own blood. I have married my own blood. I have begotten my own blood. It is clear — as light.

He goes out.

Creon signals the Shepherd off.

TIRESIAS. A linen maid! Women cannot control their tongues. Jocasta must have blamed her crime on a servant to see how he would be affected.

He takes Creon's arm and listens, his head on one side. There is a forbidding murmur. Antigone, hair in disarray, appears on the balcony.

ANTIGONE. Uncle Creon! Tiresias! Please come up, please! My mother . . . she isn't moving. And my father is stabbing her gold brooch into his eyes. There's blood. Please come, quickly!

She goes in.

CREON. This time nobody shall stop me.

TIRESIAS. I will. I warn you, Creon. This is the last touch to a masterpiece of horror. Not a movement, not a word, not even our shadow must intrude.

CREON. This is pure madness.

TIRESIAS. This is pure wisdom!

CREON. No. I am in power again, and I shall restore order.

He breaks free. As he pushes forward, Oedipus appears in the doorway, blinded. Antigone is clutching his robe.

Why . . . why that? Death would have been better.

TIRESIAS. He is still proud. He wanted to be the happiest of men; now he wants to be the unhappiest.

OEDIPUS. Stone me! Strike down the unclean beast. Drive him out of your city!

ANTIGONE. Father!

OEDIPUS. Don't touch my hands.

TIRESIAS. Antigone. Here is my staff. Offer it to him for me.

ANTIGONE. Tiresias offers you his staff.

She takes the staff and gives it to Oedipus, after kissing Tiresias' hand.

OEDIPUS. Is he there? Thank you, Tiresias, I accept it. Do you remember how, eighteen years ago, I saw it in your eyes — that I would become blind — and could not understand? It is clear now, Tiresias, but I am in pain. The journey will be hard.

CREON. We cannot let him cross Thebes. It would start a terrible scandal.

TIRESIAS. No, they are used to seeing King Oedipus as he wished to be. They will not see him as he is.

CREON. You think he will be invisible because he is blind!

TIRESIAS. Yes . . . and no.

CREON. I've had enough of your riddles and symbols. My head is on my shoulders and my feet are on the ground. And I am giving the orders.

TIRESIAS. Where this man is going, Creon, he will be beyond the power of your police.

Jocasta's ghost appears in the doorway, white and beautiful, with the long red scarf wound around her neck and her eyes closed.

OEDIPUS. Jocasta, you're alive!

JOCASTA. No, Oedipus. I am dead. You see me because you are blind. The others do not see me.

OEDIPUS. Tiresias, too, is blind.

JOCASTA. Perhaps he sees me faintly; but he loves me. He won't say anything.

OEDIPUS. Do not touch me, wife.

JOCASTA. Your wife is dead, Oedipus . . . hanged. I am your mother. I have come to help you. How would you ever get down these steps alone, my poor child?

OEDIPUS. Mother!

JOCASTA. Yes, my child. Things that seem monstrous to men are not important in my world. If you only knew how trivial they are.

OEDIPUS. But I am still on earth.

JOCASTA. Only just . . .

CREON. He's delirious . . . speaking to himself. I won't allow the child to go with him.

TIRESIAS. They are both in good care.

CREON. Antigone, Antigone! Come here!

ANTIGONE. I don't want to stay with Uncle Creon. I don't want to stay in this house. Father, don't go without me. I can lead you; I can guide you.

CREON. Ungrateful child.

OEDIPUS. No, Antigone. You must be good. I can't take you with me.

ANTIGONE. You can, you can!

OEDIPUS. Are you going to leave your sister, Ismene?

ANTIGONE. She must stay with Eteocles and Polynices. Please take me with you, Father, please! Don't leave me alone with Uncle Creon . . . don't leave me at home and alone.

JOCASTA. Antigone is proud: she wants to be your guide. Let her think she is. Take her with you. I'll look after you both.

OEDIPUS, *putting his hand to his head.* Oh!

JOCASTA. Are you in pain?

OEDIPUS. Yes, my neck, my arms, and my eyes.

JOCASTA. I'll bathe your wounds at the fountain.

OEDIPUS, *sobbing.* Mother!

JOCASTA. The scarf and the brooch! I knew. I said so, many times.

CREON. I will not let Antigone leave with this madman. It *is* my duty to . . .

TIRESIAS. Your duty! They are outside your authority. They do not belong to you now.

CREON. Whom do they belong to then?

TIRESIAS. To the people, to poets, to pure hearts.

JOCASTA. Let us leave. Take hold of my dress. Don't be afraid.

They go forward.

ANTIGONE. Come along, Father. Come along.

OEDIPUS. Where do the steps begin?

JOCASTA AND ANTIGONE, *in unison.* We have the platform to cross first . . .

They disappear. We still hear Jocasta and Antigone speaking in perfect unison.

Carefully . . . Count the steps. One, two, three, four, five . . .

CREON. And if they do pass safely through the city, who will be responsible for them, who will give them shelter?

TIRESIAS. Glory.

CREON. More likely, dishonor . . . shame.

TIRESIAS. Who can say?

CURTAIN

ORPHEUS
translated by
JOHN SAVACOOL

CHARACTERS

ORPHEUS
EURYDICE
THE HORSE
HEURTEBISE
DEATH
AZRAEL, *Death's First Assistant*
RAPHAEL, *Death's Second Assistant*
POSTMAN'S VOICE
COMMISSIONER
CLERK

The scene is laid in Thrace.

Orpheus was first performed at the Théâtre des Arts in Paris on June 17, 1926, with Georges Pitoeff in the title role

COSTUMES

Costumes for this play should conform with the place and period in which the play is presented.

Orpheus and Eurydice wear simple country clothes, as far as possible in no identifiable style.

Heurtebise wears a blue workman's jacket, a dark scarf around his neck, a pair of sandals on his feet. He is tanned and hatless; and never removes the glazier's pack of windowpanes strapped like a mountaineer's pack onto his back.

The Commissioner and his clerk wear black morning coats. They have panama hats, goatees, and spats.

Death is a beautiful young woman in a bright pink evening gown and fur wrap. Her hair, gown, wrap, shoes, gestures, and manner of walking are in accord with the latest high fashion. She wears a mask on which is painted a pair of big blue eyes. She talks rapidly in a mechanical manner and never quite seems to establish contact with the rest of us. Even her surgeon's jacket should be of an elegant cut.

Death's assistants wear the white coats and rubber gloves we associate with the operating room of a hospital.

DÉCOR

A room in Orpheus' country cottage. It is a curious room, reminiscent of a magician's parlor. Despite the clear light of an April sky seen through the window, one senses here the presence of occult forces. In this room even the most ordinary objects take on a mysterious glow.

In the center of the rear wall, in a stall which is really no more than a cubbyhole, we see a white horse. This horse has legs which might be human. Stage right of the horse, in another laurel-wreathed cubbyhole, is a pedestal waiting to receive a bust or small statue.

Next to the pedestal, at the extreme right of the upstage wall, is a door which opens onto a garden. When this door opens it swings back and blocks our view of the pedestal. Stage left of the horse is a porcelain washstand. On the extreme left of this upstage wall is a glass doorway opening onto a balcony.

Downstage right, against the wall, is a large mirror. Upstage of the mirror is a bookcase. Across from the bookcase, on the stage-left wall, is the doorway to Eurydice's room. A canted ceiling encloses the set like a box.

This room is furnished with two tables and three white chairs. One of the tables is used as a writing desk and, with one of the chairs, is placed stage right near the mirror.

The second table, stage left, is set with fruit, plates, a decanter, glasses (all of which resemble the gadgets on a magician's worktable). It is covered with a cloth which drops to the floor. Behind the table is a white chair, facing the audience. The third white chair is to the left of the table, offering the audience a profile view of the sitter.

In staging this play the director must neither add nor subtract a chair or change the disposition of doorways and windows. The set, as described by the author, is a part of the text and every element, down to the last detail, plays its part in the action — just as every rope in an acrobat's paraphernalia lends its bit of tension necessary to the balance of the trapezes as they fly through the air.

There are no colors in this room, except for the blue of the sky and a band of dark red velvet stretched at waist height across the entrance of the horse's stall; covering the middle of the animal's body.

This set should remind one of those airplane or ship interiors which side-show photographers offer as painted backdrops for their bargain-priced snapshots.

What's more, this set matches the people and actions of the play in the same hard, naive manner as the fake perspective of the photographer's backdrop matches the subjects of his pictures.

PROLOGUE

The actor who will play Orpheus appears in front of the curtain.

Ladies and gentlemen, this prologue is not in the script. Doubtless the author, if he's here tonight, will be surprised to see me in front of the curtain. But I have a request to make. This tragedy he has given us to perform is a ticklish affair, and so I'm asking that you wait until the very end to express any objections to the way we play it. You see, we'll be performing very high with no nets to catch us if we fall. The slightest distraction from the house might make us lose our balance. That means death for me and my fellow actors.

He disappears behind the curtain.

ORPHEUS

Orpheus is seated at the table, stage right. He is inter-
rogating the spirit world by means of taps representing let-
ters of the alphabet. Eurydice is seated, stage left, at the
table set for lunch.

EURYDICE. Can I move now?

ORPHEUS. Hold it one second.

EURYDICE. But he's not tapping any more.

ORPHEUS. Sometimes there is a long wait between the
first letter and the rest of the word.

EURYDICE. I can guess what's coming.

ORPHEUS. Well, don't!

EURYDICE. But it's always the same word, over and over
again.

ORPHEUS. M, M... Come on, horse. What comes after the
letter M? ... I'm waiting.

EURYDICE. How long before you learn that the horse's
head is just as empty as yours is?

ORPHEUS. Come on now, I'm listening! M! M! What
comes after M?

The horse moves.

What's that? Did you say something? Tell me what letter comes after M.

The horse stamps its hoof. Orpheus counts.

A. B. C. D. E. E? Is it the letter E?

The horse shakes its head up and down.

EURYDICE. What did you think it would be?

ORPHEUS, *furious.* Sh-sh!

The horse starts stamping its hoof.

A B C D E F G H I J K L M N O P Q R.

To Eurydice

And don't you dare laugh. R? Is it really the letter R? M - E - R, mer? Did I miscount? Horse, tell me! Is it really the letter R? If it is, knock once. Knock twice if I'm wrong.

The horse knocks once.

EURYDICE. How many times do you have to ask him?

ORPHEUS. Quiet, please. You'll make him nervous. The horse gets upset when people are skeptical. Either be quiet or go to your room.

EURYDICE. I won't open my mouth.

ORPHEUS. That's more like it!

To the horse.

Now, M - E - R, mer . . . Speak, horse, I'm listening. Speak to me, horse. Horse! Come on, try! What comes after the letter R?

The horse knocks. Orpheus counts.

A. B. C.

Silence.

C. The letter C. Did you hear that, young lady!

The horse knocks.

A. B. C. D. E. F. G. H. I. *Merci! Merci!* That's French for "thank you." He was spelling out "thank you"! Is that all? Is that all there is to it?

The horse shakes its head "yes."

This is stu-pen-dous! You see, Eurydice, if I'd listened to you I'd never have known. *"Merci,"* and that's all there is to it. Stu-pen-dous!

EURYDICE. Why?

ORPHEUS. What do you mean, why?

EURYDICE. Why is it stupendous? Of course *merci* means "thank you" — but so what?

ORPHEUS. So what! Last week this horse gave me one of the most astonishing sentences the world has ever heard.

EURYDICE. Really now . . .

ORPHEUS . . . . one of the most astonishing sentences the world has ever heard. And I intend to use it to change the face of poetry. Here I am immortalizing my horse and you wonder why he says, "thank you." Why the very fact that he said it in French shows how tactful he is. And all the while I thought . . .

He throws his arms around the horse.

EURYDICE. Orpheus, darling, try to be fair. Admit that since the horse gave you that astonishing sentence you've received one word, one single word — and not a very poetic word at that.

ORPHEUS. Who's to say what is poetic and what isn't?

EURYDICE. When Aglaonice had séances her table always tapped out the same thing.

ORPHEUS. Leave that woman out of this. I told you not to mention her name again. She almost ruined you, didn't she? A woman who drinks, who walks the streets with a tiger on a leash, who puts ideas in our wives' heads and scares young girls out of marriage.

EURYDICE. But that's her religion. It's moon worship!

ORPHEUS. All right, defend her! Why don't you go back to the Bacchantes, if you like the way they live?

EURYDICE. I was only teasing. You know it's you I love. One look from you and I turned my back on those people.

ORPHEUS. Fine company for a young girl! I'll never forget Aglaonice's voice when she said: "Take the girl, since she wants to go. Silly women are mad for artists ... but I'll have the last laugh, young fellow, you'll see."

EURYDICE. It gave me the chills.

ORPHEUS. If I ever meet that creature again ...

He bangs the inkwell on the table.

EURYDICE. See how nervous the horse has made you! You used to laugh, kiss me, throw your arms around me. You had a good job. The world was in the palm of your hand. Why, they couldn't wait to read your poems and everybody in Thrace knew them by heart as soon as you wrote them down. That's because you sang of the sun, because you were a priest singing of the gods. But then that horse came into your life. We moved to the country. You quit your job and stopped writing. Now you spend your time petting that horse, interrogating that horse, waiting for that horse to answer you. It's ridiculous!

ORPHEUS. Ridiculous? I was so successful I was overripe, beginning to rot, and I stunk of it. The sun and the moon, they're all the same to me. I wanted to be in the dark-deep in the night. Not your night, or theirs, but mine! This horse knows the way. He insinuates himself into my private darkness and comes up like a skin diver bearing a few sentences.

Can't you see that a single one of those sentences is more astonishing than any poem I ever wrote? Why, I'd give every word I ever put on paper for one of those sentences in which I can hear myself purr the way you hear the ocean in a seashell. Ridiculous! What do you want out of life? I'm turning myself inside out to discover a world. I'm on the trail of the unknown.

EURYDICE. And now we get the famous words . . .

ORPHEUS, *seriously.* Yes, here comes the sentence.

He walks to the horse and recites his sentence.

"Lady Eurydice shall return from the underworld."

EURYDICE. That doesn't make sense.

ORPHEUS. Who cares if the words make sense! Glue your ear to them. Listen to their mystery. "Eurydice shall return" . . . now that'd be quite ordinary. But "Lady" Eurydice! "Lady Eurydice shall return . . ." *Shall* return. Can't you hear the vibrations in that future tense? And then the twist — "from the underworld." Why, you should be flattered that it's *you* I'm talking about.

EURYDICE. But it's not you who's talking . . .

Pointing.

It's him!

ORPHEUS. Who's to say who's talking — him, me, or nobody at all. We bump into each other in the dark; we're up to our necks in the supernatural, playing hide-and-seek with the gods. Who really knows anything at all? "Lady Eurydice shall return from the underworld." That isn't a statement at all. It's a poem, a poem of a dream, a flower plucked from the backyard of death.

EURYDICE. Tell it to your public. They'll never admit that poetry consists in just writing down words — and that your biggest success was a whole sentence copied from a horse.

ORPHEUS. Who cares about success or the horse or what the public thinks. Besides, I'm no longer alone.

EURYDICE. Oh, I forgot your fans! Four or five insensitive rowdies who think you're an anarchist and a dozen adolescent morons trying to show off.

ORPHEUS. Just wait! Some day these poems of mine will charm the beasts — the real ones.

EURYDICE. If you scorn success so much then why did you enter your sentence in the poetry contest? The fact that you submitted a poem to the All-Thrace poetry contest means that you attach some importance to the prize.

ORPHEUS. Someone has to make a scandal, throw a bomb. Someone has to clear the air or we'll all suffocate. I can't breathe any more.

EURYDICE. But we were getting along so nicely.

ORPHEUS. Too nicely.

EURYDICE. You were in love with me.

ORPHEUS. I am in love with you.

EURYDICE. You're in love with the horse.

ORPHEUS. Don't be stupid. The horse has nothing to do with it.

Halfheartedly, he kisses Eurydice and then walks toward the horse.

Isn't that right, old fellow. Isn't that right, buddy? What's that? You love me, do you? Oh, you want some sugar? Well then, give me a kiss, Come on, you can do better than that. Isn't he beautiful! Here.

He takes a lump of sugar out of his pocket and gives it to the horse.

There's a good boy.

EURYDICE. I don't count any more. I could die, and you wouldn't even notice.

ORPHEUS. We were already dead without noticing it.

EURYDICE. Orpheus, put your arms around me.

ORPHEUS. Sorry, I haven't time. I'm going into town. But, Eurydice, tomorrow's the deadline and I still haven't signed up for the contest.

EURYDICE, *in a burst of emotion*. Orpheus, please!

ORPHEUS. Do you see that pedestal? There's nothing on it. And there won't be anything on it until I've made my masterpiece.

EURYDICE. They'll throw stones at you.

ORPHEUS. I'll convert those stones into my own image — mold them into a bust for the pedestal.

EURYDICE. The Bacchantes will get you.

ORPHEUS. I don't even know them.

EURYDICE. You should. They're attractive. Aglaonice hates you. And she's entering a poem in the contest too.

ORPHEUS. There's that woman again!

EURYDICE. Be fair, Orpheus. She *is* talented.

ORPHEUS. You don't say!

EURYDICE. In an unpleasant way, of course. But in a sense, from one point of view, she does have talent. She does make some striking images.

ORPHEUS. "In a sense ... from one point of view"! Did the Bacchantes teach you to talk that way? So you admit that, in a sense, you find her images striking, that from one point of view my mortal enemies have talent. Yet you claim you love me. Well, young lady, in that sense and from that point of view, let me tell you I've had all I can take. This horse is the only person in the house who understands me.

He bangs his fist on the table.

EURYDICE. You don't have to break the furniture.

ORPHEUS. Break the furniture! Listen to who's talking! My wife smashes a window every day and now she tells me I'm too rough on the furniture.

EURYDICE. In the first place . . .

ORPHEUS, *pacing.* I know, you still haven't broken one today.

EURYDICE. But . . .

ORPHEUS. Well, break it! Go ahead and break a window!

EURYDICE. Why must you get so upset over something so . . .

ORPHEUS. She's a sly one, she is! If you haven't broken one today, that's because you know I won't be home . . .

EURYDICE. What are you hinting at?

ORPHEUS. Do you think I'm blind? You break one windowpane a day so that the glazier will come to fix it.

EURYDICE. What if I do! He's a fine young man, and very sensitive. And he adores you.

ORPHEUS. How nice of him!

EURYDICE. I have to do something while you talk to your horse, so I smash a window. You're not jealous, are you, Orpheus?

ORPHEUS. Who, me, jealous? Jealous of a mere boy who fixes broken windows? I might as well be jealous of old Aglaonice. Look, if you won't break one, I will. It'll make me feel better.

He smashes a windowpane.

Outside we hear: "New windows for old! New windows for old!"

Hey, glazier! Up here! Now, who's jealous?

Heurtebise enters. He appears on the balcony. The sunlight strikes the panes of glass strapped to his back. He comes in the room, bends a knee, and crosses his arms on his chest.

HEURTEBISE. Ladies and gentlemen — good afternoon.

ORPHEUS. Come in, young fellow. It was I, *I*, who broke the window, and I want you to replace the glass while I'm gone.

To Eurydice. Darling, you'll see that he does a good job, won't you?

To the horse. Does he love his poet?

He kisses the horse.

Until tonight.

Orpheus leaves.

EURYDICE, *to Heurtebise.* You see, I wasn't imagining things.

HEURTEBISE. It's unheard of.

EURYDICE. Now you understand.

HEURTEBISE. You poor lady . . .

EURYDICE. Ever since the night he brought home that horse, ever since they've been talking together . . .

HEURTEBISE. Has the horse answered him yet?

EURYDICE. It says "thank you" — in French.

HEURTEBISE. *Merci* is a lovely word.

EURYDICE. For a month now we've been torturing each other.

HEURTEBISE. It doesn't make sense to be jealous of a horse.

EURYDICE. I'd rather know he had a mistress in town.

HEURTEBISE. You just say that . . .

EURYDICE. If it weren't for my friendship with you, I'd have given up long ago.

HEURTEBISE. Eurydice . . .

EURYDICE. *She looks at herself in the mirror and smiles.* Just think, I've done something clever. He's finally noticed that I've been breaking a window every day. Instead of telling him I was breaking glass to bring good luck, I said it was to get you in the house.

HEURTEBISE. I'd have thought that . . .

EURYDICE. Let me finish. We quarreled, of course, and he smashed a window himself. Heurtebise, I think he's jealous.

HEURTEBISE. Then since you love him . . .

EURYDICE. The worse he treats me the more I love him. You know, I think he was even jealous of Aglaonice.

HEURTEBISE. Aglaonice?

EURYDICE. He has a horror of everything that suggests the people I used to know. That's why I'm afraid we're taking an awful chance. Sh-sh! I can't help feeling that horse is listening to us.

They tiptoe to the horse's stall.

HEURTEBISE. He's asleep.

They tiptoe downstage.

EURYDICE. Did you see Aglaonice?

HEURTEBISE. Yes.

EURYDICE. Orpheus would kill you if he found out.

HEURTEBISE. He won't find out.

EURYDICE, *pulling Heurtebise further from the horse, toward her room.* Do you have it . . . it?

HEURTEBISE. I have it.

EURYDICE. What did she put it in?

HEURTEBISE. A lump of sugar.

EURYDICE. Was she in a good mood?

HEURTEBISE. No mood at all. She simply said, "Here's the poison. Bring me back the letter."

EURYDICE. She won't like what I wrote.

HEURTEBISE. Then she said: "Just to make sure nobody knows, here's a self-addressed envelope, written in my own hand. All she'll have to do is insert the letter and seal it. No one will ever know she's written me.

EURYDICE. No matter what Orpheus thinks, Aglaonice can be very thoughtful. Was she alone?

HEURTEBISE. There was a girl with her. Those were no people for you to run around with.

EURYDICE. Of course, they weren't. But I still think Aglaonice is a very sweet person.

HEURTEBISE. Don't trust those sweet persons and well-meaning men. Here's the sugar.

EURYDICE. Thank you . . .

She takes the sugar and fearfully walks to the horse.

I'm afraid.

HEURTEBISE. Are you backing out?

EURYDICE. Not backing out, just afraid. Now that it's time to act, I don't think I can go through with it.

She walks downstage to the writing table. Heurtebise?

HEURTEBISE. What?

EURYDICE. Heurtebise, you're sweet. You wouldn't . . .

HEURTEBISE. Come, come. That's a very big thing to ask.

EURYDICE. You said you'd do anything to help.

HEURTEBISE. And I'll say it again, but . . .

EURYDICE. Of course, if it inconveniences you in the slightest, I wouldn't think of it.

HEURTEBISE. Give me the sugar.

EURYDICE. Thank you. I think you're very brave.

HEURTEBISE. What if he won't take it from me?

EURYDICE. Try.

HEURTEBISE, *near the horse.* I confess my legs are a little shaky.

EURYDICE. Be a man!

She crosses left and stops at the door of her room.

HEURTEBISE. Here goes!

In a weak voice.

Horse . . . Horse . . .

EURYDICE, *looking out the window.* Heavens, it's Orpheus! He's coming through the garden. Quick, pretend you're working.

Heurtebise tosses the lump of sugar onto the table and then pushes the table against the wall between the rear window and the door to Eurydice's room.

Climb on the chair!

Heurtebise climbs on the chair and pretends to take measurements of the window frames in the glass doorway. Eurydice slumps onto the chair at the writing table. Orpheus enters.

ORPHEUS. I forgot my birth certificate. Where did I put it?

EURYDICE. In the bookcase, top shelf on the left. Shall I get it for you?

ORPHEUS. Stay where you are. I'll get it myself.

He passes in front of the horse, stopping just long enough to pat it. He takes the chair on which Heurtebise is standing and carries it to the bookcase. Heurtebise remains in position, suspended in mid-air. Eurydice stifles a cry of surprise. Orpheus, who notices nothing strange, climbs onto the chair and rummages on the top shelf of the bookcase.

Here it is.

Orpheus puts the birth certificate in his pocket, climbs off the chair, carries the chair back to the window, slides it under Heurtebise's feet, and leaves the room without saying a word.

EURYDICE. Heurtebise, you're a magician!

HEURTEBISE. A magician?

EURYDICE. Nobody but a magician could remain suspended in mid-air while someone slides a chair from under his feet.

HEURTEBISE. Who's suspended in mid-air?

EURYDICE. Don't deny it, I saw you. You were standing on air — three feet off the ground, with nothing underneath to hold you up.

HEURTEBISE. Sometimes you amaze me.

EURYDICE. For a full minute you were dangling between heaven and earth.

HEURTEBISE. Impossible.

EURYDICE. Of course it was impossible, that's why I want an explanation.

HEURTEBISE. You claim I was standing there with nothing to hold me up, halfway between the ceiling and the floor?

EURYDICE. Heurtebise, I saw you — with my own eyes. Even if I do live with a talking horse, I still think something's wrong when a friend starts to float in the air in front of me. Stay where you are! Until I know what happened, even the light on your back gives me the creeps. All right, Heurtebise, explain yourself.

HEURTEBISE. But I haven't done anything to explain. Either I'm dreaming or you were dreaming.

EURYDICE. In dreams I've done exactly the same thing, I admit it. But we weren't asleep, either of us.

HEURTEBISE. It must have been an optical illusion — the light reflected from the glass on my back to the window. Objects sometimes fool us that way. Once at a fair I saw a naked woman walking on the ceiling.

EURYDICE. This was no trick contrived by a magician. It was beautiful and at the same time it was chilling. In one second I saw you as spine-chilling as an accident and as lovely as a rainbow. You were the shriek of a man falling out the window and the silence of the stars. And now I'm afraid of you — and I'm honest enough to admit it. If you don't want to talk, don't; but things will never be the same between us. I thought you were simple, like me. But no, you're complicated. I thought we belonged to the same race of people. But no, you're like the horse.

HEURTEBISE. Eurydice, this hurts me. It's as if you were talking in your sleep.

EURYDICE. Now you sound like Orpheus. Stay in character. Don't *you* try to drive me out of my mind.

HEURTEBISE. Eurydice, I swear . . .

EURYDICE. It's no use, Heurtebise. I've lost faith in you.

HEURTEBISE. What can we do about it?

EURYDICE. Wait a minute.

She walks to the bookshelf, climbs on a chair, takes a book, opens it, removes a letter, and puts the book back in place.

Hand me the envelope you got from Aglaonice.

He hands it to her.

Thank you.

She puts the letter in the envelope and licks the flap.

Oh dear!

HEURTEBISE. Did you cut your tongue?

EURYDICE. No, but the glue has a funny taste. Here's the envelope. Take it to Aglaonice right away.

HEURTEBISE. But I haven't fixed the window.

EURYDICE. The window can wait.

HEURTEBISE. You want to get rid of me, don't you?

EURYDICE. I need to be alone.

HEURTEBISE. You're being nasty.

EURYDICE. I don't like tradesmen with light fingers — or light feet.

HEURTEBISE. And now you're making bad puns.

EURYDICE. That was not a pun.

HEURTEBISE, *picking up his bag.* You'll be sorry you hurt me.

Silence.

Are you sending me away?

EURYDICE. I hate mysteries. I've decided to assert myself.

HEURTEBISE. Good-by, Madame. I trust at least that my obedience pleases you.

EURYDICE. Good by.

They cross paths on stage. Eurydice moves toward her room, Heurtebise opens the door and walks out, leaving the door open. As he steps into the garden we catch the rays of sunshine reflected off his back. Eurydice suddenly stops, changes countenance. She reels, clasps a hand to her heart, and shouts.

Heurtebise! Heurtebise! Don't go yet!

HEURTEBISE, *coming back.* What's wrong?

EURYDICE. Help . . .

HEURTEBISE. You're shivering. Your face is green.

EURYDICE. I can't move. My heart's skipping a beat. My stomach burns.

HEURTEBISE. The envelope!

EURYDICE. What about the envelope?

HEURTEBISE, *shouting.* The envelope from Aglaonice. You licked it. You said it had a strange taste.

EURYDICE. The witch! Hurry, find Orpheus for me. I'm going to die. I want to see Orpheus once more. Orpheus! Orpheus!

HEURTEBISE. But I can't leave you alone. There must be some antidote.

EURYDICE. I know this posion. The Bacchantes brew it. Nothing can save me. Run quick, bring back Orpheus. I want to see him again and ask him to forgive me. I love him, Heurtebise. Hurry or it will be too late. Please, Heurtebise! You're good, you're kind. Oh, they're driving needles between my ribs! Quick, run, fly! Take the short cut. If he's on his way back you'll meet him on the road. I'll be in my room, waiting. Help me.

Heurtebise helps her to the door of her room.

Hurry, hurry, hurry.

At the very moment that Heurtebise reaches the outside door, Eurydice reappears.

Heurtebise, listen to me, if you can really do things . . . well . . . things like a little while ago . . . that let you sail through space . . . don't be angry with me, I was upset, I was being stupid . . . I really do like you, Heurtebise . . . Try anything, but bring back Orpheus. Oh!

She goes back into her room.

HEURTEBISE. I'll bring him back, I promise.

He leaves.

The stage remains empty for a moment. The lights change. Low syncopated drumbeats accompany the dialogue of the following scene. Death enters through the mirror, followed by her two assistants. She wears a formal gown and evening wrap. Her assistants are dressed in surgeon's uniforms. We see only their eyes; the rest of their faces is covered with gauze. Rubber gloves. Each carries a large and expensive-looking black suitcase. Death walks in rapidly and stops abruptly in the center of the room.

DEATH. Get to work right away.

RAPHAEL. Where does Madame wish us to place the luggage?

DEATH. On the floor, anywhere. Azrael will tell you what to do. Azrael, my coat.

He takes off her wrap.

RAPHAEL. I'm so afraid of making a mistake.

DEATH. You can't expect to learn as much as Azrael in two days, young man. Azrael has been with me for centuries. He was clumsy, too, in the beginning. My jacket, please.

Azrael takes a white surgeon's jacket out of one of the bags and helps Death slip it on over her evening gown.

AZRAEL, *to Raphael.* Put the metal boxes on the table. No, not that way. First, the napkins. First cover the table with napkins.

DEATH, *moving to the washstand.* Azrael will tell you that I demand absolute cleanliness — like on a ship.

RAPHAEL. Yes, Madame. I hope Madame will forgive me, but I was looking at the horse.

DEATH. Do you like that horse?

RAPHAEL. Oh yes, Madame, very much.

DEATH. What a child! And you wish he were yours, don't you. Very well, I'll give him to you. Azrael, the alcohol.

To Raphael.

You'll find a piece of sugar on the table.

RAPHAEL. Yes, Madame. I see it.

DEATH. Give it to the horse. If he refuses, I'll give it to him myself. Azrael, my rubber gloves. Thank you.

She puts a glove on her right hand.

RAPHAEL. Madame, the horse won't eat the sugar.

DEATH, *takes the sugar from Raphael.* Eat it, horse, I want you to eat it.

The horse takes the sugar, backs up in his stall, and disappears from view. A black curtain is drawn over the opening.

There!

To Raphael. Now he's yours.

RAPHAEL. Madame is too generous!

DEATH, *pulling on her left glove.* A week ago you still thought I was a skeleton wrapped in a shroud, carrying a scythe. A kind of bogeyman with wrinkles and scars on my face.

RAPHAEL. Oh, Madame! . . .

During this dialogue, Azrael drapes a piece of cloth over the mirror.

DEATH. Oh yes, you did. They all do. The truth is, my dear boy, that if I were really the way people picture me, then they would recognize me when I come to them. And it is essential that I slip into their lives unnoticed.

She places a chair downstage center.

Azrael, try the switch.

AZRAEL. It works, Madame.

There is a rumbling sound of an electrical apparatus.

DEATH, *taking a handkerchief out of the jacket pocket.* Excellent! Now, Raphael, if you'll tie this handkerchief over my eyes . . .

While Raphael is blindfolding her.

We're on one-wave-seven and one-zone-seven-twelve. Set the control dial on four. If I call for more current turn it up to five, but no further. Tighter, please, and make a double knot. Thank you. Are you both in position?

Azarel and Raphael stand side by side behind the table. Their hands are in the instrument boxes on the table.

I shall begin.

Death moves to the chair. With slow, caressing motions she seems to be hypnotizing an invisible head.

RAPHAEL, *low.* Azrael . . .

AZRAEL. Sh-sh!

DEATH. Go on, talk. You are not disturbing me.

RAPHAEL. Azrael, where is Eurydice?

DEATH. I expected that. Always the same question, isn't it, Azrael? Explain it to him.

AZRAEL. When Death wants to touch a living object she operates through a neutral element which changes its position in space. These machines enable her to touch things where she sees them. That eliminates mathematical calculations and saves us considerable time.

RAPHAEL. It's like spearing fish in the water. If you aim straight at the fish, you'll never hit it.

DEATH, *laughing.* If you like.

Seriously.

Azrael, prepare the spool.

AZRAEL. Yes, Madame ... Does Madame know what has happened to Heurtebise?

DEATH. He's bringing Orpheus back from town.

RAPHAEL. What if they come in before we finish?

DEATH. That's up to Azrael. He controls the time gears. One minute to them is a whole hour for me.

AZRAEL. The needle's moving past number five. Is Madame ready for the spool?

DEATH. Tie it appropriately and give me one end.

Azrael disappears into Eurydice's room and then returns with the spool. Death counts the number of steps between her chair and the door to Eurydice's room. At the doorway, she stops. Azrael hands her the spool which is shaped like a circular tape measure and wound with a white thread, one end of which is now anchored in Eurydice's room.

AZRAEL. Raphael, the chronometer.

RAPHAEL. I forgot to bring it with me!

AZRAEL. Now we're in a fix.

DEATH. Don't get excited. There's another way . . .

She whispers to Azrael.

AZRAEL, *stepping down to the footlights.* Ladies and gentlemen. Death has requested me to ask the audience if there isn't someone in the theater who would kindly lend us a watch.

A man in the first row raises his hand.

Thank you, sir. Raphael, would you hand me the gentlemen's watch?

Raphael walks into the audience and takes the watch.

DEATH. Are you ready?

AZRAEL. Ready, Madame.

A drum rolls, The thread is wound on the spool; slowly it inches its way out of Eurydice's room into the metal box which Death holds in her hands. Azrael and Raphael stand behind Death, their backs turned. Azrael is counting. He holds one hand in the air like a referee at a boxing match. Raphael slowly goes through a set of hand signals, like a sailor practicing semaphore.

Enough!

The drum rolls cease. Raphael freezes in position. The thread is taut. Death rushes into Eurydice's room. When she returns the bandage is no longer on her eyes and she carries a live dove which is attached to the end of the thread. The electric apparatus is no longer buzzing.

DEATH. Quick now. Quick, Raphael, the scissors!

She runs to the balcony.

Out here. Now, cut!

He cuts the thread. The dove flies into space.

Adjust the bandages. Azrael, show him how. It's very simple. No, let him do it. He's got to learn.

Azrael and Raphael close the metal boxes. They pack them in the suitcases along with the jackets, etc. Death leans on the table stage left. She passes one hand across her forehead, like someone waking from a deep sleep or hypnotic trance.

AZRAEL. Everything is in order, Madame.

DEATH. Then close the lids. Lock them. My cloak.

Azrael puts the cloak on her shoulders while Raphael closes the suitcases.

Have we forgotten anything?

AZRAEL. No, Madame.

DEATH. Then let's go.

GENTLEMAN IN THE FIRST ROW. Psst!

AZRAEL. Oh, excuse me.

DEATH. What's wrong?

AZRAEL. The watch! Raphael, give the gentleman back his watch, and don't forget to thank him.

Raphael returns the watch.

DEATH. Hurry, Raphael, hurry.

RAPHAEL. I'm hurrying, Madame. I'm ready.

Death moves rapidly. She extends her arms and stands motionless in front of the mirror. Then she walks right into it, followed by her assistants who go through the same ritual. On the table, stage left, in full view of the audience are the rubber gloves which Death forgot to take with her. Immediately following Death's last order to Raphael, we hear Orpheus in the garden.

ORPHEUS. You don't know her the way I do. She makes an act out of it to get me back in the house.

The door opens. They enter. Heurtebise rushes to Eurydice's room, looks in, steps back, and falls to his knees in the doorway.

Where is she? Eurydice! ... I bet she's sulking again. That woman will drive me out of my mind. The horse! Where's the horse?

He uncovers the stall.

Gone! Someone must have opened the door. Someone must have frightened him away. I'll make Eurydice pay for this!

He swings around and starts for Eurydice's room.

HEURTEBISE. Stop!

ORPHEUS. You're not going to keep me out of my own wife's room!

HEURTEBISE. Look.

ORPHEUS. Where?

HEURTEBISE. Look through the glass on my back.

ORPHEUS, *looks through one of the glass panes.* She's fallen asleep in the chair.

HEURTEBISE. She's dead.

ORPHEUS. What?

HEURTEBISE. Dead. We arrived too late.

ORPHEUS. I don't believe it.

He bangs on the glass.

Eurydice, darling! Wake up!

HEURTEBISE. It's no use, I tell you.

ORPHEUS. Get out of the way. I'm going in.

He pushes Heurtebise aside.

Where is she?

Off stage.

She was here, I saw her, sitting in the chair next to the bed. The room's empty!

He returns from Eurydice's room.

Eurydice!

HEURTEBISE. You only thought you saw her. Eurydice has left this house. She's gone to live with Death.

ORPHEUS. I don't care about the horse. I want Eurydice. I want her to forgive me. Help me, Heurtebise. What can I do?

HEURTEBISE. Those few kind words have already helped you, Orpheus . . .

ORPHEUS, *slumps to the table, sobbing.* Dead! Eurydice's dead!

He rises.

Well, I'll get her back, I'll find her again if I have to go all the way to the underworld.

HEURTEBISE. Orpheus . . . Listen to me. Calm yourself and listen to what I have to say.

ORPHEUS. Yes . . . I'll be calm. But think, think of a way . . .

HEURTEBISE. I know one way to do it.

ORPHEUS. You do!

HEURTEBISE. But you'll have to obey me to the letter.

ORPHEUS. I will. I swear I will.

During this dialogue Orpheus answers with a kind of docile fervor. The scene should be played very rapidly.

HEURTEBISE. Death came into your house to take Eurydice.

ORPHEUS. Yes . . .

HEURTEBISE. She forgot her rubber gloves.

A silence. Heurtebise walks to the table. Hesitates. Picks up the gloves gingerly — the way one might handle a holy relic.

ORPHEUS, *terrified.* Oh!

HEURTEBISE. You're going to put them on.

ORPHEUS. If you say so . . .

HEURTEBISE. Put them on, Orpheus.

He hands the gloves to Orpheus who puts them on.

Now you are going to return these gloves to their owner, give them to her yourself.

ORPHEUS. If you say so . . .

HEURTEBISE. Death will be looking for her gloves. If you return them to her, she'll offer a reward. Fundamentally, she's a rather stingy person, she'd rather take away than give; and, since she's had no experience with giving up what people have let her take away, she'll be quite astonished by your gesture. Of course, she won't offer much, but it'll be something.

ORPHEUS. As you say.

HEURTEBISE, *leads Orpheus to the mirror.* Through here.

ORPHEUS. Through the mirror?

HEURTEBISE. For you, Orpheus, I am going to unwrap the secret of secrets. Mirrors are doors. It's through them that Death moves back and forth into life. You're not to tell anyone. Besides, spend your life looking at yourself in a mirror, and you'll see Death at work like a swarm of bees storing up honey in a hive of glass. Good-by. And good luck!

ORPHEUS. But mirrors are solid glass.

HEURTEBISE, *hand held high.* With those gloves you'll pass through mirrors as if they were water.

ORPHEUS. Where did you learn all this?

HEURTEBISE, *hand drops to his side.* Mirrors, you know, are only a special kind of glass. And glass is my business.

ORPHEUS. But once I go through that . . . that door . . .

HEURTEBISE. Take deep rhythmic breaths. Walk fearlessly straight ahead. Turn right, then left, then right, then straight ahead. After that I can't explain . . . except that there are no more directions . . . you just keep on turning. It's quite confusing at first.

ORPHEUS. And then where do I go?

HEURTEBISE. Then? No one can tell you what to do after that. That's where Death begins.

ORPHEUS. I'm not afraid of her.

HEURTEBISE. Good-by, Orpheus. I'll be waiting for your return.

ORPHEUS. I may be gone for a long time.

HEURTEBISE. Long . . . for you. For us it will be only a matter of seeing you walk in and walk out again.

ORPHEUS. I can't believe the mirror's really like water. Well, here goes.

HEURTEBISE, *as Orpheus moves toward the mirror.* Lead with your hands!

Walking with his hands outstretched in front of him, Orpheus plunges into the mirror.

ORPHEUS. Eurydice! . . .

He disappears from view.

Heurtebise remains alone, kneeling in front of the horse's empty stall. There is a knock at the door.

HEURTEBISE. Who is it?

VOICE. The postman. I have a letter for you.

HEURTEBISE. Orpheus isn't home.

VOICE. What about his wife?

HEURTEBISE. She's not home either. Slip the letter under the door.

Someone slides a letter under the door.

VOICE. Where did they go?

HEURTEBISE. Nowhere. They're asleep.

THE ACT CURTAIN FALLS SLOWLY
AND
IMMEDIATELY RISES AGAIN

HEURTEBISE. Who is it?

VOICE. The postman. I have a letter for you.

HEURTEBISE. Orpheus isn't home.

VOICE. What about his wife?

HEURTEBISE. She's not home either. Slip the letter under the door.

VOICE. Where did they go?

HEURTEBISE. Nowhere. They're asleep.

Orpheus steps out of the mirror.

ORPHEUS. Are you still here?

HEURTEBISE. Quick, tell me what happened.

ORPHEUS. My friend, you're an angel.

HEURTEBISE. Not at all.

ORPHEUS. Oh, yes, you are, a real angel. You've saved the day for me.

HEURTEBISE. And Eurydice?

ORPHEUS. Look!

HEURTEBISE. Where?

ORPHEUS. In the mirror. One, two, three.

Eurydice steps out of the mirror.

HEURTEBISE. Eurydice!

EURYDICE. Yes, it's me, the first woman whose husband's love was strong enough to wrest her from the dead.

ORPHEUS. "Lady Eurydice shall return from the underworld." And we thought the horse was talking nonsense.

EURYDICE. Careful, dear. Remember your promise. You are never to mention that horse again.

ORPHEUS. What was I thinking of?

EURYDICE. And you know, Heurtebise, he found the way all by himself, didn't hesitate one second. Wasn't it ingenious of him to think of putting on those rubber gloves?

HEURTEBISE. Yes, wasn't it ingenious?

ORPHEUS, *quickly.* The important thing was to get there, no matter how.

He starts to face Eurydice.

EURYDICE. Watch out!

ORPHEUS. Oh dear!

He freezes.

HEURTEBISE. What's wrong?

ORPHEUS. Nothing important, really. At first I thought I couldn't stand it, but with a little caution we'll make out.

EURYDICE. We'll soon get used to it.

HEURTEBISE. Used to what?

ORPHEUS. I made a pact with them. They let me bring Eurydice back from the underworld, but I must never look at her. If I look at her, she'll disappear.

HEURTEBISE. That's terrible!

EURYDICE. Now don't you discourage my husband!

ORPHEUS, *pulling Heurtebise in front of him.* Let him talk. He won't discourage me. We went through the same thing. You can imagine how upset we were after making the pact — because we had to make it, no matter what. But it is feasible. Not easy, but feasible. Certainly it's better than going completely blind.

EURYDICE. Or losing a leg.

ORPHEUS. You see, we had no choice.

EURYDICE. And there *are* certain advantages. Orpheus will never see me grow old and wrinkled.

HEURTEBISE. Bravo! Then all I have to do is wish you good luck.

ORPHEUS. You're not leaving?

HEURTEBISE. I suddenly feel as if there is one person too many in this room. You must have lots to tell each other.

ORPHEUS. After lunch. The table is set. I'm hungry. You're too much a part of this affair not to have lunch with us.

HEURTEBISE. Are you sure your wife won't object to a third person at the table?

EURYDICE. Not at all, Heurtebise.

Weighing her words.

My travels have changed the face of the earth for me. I've learned a lot, and I'm ashamed of what I was. From now on I intend to be a model wife. Orpheus and I will be living one long honeymoon.

ORPHEUS. Eurydice, remember your promise! You're not supposed to mention the moon again.

EURYDICE. Oh dear, it was my turn to forget. Let's eat lunch! Heurtebise, you sit here, on my right. Sit down, please. Orpheus, across the table.

HEURTEBISE. Not where he can see you!

ORPHEUS. By the gods, I'm glad we invited you, Heurtebise. I'll sit on your left with my back turned. So what, I'll hold the plate on my knees.

Eurydice serves them.

HEURTEBISE. I'm dying to hear about your trip.

ORPHEUS. It's not easy to put into words. I still feel like a man just out of the hospital after a major operation. I vaguely remember reciting one of my poems to stay awake, and then there were all those disgusting beasts dozing away. Then a big black pit. Then there I was, talking to a lady who wasn't there. She thanked me for her gloves, though. A kind of surgeon took them from me and showed me the way out. He said that Eurydice would follow me and that I was not, under any circumstances, to look at her. I'm thirsty!

He picks up his glass and turns around.

EURYDICE AND HEURTEBISE. Watch out!

EURYDICE. What a scare! Darling, without turning around, just feel my heart pounding.

ORPHEUS. This is ridiculous. Maybe I should bandage my eyes.

HEURTEBISE. I'd advise you not to do that. It's against the rules. If you cheat, you lose everything.

ORPHEUS. You can't imagine the effort it takes to carry out those stupid rules.

EURYDICE. But darling, if you'd just stop mooning . . .

ORPHEUS. There's that moon again! You might as well call me nuts.

EURYDICE. Orpheus!

ORPHEUS. Save the moon-talk for your old playmates.

Silence.

HEURTEBISE. Orpheus!

ORPHEUS. I'm a priest of the sun.

EURYDICE. Not any more, my dear.

ORPHEUS. As you like. Anyway, don't mention the moon in my house again.

Silence.

EURYDICE. If you knew how insignificant all this talk is about the sun and the moon.

ORPHEUS. It's beneath you, I suppose.

EURYDICE. If only I could find the words to . . .

ORPHEUS. It seems to me that for someone who can't find the words you're using an awful lot of them.

Eurydice starts to cry. Silence.

HEURTEBISE. Now you've made her cry.

ORPHEUS. You stay out of this.

He swings around.

EURYDICE. Don't!

HEURTEBISE. Careful!

ORPHEUS. It's her own fault. She'd make the dead sit up and wail.

EURYDICE. I should have stayed dead.

Silence.

ORPHEUS. As for the moon! If I let her go on about that, you know where we'd be. It'd be the horse affair all over again.

HEURTEBISE. Don't exaggerate . . .

ORPHEUS. So I'm exaggerating?

HEURTEBISE. Yes.

ORPHEUS. Well, what if I am exaggerating.

He swings around.

EURYDICE. Watch out!

HEURTEBISE, *to Eurydice.* Don't cry. Orpheus, you are going to spoil everything.

ORPHEUS. Well, what if I am exaggerating! Who started it?

EURYDICE. Not me.

ORPHEUS. Not you! Not you!

He swings around again.

EURYDICE AND HEURTEBISE. Careful!

HEURTEBISE. You're a dangerous man, my friend.

ORPHEUS. Correct. And in that case the best thing for me to do is to leave you alone.

He rises. Eurydice and Heurtebise grab his coat and prevent him from leaving.

EURYDICE. Darling . . .

HEURTEBISE. Orpheus . . .

ORPHEUS. No, no. Let me go.

HEURTEBISE. Be sensible.

ORPHEUS. I'll be anything I want.

EURYDICE. Don't leave me.

She tugs on his coat. He trips, loses his balance, turns, and stares at her. He cries out. Terrified, Eurydice rises to full height. On her face we read horror. The light dims as Eurydice slowly collapses and disappears. The lights come up again.

HEURTEBISE. It was inevitable.

ORPHEUS, *pale, weak, forcing a kind of carefree attitude.* Oof! Now I feel better.

HEURTEBISE. What did you say?

ORPHEUS, *with the same fake nonchalance.* Now we can breathe freely.

HEURTEBISE. He's out of his mind.

ORPHEUS, *covering his discomfort with anger.* A man has to be firm with women, show he can get along without them. Otherwise, they lead you around by the nose.

HEURTEBISE. Are you trying to say that you looked at her on purpose?

ORPHEUS. How else would I look at her?

HEURTEBISE. But you lost your balance; it wasn't **your** fault you turned your head. I saw it happen.

ORPHEUS. I lost my balance on purpose. I turned my head on purpose. And don't contradict me.

Silence.

HEURTEBISE. You don't expect me to congratulate you, I hope.

ORPHEUS. I can do without your congratulations. I'm quite capable of congratulating myself for having looked my wife in the face. Well, it's better than staring at other men's wives, isn't it?

HEURTEBISE. Is that intended for me?

ORPHEUS. Take it any way you like.

HEURTEBISE. You're unfair, Opheus. I never made love to your wife and she would never have permitted it. She was a perfect lady. You didn't realize it until you lost her for the first time, and now you've lost her again — stupidly, tragically lost her, lost yourself, killed her when she was already dead, played with life and death as if you were playing just another game. Because she *is* dead, twice dead. And she won't come back again.

ORPHEUS. That's what you think!

HEURTEBISE. That's what I think.

ORPHEUS. Did you ever see a woman leave the table, swearing she'd never come back, who didn't return meek as a lamb in time for dessert?

HEURTEBISE. I'll give you five minutes to come to your senses.

Orpheus throws his napkin on the floor. Rises. Walks around the table. Looks at the mirror, crosses to the door, and picks up the letter.

ORPHEUS, *opening the letter.* What's this?

HEURTEBISE. Bad news?

ORPHEUS. I can't read it. It's written backward.

HEURTEBISE. That's an old trick to disguise the writing. Hold it up to the mirror. Now, read what it says.

ORPHEUS, *holding letter in front of the mirror and reading*. "Dear Sir: Excuse me if I choose to remain anonymous, but someone should inform you of the danger you're in. Aglaonice has discovered that if you translated into French your sentence about Lady Eurydice returning from the underworld and take the first letter of each word, the result is a four-letter sentiment which may be construed as an insult to the judges of the poetry contest. By translating your sentence into French and capitalizing the initial letters, Aglaonice has convinced the judges that you are a phony. She has roused half the women in town against you. In fact, there is a crowd of raving females on its way to your house now. The Bacchantes are with them, fanning their anger, screaming for your head. If you want to save yourself, you must hide from them. There's not a minute to lose. An unknown friend . . ."

HEURTEBISE. I don't believe a word of it.

In the distance, we hear wild rhythms of drums beating.

ORPHEUS. Listen . . .

HEURTEBISE. Drums.

ORPHEUS. *Their* drums. Eurydice was right. The horse was bait in a trap they set to catch me.

HEURTEBISE. They can't string up a man for a word.

ORPHEUS. The word's only an excuse. Their hate runs so deep it's a religion to them. Aglaonice was waiting for her chance and now she's got it.

HEURTEBISE. The drums are coming nearer.

ORPHEUS. Why didn't I see that letter before? How long has it been on the floor?

HEURTEBISE. It's my fault, Orpheus. The postman slipped the letter under the door while you were traveling in the underworld. I was so excited by your wife's return that I forgot to tell you about it. Do what the unknown friend advises: hide yourself.

ORPHEUS. It's too late.

The horse magic has completely disappeared. Orpheus is a changed man.

HEURTEBISE. You can hide in the caves behind the house. I'll tell them you're away on a trip.

ORPHEUS. It's no use, Heurtebise. It's no use trying to avoid the inevitable.

HEURTEBISE. I'll save you despite yourself.

ORPHEUS. I won't let you.

HEURTEBISE. But it makes no sense.

ORPHEUS. The mirror is solid now. It read the letter for me. There's only one thing left for me to do.

HEURTEBISE. What's that?

ORPHEUS. Join Eurydice.

HEURTEBISE. But you can't do that again.

ORPHEUS. Oh, yes, I can.

HEURTEBISE. And even if you do find her, it will be the same old quarrel all over again.

ORPHEUS, *ecstatic.* Not in the place she's calling from.

HEURTEBISE. Look at your face, it's contracted with pain. I won't let you throw yourself away like this.

ORPHEUS. It's those drums! Those drums! They're coming for me, Heurtebise. They'll soon be here.

HEURTEBISE. You've done the impossible before.

ORPHEUS. The impossible is what I've lived for.

HEURTEBISE. You've survived other conspiracies.

ORPHEUS. But I've never fought to the last drop of blood.

HEURTEBISE, *his face illuminated with a supernatural joy.* Orpheus, you frighten me . . .

ORPHEUS. What thoughts does the marble think while the sculptor chisels its veins to make a masterpiece? The marble thinks: someone's striking me, destroying me, insulting me, breaking me — I'm doomed to die. The marble is wrong to think those thoughts. It's life that's chipping away at my veins, chiseling a new form, Heurtebise. She'll make me into a work of art. It's my duty to let her hammer away — without trying to understand. Make myself hard. Accept the blows as they come, try to help her, work along with her, but let her finish the task herself.

HEURTEBISE. Watch out for the stones!

Stones come crashing through the windows.

ORPHEUS. Glass! Luck's on my side. I'll have the image I've always dreamed of.

A stone breaks the mirror.

HEURTEBISE. The mirror!

ORPHEUS. Oh no, they mustn't break the mirror!

He rushes onto the balcony.

HEURTEBISE. They'll cut you to pieces.

ORPHEUS, *on the balcony, back to the audience, he leans on the balustrade.* Ladies!

Drum roll.

Ladies!

Drum roll.

Ladies!

Drum roll.

Orpheus moves left on the balcony, out of view. His voice is drowned in the noise of drums. A shadow moves across the stage. Heurtebise covers his face and kneels.

Suddenly an object comes hurtling through the window. It is Orpheus' head. It falls to the floor and rolls toward the footlights. Heurtebise lets out a feeble cry. Drums fade in the distance.

ORPHEUS' HEAD, *the voice of a wounded man.* Where am I? It's dark in here. My head aches. My whole body hurts. I must have fallen off the balcony. I must have fallen from way up high, way up high . . . Where's my head? Oh, of course, that's what's talking — my head. But where is it? Where's my head? Eurydice! Heurtebise! Help! Put on the lights, Eurydice, I can't see my legs. I can't feel my head any more. They've gone, both of them — no head, no body. I'm empty now, empty all over. Help! Help! Somebody wake me up! Eurydice!

A moan.

Eurydice . . . Eurydice . . . Eurydice . . .

Eurydice steps out of the mirror. She stands motionless.

EURYDICE. Did you call me, darling?

ORPHEUS' HEAD. Is that you, Eurydice?

EURYDICE. It's me.

ORPHEUS' HEAD. Where's the rest of me? Where did I put my body?

EURYDICE. You mustn't get upset. Just give me your hand.

ORPHEUS' HEAD. Where's my head?

EURYDICE, *taking an invisible body by the hand.* There, hand in hand. Now, walk. You mustn't be afraid. Just come along with me ...

ORPHEUS' HEAD. But where's my body?

EURYDICE. Next to mine, pressed close. Now that you can't see me any more, I can take you back with me.

ORPHEUS' HEAD. But my head, Eurydice . . . my head ... where did I put it?

EURYDICE. Forget your head, darling. You'll never have to worry about your head again ...

Eurydice leads the invisible body through the mirror and disappears.

A knock at the door. Silence. Heurtebise looks up but does not answer. Knocks. Still no answer.

COMMISSIONER'S VOICE. Open in the name of the law.

HEURTEBISE. Who's there?

COMMISSIONER'S VOICE. The police. Open the door or we'll force our way in.

HEURTEBISE, I'm coming.

He moves quickly to Orpheus' head. Picks it up. Places the head on the pedestal and then opens the door wide so that it covers the pedestal from view. It is at this moment that the actor playing Orpheus substitutes his own head for the papier-mâché replica. The Commissioner enters, followed by his clerk.

COMMISSIONER. Why didn't you answer the first time I knocked?

HEURTEBISE. But. Judge, I ...

COMMISSIONER. Commissioner, please.

HEURTEBISE. But, Commissioner, I'm a friend of the family . . . I was still recovering from the shock . . .

COMMISSIONER. Shock? What shock?

HEURTEBISE. I was alone with Orpheus when it happened.

COMMISSIONER. When what happened?

HEURTEBISE. The murder . . . When Orpheus was murdered by the Bacchantes.

COMMISSIONER, *turning to his Clerk.* Just what we expected him to say. And the victim's wife . . . where is she? We'll see what she says about your story.

HEURTEBISE. She's gone.

COMMISSIONER. How convenient!

HEURTEBISE. She'd already left her husband before the crime was committed.

COMMISSIONER. You don't say!

To Clerk.

Why don't you sit at the table so you can take notes.

The Clerk sits at the writing table where pen and paper are waiting for him. The Clerk starts to sit, his back to the mirror, but Heurtebise is in his way so he has to drag the table upstage where it blocks the exit.

HEURTEBISE. But I . . .

CLERK. Quiet, you!

COMMISSIONER. Now, one thing at a time. And don't speak unless you're spoken to. Where's the body?

HEURTEBISE. What body?

COMMISSIONER. When there's a crime there's always a body. Where is it?

HEURTEBISE. But, Commissioner, there is no body. It was torn to pieces, decapitated, and carried away by those raving women.

COMMISSIONER. *Primo,* you are not to insult those ladies. They were performing a holy duty. *Secondo,* I have five hundred eyewitnesses who will say you're not telling the truth.

HEURTEBISE: You mean ... ?

COMMISSIONER. Quiet!

HEURTEBISE. But I ...

COMMISSIONER, *pompously.* Quiet, I said. Now listen carefully, young man. This afternoon there was an eclipse of the sun. This eclipse has brought about a reversal of public sentiment in favor of Orpheus. The whole town is in mourning. We're going to have a state funeral and the authorities want to take possession of his mortal remains. Now it so happens that the Bacchantes saw Orpheus walk out onto the balcony, smeared with blood and crying for help. I know they had come to make trouble for him, but they (and five hundred other witnesses) would have flown to his side if he hadn't fallen to the ground, dead, right in front of their eyes.

I repeat. The ladies had organized a mass protest, they were out to make trouble by shouting "Down with Orpheus" when suddenly the window opened and a blood-drenched Orpheus rushed onto the balcony screaming for help. The ladies would have rushed to his side, but it was too late. Orpheus tumbled to the ground, and all five hundred of them (don't forget that these were women ... and women make a lot of noise, but they can't stand the sight of blood), all five hundred of them took to their heels and ran. And then an eclipse of the sun. In town they interpret the eclipse as a sign that the sun is angry at this lack of respect for one of its former priests. The authorities assembled and went out to meet the crowd returning from Orpheus' house. Speaking for the women, all five hundred of them, Aglaonice described the strange crime they had witnessed outside

that window. The whole town is up in arms. We have riot
squads patrolling the streets. And they've sent *me*, the Chief
of Police, to interrogate you on the scene of the crime. So
you see, I do not expect to be treated like any ordinary cop
on the beat. Enough said.

HEURTEBISE. But I didn't mean to . . .

CLERK. Quiet! Nobody asked your opinion.

COMMISSIONER. Now, one thing at a time.

To Clerk.

Where was I?

CLERK. The head. May I remind you, sir, about the head?

COMMISSIONER. Oh yes, the bust of Orpheus.

To Heurtebise.

Do you live here?

HEURTEBISE. I'm a friend of the family.

COMMISSIONER. The town fathers want a bust of Orpheus
to carry in the procession. Is there one in the house?

*Heurtebise walks to the door, closes it. We see the head
on the pedestal. The Commissioner and the Clerk turn to
look at it.*

COMMISSIONER. It doesn't look much like him.

HEURTEBISE. I find it quite beautiful.

COMMISSIONER. Who's it by?

HEURTEBISE. I don't know.

COMMISSIONER. Didn't the artist sign it?

HEURTEBISE. No.

COMMISSIONER. Take this down: one bust, presumed to be
head of Orpheus.

HEURTEBISE. It's Orpheus, all right, I'm sure of that. What's in doubt is the sculptor.

COMMISSIONER. Cross that out. Write: one head of Orpheus, artist unknown.

To Heurtebise.

Name?

HEURTEBISE. Pardon?

CLERK. He asked for your name? Last name first, please.

COMMISSIONER. A matter of form, that's all; I know whom I'm dealing with.

He walks to window and taps the panes.

Young man, you're the glazier.

HEURTEBISE, *smiling.* I admit it.

COMMISSIONER. Admit everything, young man. That will be your best defense.

CLERK. Excuse me, Commissioner, but wouldn't it save time if we just asked for his papers?

COMMISSIONER. Give the clerk your papers, young man.

HEURTEBISE. But I . . . I don't have any.

COMMISSIONER. What's that?

CLERK. Oh-oh!

COMMISSIONER. You've been walking around with no papers? Where are they? Where do you live?

HEURTEBISE. I live . . . that is, I used to live . . .

COMMISSIONER. I don't care where you used to live. I want your present address.

HEURTEBISE. Right now I don't have any.

COMMISSIONER. No papers. No residence. A clear case of vagrancy. How old are you?

HEURTEBISE, *hesitating*, I . . .

COMMISSIONER, *turning away, eyes to the ceiling, in the manner of a professional cross-examiner.* I suppose you do have an age . . .

ORPHEUS' HEAD. Eighteen.

CLERK, *writing.* Seventeen.

ORPHEUS' HEAD. Eighteen.

COMMISSIONER. Place of birth?

CLERK. Not so fast, Commissioner. I've got to erase something.

Eurydice appears in the mirror and puts one foot into the room.

EURYDICE. Heurtebise . . . Heurtebise . . . I've found out who you are. Come with us, we're waiting for you.

Heurtebise hesitates.

ORPHEUS' HEAD. Hurry, Heurtebise. Go with my wife. I'll answer his questions — even if I have to make something up.

Heurtebise disappears into the mirror.

CLERK. I'm ready, Commissioner.

COMMISSIONER. Place of birth?

ORPHEUS' HEAD. Maisons-Laffitte.

CLERK. What's that?

ORPHEUS' HEAD. Maisons-Laffitte. Two *f*'s and two *t*'s.

COMMISSIONER. Well, now that you've told us where you were born, maybe you can remember your name . . .

ORPHEUS' HEAD. Jean.

COMMISSIONER. Jean what?

ORPHEUS' HEAD. Jean Cocteau.

COMMISSIONER. Coc . . .

ORPHEUS' HEAD. C - O - C - T - E - A - U. Cocteau.

COMMISSIONER. That's a name to walk the streets with. Unless, of course, you've changed your mind and will tell us where you live . . .

ORPHEUS' HEAD. Number 10, Rue d'Anjou.

COMMISSIONER. That's more like it.

CLERK. Sign here, please . . .

COMMISSIONER. Give him the pen.

To Heurtebise.

Over here, young man. Over here. He won't eat you.

He turns around.

Well!

CLERK. What's wrong?

COMMISSIONER. Thunder in heaven, the accused has disappeared!

CLERK. Magic!

COMMISSIONER. Magic . . . magic! There's no such thing.

He paces the stage.

I refuse to believe in magic. An eclipse is an eclipse. A table is a table. An accused is an accused. Now, one thing at a time. That door . . .

CLERK. Impossible, sir. If he went out that door he'd have jostled my chair.

COMMISSIONER. That leaves the window.

CLERK. If he went out that window he'd have walked in front of us. Besides, he was answering questions until you turned around.

COMMISSIONER. Well then?

CLERK. I can't imagine what happened to him.

COMMISSIONER. Then the murderer must have escaped through a secret door. Anyway, we have our proof. If he ran away that proves he's the criminal. Tap the walls, see if they're solid.

The clerk taps the walls.

CLERK. They sound solid to me.

COMMISSIONER. Good. That means he's hiding somewhere in this room. And I don't intend to give him the satisfaction of watching us search.

In a loud voice.

I have the house surrounded. If he goes into the garden he'll be caught. If he stays inside he'll starve to death.

CLERK. This is scandalous.

COMMISSIONER. What's scandalous about it? You see a scandal everywhere you look.

They leave. When the door opens it covers the bust and the actor substitutes a papier-mâché head for his own on the pedestal. The stage remains empty for a moment. Then the Commissioner returns.

We forgot the bust of Orpheus.

CLERK. It wouldn't do to go back empty-handed.

COMMISSIONER. There it is. Take it.

The clerk takes the head off the pedestal and follows the Commissioner from the room.

The walls of the room fly upward, out of view. Orpheus and Eurydice, guided by Heurtebise, step out of the mirror. They look around, as if seeing the room for the first time. They sit at the table. Eurydice motions to Heurtebise to sit on her right. All smile. They are the image of contentment.

EURYDICE. Shall I pour the wine, dear?

ORPHEUS. Not yet. First let's say grace.

The three of them stand while Orpheus recites his prayer.

Dear God, we thank you for having made heaven of our home and for revealing your heaven to us. We thank you for having sent Heurtebise to guide us, and we are ashamed for not having recognized him as our guardian angel. We thank you for having saved Eurydice — since, for love of me, she killed the devil in the form of a horse and died a horrible death. We thank you for having saved me — since I worship poetry and poetry is what you are. Amen.

They sit down.

HEURTEBISE. Shall I serve the wine?

ORPHEUS, *respectfully*. Let Eurydice do it . . .

Eurydice pours him a glass of wine.

HEURTEBISE. And maybe at last we'll get something to eat.

CURTAIN

THE
EIFFEL
TOWER
WEDDING
PARTY
translated by
DUDLEY FITTS

PREFACE

Every work of the poetic order contains what Gide, in his preface to *Paludes,* so aptly calls "God's share." This "Share," which eludes the poet himself, can surprise him. Such and such a phrase or gesture, which originally meant no more to him than the third dimension means to a painter, has a hidden meaning that each person will interpret in his own way. The true Symbol is never planned: it emerges by itself, so long as the bizarre, the unreal, do not enter into the reckoning.

In a fairyland, the fairies do not appear. They walk invisibly there. To mortal eyes they can appear only on the terra firma of everyday. The unsophisticated mind is more likely than the others to see the fairies, for it will not oppose to the marvelous the resistance of the hardheaded. I might almost say that the Chief Electrician, with his reflections, has often illuminated a piece for me.

I have been reading in Antoine's memoirs of the scandal provoked by the presence on the stage of real quarters of beef and a fountain of real water. But now, thanks to Antoine, we have come to such a pass that the audience is displeased if real objects are *not* used on the stage, and if it is not subjected to a plot precisely as complex, precisely as tedious, as those from which the theater should serve as a distraction.*

*Writing of *Orphée* in 1926, Antoine called it "a studio-farce, not even funny" (sic).

The Eiffel Tower Wedding Party, because of its candor, was first of all mistaken for a bit of esoteric writing. The mysterious inspires in the public a sort of fear. Here, I renounce mystery. I illuminate everything, I underline everything. Sunday vacuity, human livestock, ready-made expressions, dissociation of ideas into flesh and bone, the fierce cruelty of childhood, the miraculous poetry of daily life: these are my play, so well understood by the young musicians who composed the score for it.

A remark of the Photographer's might do well for my epigraph: "Since these mysteries are beyond me, let's pretend that I arranged them all the time." This is our motto, par excellence. Your prig always finds a last refuge in responsibility. Thus, for example, he will go on fighting a war after the end has been reached.

In *Wedding Party,* God's share is considerable. To the right and left of the scene the human phonographs (like the ancient Chorus, like the *compère* and *commère* of our music-hall stage), describe, without the least "literature," the absurd action which is unfolded, danced, and pantomimed between them. I say "absurd" because instead of trying to keep this side of the absurdity of life, to lessen it, to arrange it as we arrange the story of an incident in which we played an uncomplimentary part, I accentuate it, I push it forward, I try to paint *more truly than the truth.*

The poet ought to disengage objects and ideas from their veiling mists; he ought to display them suddenly, so nakedly and so quickly that they are scarcely recognizable. It is then that they strike us with their youth, as though they had never become official dotards.

This is the case with commonplaces — old, powerful, generally esteemed after the manner of masterpieces, but whose original beauty, because of long use, no longer surprises us.

In my play I rejuvenate the commonplace. It is my concern to present it in such a light that it recaptures its teens.

A generation devoted to obscurity, to jaded realism, does not give way before the shrug of a shoulder. I know that my text has too "obvious" an air, that it is too *readably writ-ten*, like the alphabets in school. But aren't we in school? Aren't we still deciphering the elementary symbols?

The young music finds itself in an analogous position. It employs a clarity, a simplicity, a good humor, that are new. The ingenuous ear is deceived: it seems to be listening to a café orchestra, but it is as mistaken as would be an eye which could not distinguish between a loud garish material and the same material copied by Ingres.

In *Wedding Party* we employ all the popular resources that France will have none of at home, but will approve whenever a musician, native or foreign, exploits them outside.

Do you think, for example, that a Russian can hear the *Pétrouchka* just as we do? In addition to the charms of that musical masterpiece he finds there his childhood, his Sundays in Petrograd, the lullabies of nurses.

Why should I deny myself this double pleasure? I assure you that the orchestra of *The Eiffel Tower Wedding Party* moves me more than any number of Russian or Spanish dances. It is not a question of honor rolls. I think I have sufficiently exalted Russian, German, and Spanish musicians (to say nothing of Negro orchestras) to permit myself this *cri du coeur*.

It is curious to observe the French everywhere repulsing bitterly whatever is truly French and embracing unreservedly the local alien spirit. It is curious, too, that in the case of *Wedding Party* an audience at a dress rehearsal should have been outraged by a classic blockhead character whose presence in the wedding cortege was neither more nor less controversial than the presence of the commonplaces in the text.

Every living work of art has its own ballyhoo, and only this is seen by those who stay outside. Now in the case of new work, this first impression so shocks, irritates, angers the spectator that he will not enter. He is repelled from its true nature by its face, by the unfamiliar outward appearance which distracts him as would a clown grimacing at the door. It is this phenomenon which deceives even those critics who are least slaves to convention. They forget that they are at a performance which must be followed just as attentively as a "popular success." They think that they are watching a sort of street carnival. A conscientious critic who would never think of writing, "The Duchess kisses the Steward" instead of "The Steward presents a letter to the Duchess" in his review of one of these "legitimate" dramas, will not hesitate, reviewing *Wedding Party,* to make the Bicycle Girl or the Collector come out of the camera — which is absurd enough. Not the organized absurdity, the desirable, the good absurdity, but simply the absurd. And he can never see the difference. Alone among the critics, M. Bidou explained to the readers of *Débats* that my piece was "a composition of active wit."*

The action of my piece is pictorial, though the text itself is not. The fact is that I am trying to substitute a "theater poetry" for the usual "poetry in the theater." "Poetry in the theater" is a delicate lace, invisible at any considerable distance. "Theater poetry" should be a coarse lace, a lace of rigging, a ship upon the sea. *Wedding Party* can be as terrifying as a drop of poetry under the microscope. The scenes fit together like the words of a poem.

The secret of theatrical success is this: you must set a decoy at the door so that part of your audience can amuse themselves there while the rest are inside. Shakspere, Molière, and the profound Chaplin know this well.

After the hisses, confusion, and applause which marked the first performance of my piece by the Swedish dancers at the Champs-Elysées, I should have set it down as a failure if the audience of the "informed" had not given place to the real public. This public always gives me a hearing.

*Only he could write of *Orphée* that it was "a meditation on death."

After the performance a lady complained to me that the piece did not carry beyond the footlights. Seeing that I was astonished by her criticism (for masks and megaphones are more effective beyond the footlights than ordinary voices and make-up), she went on to explain that she so greatly admired the ceiling of Maurice Denis, who decorated the theater, that she had engaged the highest seats in the house — which necessarily lessened her command of what was going on on the stage.

I cite this as an example of the criticism offered by that little group with neither intelligence nor sympathy, the little group that the newspapers call "the élite."

Moreover, our senses are so unused to reacting together that the critics — even my publishers — found it hard to believe that this complicated machinery did not entail two or three pages of text. This faulty perspective must also be blamed upon the absence of the development of ideas: a development that the ear customarily perceives, since the symbolic drama and the drama à thèse. (Jarry's Ubu and Apollinaire's Les mamelles de Tirésias are both symbolic dramas and dramas à thèse).

The diction of my human phonographs, Pierre Bertin and Marcel Herrand, also comes in for its share in the general misunderstanding: a diction black as ink, immense and clear as the lettering of a billboard. Here, surprisingly enough, are actors who are content to follow the text, rather than force the text to follow them: still another lyric novelty to which the audience is not accustomed!

Let us touch on the accusation of buffoonery, which has often been hurled at me by our age — an age preoccupied with the false-sublime, an age (let's admit it) still in love with Wagner.

If Cold means Night, and Hot means Light, Lukewarm means Dusk. Ghosts love the dusk. The crowd loves the lukewarm. Very well: aside from the fact that the buffoon attitude brings with it a clarity that is ill-suited to ghosts

(by "ghosts" I mean what the crowd calls "poems"); aside
from the fact that Molière proved himself more of a poet
in his *Pourceaugnac* and *Le bourgeois gentilhomme* than
in his poetic dramas: the buffoon attitude is the only one
that permits certain audacities.

People come to the theater for relaxation. It is easy to
amuse them with the dancing dolls, to tickle them with the
candies that one gives recalcitrant children to make them
take their medicine. But once the medicine is taken, we
shall pass on to other exercises.

Thanks to people like Sergei Diaghilev and Rolf de
Maré, little by little there is coming into being in France a
theatrical form which is not properly the Ballet, and which
has no place in the Opéra, the Opéra-Comique, or the fashionable theaters. The future is indicated on the fringe of
these conventional forms. Our friend Lugné-Poë has admitted this with considerable apprehension in one of his arti-
cles. This new form, more consonant with the modern spirit,
remains still an unexplored land, rich in possibilities.

Revolution which flings the doors wide open for the ex-
perimentalists! The new generation will continue to experiment with forms in which the fairy, the dance, acrobatics,
pantomime, drama, satire, music, and the spoken word all
combine to produce a novel genre: and unaided, they will
stage pieces which the official "artists" will take for studio-
farces, pieces which for all that will be no less the plastic
expression of poetry.

The mixture of good humor and bad humor in Paris cre-
ates the most vital atmosphere in the world. Sergei Diaghilev told me one day that he had felt nothing like it in any
other capital. Hisses and cheers; nasty reviews, with here
and there an unexpected approval: and three years later
the scoffers are applauding and cannot remember having
once hissed. Such is the history of my *Parade*, and of any
other piece that alters the rules of the game.

A theatrical piece ought to be written, mounted, costumed, furnished with musical accompaniment, played, and

danced, all by one and the same man. Such a universal athlete does not exist, and the next best thing is to replace the individual by what is most like an individual: a friendly group.

There are many cliques, but few such groups. I am fortunate enough to belong to one made up of various young musicians, poets, and painters. *The Eiffel Tower Wedding Party,* taken as a whole, is the manifesto of a poetic spirit to which I am proud to have contributed already a great deal.

Thanks to Jean Victor-Hugo, my characters, instead of being (as is so often the case in the theater) too small, too true to life to be able to support the mass of lighting and décor, were constructed, corrected, built up, raised by every device of artistry to a likeness on an epic scale. I find in Jean Victor-Hugo a certain atavism of monstrous reality.

Thanks to Irène Lagut, our Eiffel Tower suggests forget-me-nots and lace valentines.

Georges Auric's Overture, *The Fourteenth of July* — marching bands whose music blares out at the street corner and moves away — calls up the strong enchantment of the sidewalk, of the popular fair, of red-festooned grandstands like guillotines, where drums and trumpets make the stenographers and the sailors and the shipping clerks dance. And his *ritournelles* accompany the pantomime just as a circus band repeats a motif during an acrobatic act.

The same atmosphere breathes through Milhaud's *Wedding March,* through Germaine Tailleferre's *Quadrille* and *Waltz of the Telegrams,* through Poulenc's *The General's Speech* and *The Trouville Bathing Beauty.* Arthur Honegger amused himself by making fun of what our musicographers gravely call: MUSIC. It is unnecessary to add that they all fell into the trap. Hardly had the first notes of the *Funeral March* sounded when all those long ears pricked up in grave attention. Not one noticed that that march was beautiful as a sarcasm, written with a taste, an extraordinary feeling for appositeness: not one of the critics, all of whom praised the piece, recognized the Waltz in *Faust* which served as its bass!

How can I express my gratitude to MM. Rolf de Maré and Borlin? The former with his generous insight, the latter with his modesty, made it possible for me to crystallize a formula with which I had been experimenting in *Parade* and in *Le Boeuf sur le toit*.

JEAN COCTEAU

1922

Les Mariés de la Tour Eiffel was first played on June 8, 1921, by Rolf de Maré's Swedish Ballet Company. The choreography was by Jean Cocteau and Jean Borlin, the décor by Irène Lagut, and the costumes and masks by Jean Victor-Hugo. The musical program was as follows:

Overture	Georges Auric
Wedding March (entrance)	Darius Milhaud
The General's Speech	Francis Poulenc
The Trouville Bathing Beauty	Francis Poulenc
The Massacre (fugue)	Darius Milhaud
Waltz of the Radiograms	Germaine Tailleferre
Funeral March	Arthur Honegger
Quadrille	Germaine Tailleferre
Wedding March (exit)	Darius Milhaud

During the course of the action there were three *ritournelles* by Georges Auric.

CHARACTERS

PHONOGRAPH I
PHONOGRAPH II
THE OSTRICH
THE HUNTER
THE MANAGER OF THE EIFFEL TOWER
THE PHOTOGRAPHER
THE BRIDE
THE BRIDEGROOM
THE MOTHER-IN-LAW
THE FATHER-IN-LAW
THE GENERAL
TWO BRIDESMAIDS
TWO USHERS
THE CYCLIST
THE CHILD
THE TROUVILLE BATHING BEAUTY
THE LION
THE COLLECTOR OF PAINTINGS
THE ART DEALER
FIVE RADIOGRAMS

DÉCOR

The first platform of the Eiffel Tower. The backdrop represents a bird's-eye view of Paris. Upstage, right, a camera at eye level: the black funnel forms a corridor extending to the wings, and the camera front opens like a door to permit the entrances and exits of the characters. Downstage, right and left, half hidden by the proscenium arch, two actors costumed as Phonographs: their bodies are the cabinets, their mouths the horns. It is these Phonographs which comment on the action and recite the lines of the characters. They should speak very loudly and quickly, pronouncing each syllable distinctly. The action is simultaneous with the comments of the Phonographs.

THE EIFFEL TOWER WEDDING PARTY

The curtain rises with the drum-roll which ends the Overture. Empty set.

PHONO I. You are on the first platform of the Eiffel Tower.

PHONO II. Look! An ostrich. She crosses the stage. She goes off. And here's the Hunter. He's tracking the ostrich. He looks up. He sees something. He raises his gun. He fires.

PHONO I. Heavens! A radiogram.

A large blue radiogram falls from above.

PHONO II. The shot wakes up the Manager of the Eiffel Tower. He appears.

PHONO I. Hey, Mac, where do you think you are — hunting?

PHONO II. I was trailing an ostrich. I thought I saw it on the cables of the Eiffel Tower.

PHONO I. And you kill me a radiogram!

PHONO II. I didn't mean to do it.

PHONO I. End of the dialogue.

PHONO II. Here comes the Photographer of the Eiffel Tower. He speaks. What is he saying?

PHONO I. You haven't seen an ostrich around here anywhere, have you?

PHONO II. I most certainly have! I'm trailing it right now!

PHONO I. Well, it's like this: my camera's out of order. Usually when I say, "Steady, now, watch for the little bird" — a little bird comes out. This morning I said to a lady,

"Watch for the little bird!" — and out came an ostrich. So now I am looking for the ostrich in order to make it get back into the camera.

PHONO II. Ladies and Gentlemen, the situation is getting complicated, for the Manager of the Eiffel Tower has suddenly discovered that the radiogram was addressed to him.

PHONO I. He opens it.

PHONO II. MANAGER EIFFEL TOWER STOP ARRIVE WEDDING BREAKFAST PLEASE RESERVE TABLE.

PHONO I. But this radiogram is dead.

PHONO II. It's precisely because it's dead that everyone can understand it.

PHONO I. Quick quick! We've just got time to set the table. I remit your fine. I appoint you Waiter of the Eiffel Tower. Photographer, on your job!

PHONO II. They set the table.

PHONO I. Wedding March.

PHONO II. Wedding Procession.

Wedding march. The Phonographs announce the members of the wedding party, who enter in pairs, strutting like trained dogs in an animal act.

PHONO I. The bride, sweet as a lamb.

PHONO II. The father-in-law, rich as Croesus.

PHONO I. The bridegroom, handsome as a matinee idol.

PHONO II. The mother-in-law, snide as a wooden nickel.

PHONO I. The General, dumb as a goose.

PHONO II. Look at him. He thinks he's on his mare Mirabelle.

PHONO I. The ushers, strong as Turks.

PHONO II. The bridesmaids, fresh as roses.

PHONO I. The manager of the Eiffel Tower is doing them the honors of the Eiffel Tower. He is giving them a bird's-eye view of Paris.

PHONO II. It makes me dizzy!

The Hunter and the Manager bring in a table with plates painted on it. The cloth sweeps the ground.

PHONO I. The General is shouting, "Sit down, Sit down!" The wedding party sits down to the table.

PHONO II. All on one side of the table, so that the audience can see them.

PHONO I. The General rises.

PHONO II. Speech by the General.

The General's discourse is orchestral. He merely gesticulates.

PHONO I. Everyone is deeply moved.

PHONO II. After his speech the General describes a mirage that deceived him in Africa.

PHONO I. I was eating pie with the Duc d'Aumale. The pie was covered with wasps. We tried to brush them away. No luck. Well, those wasps were tigers.

PHONO II. What?

PHONO I. Tigers. Thousands of them, all stalking around. A mirage had projected their image, much reduced, onto our pie, and we took them for wasps.

PHONO II. You would never think he was seventy-four years old.

PHONO I. But who is this charming bicycle girl in shorts?

Enter Cyclist in shorts. She dismounts.

PHONO II, *girl's voice*. Excuse me, gentlemen. . . .

PHONO I. Madam, in what way can we be of service to you?

PHONO II. Am I on the right road for Chatou?

PHONO I. You. are, Madam. You have only to follow the car line.

PHONO II. It is the General who answers her, for he has just recognized her as a mirage.

The Cyclist remounts and rides off.

PHONO I. Ladies and Gentlemen, we have just been fortunate enough to witness a mirage. They often occur on the Eiffel Tower. That bicycle girl is actually pedaling along the Chatou road.

PHONO II. After this instructive interlude the Photographer appears. What is he saying?

PHONO I. I am the Photographer of the Eiffel Tower and I am going to take your picture.

PHONOS I AND II. Yes! Yes! Yes! Yes!

PHONO I. Arrange yourselves in a group.

The party groups itself behind the table.

PHONO II. You are wondering what has happened to the ostrich hunter and the Manager of the Eiffel Tower. The Hunter is trailing the ostrich up through every platform. The manager is trailing the Hunter, and running the Eiffel Tower. This is no sinecure. The Eiffel Tower is a world, like Notre-Dame. It is the Notre-Dame of the Left Bank.

PHONO I. It is the Queen of Paris.

PHONO II. It *was* the Queen of Paris. Now it is a telegraph girl.

PHONO I. After all, a man's got to live!

PHONO II. Now, don't move. Look pleasant, please. Look straight into the camera. A little bird's going to come out.

A Trouville Bathing Beauty comes out of the camera. She wears a one-piece bathing suit, carries a butterfly net in which there is a heart, and has a picnic basket slung over one shoulder. Colored lights. The wedding party lifts its hands in admiration.

PHONO I. Oh the pretty postcard!

Dance of the Bathing Beauty.

But the Photographer does not share the delight of the wedding party. This is the second time today that his camera has gone back on him. He is trying to make the Trouville Bathing Beauty get back into the camera.

PHONO II. Finally the Bathing Beauty goes back into the camera. The Photographer has convinced her that it is a bathhouse.

End of the dance. The photographer throws a bathrobe over the girl's shoulders; she exits into the camera, skipping, throwing kisses.

PHONOS I AND II. Bravo! Bravo! Bis! Bis! Bis!

PHONO I. If only I could tell beforehand what surprise this crazy camera had in store for me, I should be able to put on a show. As it is, dear Lord! — I shudder every time I pronounce the fatal words. God knows *what* is coming next! Since these mysteries are beyond me, let's pretend that I arranged them all the time.

He bows profoundly.

PHONOS I AND II. Bravo! Bravo! Bravo!

PHONO II. Ladies and Gentlemen, in spite of my earnest desire to please you one and all, I regret that the lateness of the hour makes it impossible for me to present a second time that popular number, "The Trouville Bathing Beauty."

PHONOS I AND II. Yes! Yes! Yes!

PHONO I. The Photographer is lying in order to save face and at the same time make a hit. He looks at his watch. Two o'clock, and that ostrich hasn't come back yet!

PHONO II. The wedding party rearranges itself. Madam, your left foot on one of the spurs. Sir, drape the veil over the corner of your mustache. Perfect. Now, don't move. One. Two. Three. Look straight into the camera. A little bird's going to come out.

He squeezes the bulb. A fat child, crowned with green paper, comes out. Under its arm it carries some prize books and a basket.

PHONO I. Hello, Mamá.

PHONO II. Hello, Papá.

PHONO I. More perils of photography.

PHONO II. This child is the very image of the wedding party.

PHONO I. And just listen to them!

PHONO II. He's the image of his mother.

PHONO I. He's the image of his father.

PHONO II. He's the image of his grandma.

PHONO I. He's the image of his grandpa.

PHONO II. He has our mouth.

PHONO I. He has our eyes.

PHONO II. My dear parents, on this auspicious occasion accept my expressions of esteem and love.

PHONO I. The same sentiment from a different point of view.

PHONO II. Accept my expressions of love and esteem.

PHONO I. He might have learned a longer sentiment!

PHONO II. Accept my expressions of esteem and love.

PHONO I. He shall be a Captain.

PHONO II. Architect.

PHONO I. Boxer.

PHONO II. Poet.

PHONO I. President of the Republic.

PHONO II. A pretty little corpse for the next war.

PHONO I. What is he looking for in his basket?

PHONO II. Bullets.

PHONO I. What does he want with bullets? It looks as though he were planning something naughty.

PHONO II. He is massacring the wedding party.

PHONO I. He is massacring his own family to get some macaroons.

The Child bombards the guests, who flee with screams of terror.

PHONO II. Mercy!

PHONO I. When I think of the trouble it cost us to bring him up.

PHONO II. All the sacrifices we made for him.

PHONO I. Wretch, I am your father!

PHONO II. Desist, for yet there is time!

PHONO I. Will you have no pity on your grandparents?

PHONO II. Will you show no respect for the Uniform?

PHONO I. Bang! Bang! Bang!

PHONO II. I forgive you.

PHONO I. Be damned.

PHONO II. No bullets left.

PHONO I. The wedding party is massacred.

PHONO II. The Photographer is chasing the child about. He is threatening it with a whip. He is ordering it to get back into the camera.

PHONO I. The child is dodging. He screams. He stamps his foot. He wants to "live his own life."

PHONO II. I want to live my own life! I want to live my own life!

PHONO I. But what is this other noise?

PHONO II. The Manager of the Eiffel Tower. What is he saying?

PHONO I. A little less noise, please. Don't scare the radiograms.

PHONO II. Papa! Papa! Look at the radiograms.

PHONO I. There are some big ones.

PHONO II. The wedding party gets up again.

PHONO I. You

PHONO II. could hear

PHONO I. a

PHONO II. pin

PHONO I. drop.

PHONO II. The trapped radiograms fall onto the stage and flutter about. The guests run after them and jump on them.

PHONO I. Look, look, I've got one! Me too! Help, it's biting me! Hold it down, hold it down!

PHONO II. The radiograms are calming down. They draw up in a line. The prettiest one steps forward and gives the military salute.

PHONO I, *burlesque comedian's voice.* Well well well! And who are you?

PHONO II. I am a wireless, and like my sister the stork I've come from New York.

PHONO I, *voice of a burlesque queen.* Ah New York! City of lovers and midday twilights!

PHONO II. Music, music!

Dance and exit of the Radiograms.

PHONO I. Son-in-law, you can thank me for all this. Whose idea was it to come to the Eiffel Tower? Whose idea was it to have the wedding on July Fourteenth?

PHONO II. The child is stamping again.

PHONO I. Papa! Papa!

PHONO II. What is he saying?

PHONO I. I want to have my picture taken with the General.

PHONO II. General, you wouldn't refuse our little Justin, would you?

PHONO I. As you like.

PHONO II. Poor Photographer! He's worried to death, but he loads his camera again.

PHONO I. The child straddles the General's saber and pretends to listen to the General, who pretends to read to him out of a book by Jules Verne.

PHONO II. Now, don't move. Perfect. A little bird's going to come out.

A Lion comes out.

PHONO I. Heavens, a lion! The Photographer is hiding behind his camera. All the guests are climbing up the cables of the Eiffel Tower. The lion is glaring at the General, for the General is the only one who has not moved. He is speaking. What is he saying?

PHONO II. No need to be afraid. There can be no lions on the Eiffel Tower. Therefore, this is a mirage, a simple mirage. Mirages are the lies of the desert, so to speak. This lion is really in Africa, just as the bicycle girl was on Chatou road. The lion sees me, and I see the lion; but to each other we are nothing more than projected reflections.

PHONO I. To confound the unbelievers, the General is approaching the lion. The lion suddenly roars. The General dodges, followed by the lion.

PHONO II. The General disappears under the table. The lion disappears after him.

PHONO I. After a minute which seems a year, the lion comes out from under the tablecloth.

PHONO II. Horror of horrors! Ahhhhhh!

PHONO I. What is he carrying in his jaws?

PHONO II. A boot, with a spur. Having eaten the General, the lion goes back into the camera.

Dirge.

PHONOS I AND II. Ahhhh! Ahhhh!

PHONO I. Poor General!

PHONO II. He was so lighthearted, so eternally youthful! Nothing would have amused him more than this death: he would have been the first to chuckle over it.

PHONO I. Funeral of the General.

Funeral march.

PHONO II. The father-in-law is pronouncing the eulogy. What is he saying?

PHONO I. Farewell farewell old friend! Since first you girded on the sword, you have given evidence of an intelligence far above your rank. Your end is worthy of your career. We have seen you brave the ferocious beast, careless of danger, nay, unaware of its very existence; and fleeing only when you began to understand at last that it *did* exist. And so once more Farewell, or, better, Till we meet again: for your kind will be with us as long as there are men upon the earth.

PHONO II. Three o'clock, and that ostrich isn't back yet!

PHONO I. She probably wanted to walk back.

PHONO II. That is stupid. Nothing is more fragile than ostrich plumes.

PHONO I. Attention! "The Eiffel Tower Wedding Party," a quadrille, played by the band of the Garde Républicaine: director, Parès.

Quadrille.

PHONOS I AND II. Bravo! Bravo! 'ray for the Garde Républicaine!

PHONO II. Oof, what a dance!

PHONO I. Your arm.

PHONO II. Mister Photographer, you wouldn't turn down a cup of champagne?

PHONO I. You are too kind. I'm overcome.

PHONO II. "When in Rome . . ." — But what does my grandson want now?

PHONO I. I want someone to buy me some bread so I can feed the Eiffel Tower.

PHONO II. They sell it down below. I am not going down.

PHONO I. Wanna feed the Eiffel Tower!

PHONO II. They feed it only at certain hours. That's why it's surrounded by wires.

PHONO I. Wanna feed the Eiffel Tower!

PHONO II. No, no, I said no!

PHONO I. The guests are beginning to shout: here comes the ostrich. She was hidden in the elevator all the time. Now she is looking for another place to hide. And here comes the Hunter. The Photographer wishes the ostrich would take advantage of the camera box.

PHONO II. Suddenly he remembers that to make an ostrich invisible all you have to do is hide its head.

PHONO I. He hides the ostrich's head under his hat. Just in time!

The Ostrich walks about invisible, the hat on its head. Enter the Hunter.

PHONO II. Have any of you seen the ostrich?

PHONOS I AND II. No. We have seen nothing.

PHONO II. Strange! I thought it jumped down onto the platform.

PHONO I. It may have been a wave, and you took it for an ostrich.

PHONO II. No, the sea is calm. Well, I shall hide behind this phonograph cabinet and wait for it.

PHONO I. No sooner said than done.

PHONO II. The Photographer is approaching the ostrich on tiptoe. What is he saying?

PHONO I. Madam, you have not a minute to lose! He has not recognized you in your veil. Make haste: I have called a cab.

PHONO II. He opens the shutter of the camera. The ostrich disappears.

PHONO I. Saved, thank God!

PHONO II. You can imagine the joy of the Photographer. He is shouting for pure delight.

PHONO I. The guests are asking him why.

PHONO II. Ladies and Gentlemen, at last I am able to photograph you in peace. My camera was out of order, but it is working now. Now, don't move!

PHONO I. But who are these two gentlemen who have come just in time to upset the Photographer again?

PHONO II. Look, the wedding party and the Photographer have frozen stiff. The guests are immobile. Do you not find it a bit. . .

PHONO I. A bit — *wedding cake?*

PHONO II. A bit — *arty?*

PHONO I. A bit — *Mona Lisa?*

PHONO II. A bit — *Old Master?*

PHONO I. The Modern Art Dealer and the Collector of Modern Paintings halt before the wedding party. What is the dealer saying?

PHONO II. I have brought you up here on the Eiffel Tower so that you may be the first to see a unique piece: *The Wedding Breakfast.*

PHONO I. And the Collector replies:

PHONO II. I follow you blindly.

PHONO I. Well, is it good, or is it not? It looks like a primitive.

PHONO II. Whose is it?

PHONO I. What! Whose is it? It's one of God's very latest things!

PHONO II. Is it signed?

PHONO I. God never signs — But I ask you: is it *painted*! And what texture! Observe the style, the nobility, the *joie de vivre*! It might almost be a funeral.

PHONO II. I see a wedding party.

PHONO I. Then you see wrong. It is more than a wedding. It is *all* weddings. It is more than all weddings. It is a cathedral.

PHONO II. What do you want for it?

PHONO I. It is not for sale, except to the Louvre or you. See here: you can have it at cost price.

PHONO II. The Dealer displays a huge placard.

The placard reads 10000000000.

PHONO I. Will the collector let himself be convinced? What is he saying?

PHONO II. I take *The Wedding Breakfast*.

The Dealer turns the placard over. The reverse reads SOLD *in huge letters. He places it against the wedding party.*

PHONO I. The Dealer addresses the Photographer.

PHONO II. Make me a picture of that wedding party, with the placard. I want to have it in all the American magazines.

PHONO I. The Collector and the Dealer leave the Eiffel Tower.

PHONO II. The Photographer is getting ready to take the picture, but — what's this! His camera is speaking to him.

PHONO I. What is it saying?

THE CAMERA, *in a distant voice.* I want . . . . I want . . . .

PHONO II. Speak out, sweet silver swan!

THE CAMERA. I want to give up the General.

PHONO II. He is perfectly capable of giving himself up.

PHONO I. The General reappears. He is pale. One boot is missing. After all, he comes from far away. He will inform them that he is returning from a mission about which he must not speak. The wedding party is motionless. Head lowered, the General crosses the platform and strikes a modest pose among the rest.

PHONO II. This will be a pleasant surprise for the Collector of masterpieces. In a masterpiece one is never through discovering unexpected details.

PHONO I. The Photographer turns away. He finds the wedding a bit stiff. If the wedding can reproach the General for being alive, he in his turn can reproach the *Wedding* for letting itself be sold.

PHONO II. The Photographer is a man of feeling.

PHONO I. He speaks. What is he saying?

PHONO II. Now, Ladies and Gentlemen, I am going to count up to five. Look straight into the camera. A little bird's going to come out.

PHONO I. A dove!

PHONO II. The machine is working.

PHONO I. Peace has been declared.

PHONO II. One.

The Bride and Bridegroom leave the group, cross the stage, and exit into the camera.

Two.

Same business for the Father-in-law and Mother-in-law.

Three.

Same business for the First Usher and Bridesmaid.

Four.

Same business for the Second Usher and Bridesmaid.

Five.

Same business for the General, alone, head hanging; and for the Child, who leads him by the hand.

PHONO I. Enter the Manager of the Eiffel Tower. He is waving a megaphone.

PHONO II. Closing time! Closing time!

PHONO I. He goes out.

PHONO II. Enter the Hunter. He is in a hurry. He rushes up to the camera. What is the Photographer saying?

PHONO I. Where do you think you're going?

PHONO II. I want to make the last train.

PHONO I. The gate is closed.

PHONO II. This is disgraceful. I shall complain to the Minister of Railroads.

PHONO I. No fault of mine. That train of yours — there she goes!

The camera starts to move to the left, its bellows stretching out after it like railway coaches. Through openings the wedding guests can be seen, waving handkerchiefs; and, underneath, feet in motion.

CURTAIN

THE KNIGHTS
OF THE
ROUND
TABLE
translated by
W. H. AUDEN

PREFACE

So many marvels have happened since Racine wrote his prefaces and thought it necessary to defend great works, so many marvels have been produced and have liberated the theatre from the rules that were limiting it on all sides — or, rather, obliging Racine not to determine his own limits and to make a moralist of himself — that I believe a different sort of preface is useful in 1937.*

The Calvaries climbed by our masters have not been transformed into a public promenade.

Calvary has changed its place, that is all. We must still climb it again, a little less lonely now perhaps, but equally attended by emptiness and insults.

For my drama *The Knights of the Round Table*, in which I seem to break with a sort of mania for Greece, it would be mad to lean on fable and exactness, the source of a work of this order being precisely inexactness, and exactness no longer winning a place for itself there except under the secret forms of numbers, equilibrium, perspectives, weights and measures, spells, and so on. . . .

It seems to me more interesting to say why this work was born. Let no one look for indirect borrowings from fact, to which I do not hold myself accountable. Inspiration does not necessarily come down from some heaven. To explain it one would have to disturb the human darkness and, without doubt, nothing flattering would emerge. The poet's role is a humble one. He is at the orders of his night.

*When the play was first performed (October 14 at the Théâtre de l'Oeuvre).

In 1934 I was ill. I awoke one morning, unaccustomed to sleeping, and I sat in on this drama from beginning to end; its plot, its period and its people were as unfamiliar to me as possible. I must add that I looked on them as being forbidding.

It was three years later, when Markevitch affectionately forced my hand, that I came to draw it out of the vagueness to which I had consigned it, as happens to us when we are sick, of a morning, from prolonging our dreams, floundering between dawn and daylight, and inventing an in-between world that keeps us from the shock of reality.

Once the play was written, I began to do research and found myself face to face with my faults as a fable-maker, and I decided to leave the play alone.

Except for "the talking flower," which came to me by way of a newspaper item (a plant grew out of the waves in Florida like a radio aerial), the whole work was given to me, I repeat, by myself. It is not necessary to see any privilege in this gift.

What strikes me in looking at *The Knights* from outside is the main character, the invisible Ginifer, the young demon and Merlin's servant.

This character appears only in the forms created by the sorcerer. Sometimes the characters are true (Gawain, the Queen, Galahad), sometimes false. It will be seen that if the false characters run the risk of causing evil, they can also assume charms that are far more dangerous, in that these charms offer only a phantom happiness. This is the case with Arthur who is enchanted by the false Gawain, and bored by the true Gawain. But living is not a dream; the play, alas, proves it; and when disenchanted — I was going to write "disintoxicated" — the castle will be less light for some, more solid for others and, in any case, uninhabitable for those souls who picture the earth as an Eden.

We entrusted the costumes to Mademoiselle Chanel, for an epoch is perceived most sharply in its fashions, and only a woman who invents fashion could unite the delicate forces of the elegant present and mythological never-present.

So this is how I was slammed — as in cards* — unexpectedly into the agonies of this dark world's approaches, where we must live together with works that are destined to live on in our place after eating us.

NOTE: It is a pure theatrical fluke if, in *The Knights*, what is conveniently called Good seems to triumph over what is conveniently called Evil. Demonstrations of this sort recall, to my way of thinking, the moralist's esthetic, and that is the worst one I know.

❖   ❖   ❖

If I had to tell the story of this play — and the difficulty of the critic's vocation must make us indulgent toward ourselves — here is how I would try to extricate myself.

ACT ONE

Arthur's castle is intoxicated, drugged. Some blame this on the Grail, the mysterious taboo, relic of the Christ who enchants or disenchants Britain; others delight in the situation or are repelled by it. The arrival of Galahad (Parsifal), the very pure soul who is responsible for the "disintoxication", leads to disaster and disorder in the crooked party.

ACT TWO

At Merlin's. We now know who has drugged Arthur's castle and found what he wanted there. It is Merlin the Sorcerer, a negative spirit who uses his young servant, the demon Ginifer, and transforms him into different characters. Galahad's magic power defeats Merlin's. Merlin is confounded. For the first time. Unmasked, he defends himself wildly.

*In French Cocteau plays on the idea of three successively higher cards being slammed down on top of one another, the last and highest taking the trick — *Translator*.

ACT THREE

Arthur's castle is "disintoxicated" and rid of the trickery or — to be more exact — the author shows it to us at the height of the "disintoxication." Truth comes to light and is hard to live with.

The truth begins with the shaming of the Queen, the double death of the wife and the friend. Arthur hunts Merlin down. And the poet, the very pure soul, leaves them. He cannot remain where he is loved. The sun and the birds are reborn. This real, violent, forgotten life exhausts Arthur. Will he have the strength for it? Merlin ironically wishes it on him. But the King says:

"I prefer true deaths to a false life."

Let us hope that he is right and that he will keep the Grail at Camelot, that token which is simply the very rare equilibrium with oneself.

It is important for me that my attentive readers realize the extent to which I remain outside this work.

The theatre public must decide whether the forces that direct the first and the last act respectively make life more or less pleasant. The final question being to know whether, according to the code of Baudelaire, life *should* be pleasant. (Letter to Jules Janin.)

PRODUCTION NOTES

I

The character of Ginifer exists only in the characters whose parts and places he takes in the play. The same actor thus interprets Gawain and the false Gawain, the same actress the Queen and the false Queen, and so on.

The Queen in Act Two is therefore inspired by Gawain's game in Act One. The false Galahad in Act Three, by the false Queen and by the false Gawain. In this way, the parts add up to an invisible role.

When Galahad meets the false Galahad in flight, during the last act, and says: "I thought I had smashed a mirror," it is understood that the same actor runs off, leaves the stage, pretends to fight, and re-enters in order to endure Arthur's anger.

II

The whole supernatural element of the drama must be staged with absolute care, so as to give the impression of realism. I recommend the director to put the movements of the chess game into the hands of a specialist in stage tricks. The chess pieces must move and re-align *themselves*, visibly and violently.

The chair that slides and falls, the serving table that comes out of the wall, the doors that open and close on their own are all equally problems that cannot be resolved at the last minute and must be given long and serious study in advance.

I recommend the actors playing the double roles of the Queen and Blandine, Lancelot and Segramor — at the end of Act Three — to make sure that the substitution does not lead to the least misunderstanding. Mere physical resemblance is not enough. Costumes, stances, hair styles and colors must all conspire to make this substitution clear.

The lighting will not change throughout the drama, except for Merlin's magic departures and, in Act Three, for the return of Life.

❖   ❖   ❖

The auditorium must be decorated with a stag's horns and pennants, and the proscenium frame be surrounded with a genealogical tree that takes root in front of the prompter's box, with its plaster foliage covering Harlequin's cloak and the balcony exits to right and left.

My settings are the walls, different for each act. The doors are fashioned like stonework and the wall, when it slides open, exposes the relief and the depth.

INCIDENTAL MUSIC

Galahad's trumpets and triumphal march (entry in Act One): a) Trumpet Voluntary. Purcell. Columbia [of England] L. 1986.

This composition, formerly thought to be Purcell's, is now generally believed to be the work of Jeremiah Clarke; it can be found on Kapp long-playing record no. 9017. — Ed.

Launcelot's chess game (Act Two): Hornpipe by Purcell. His Master's Voice recording C.1656 (at the end of a Mozart record.)

This is the Hornpipe #2, in C Major, from Purcell's The Married Beau; no recording of it is available at the present time. — Ed.

Death of the Queen (Act Three): Solemn Melody. Purcell. Columbia L.1986. [*Note: This was the reverse side of the Trumpet Voluntary on Columbia L.1986; it is actually by Davies, and can presently be obtained on London Stereo Recording no. CS 6102. — Ed.*]

Preface and Notes translated by Albert Bermel

CHARACTERS

ARTHUR, *The King*
MERLIN, *The Magician*
THE FALSE GAWAIN (*Ginifer, a demon*)
BLANDINE, *The King's Daughter*
GUINEVERE, *The Queen*
SEGRAMOR, *The King's Son*
LAUNCELOT, *A Knight*
GALAHAD, *A Knight*
THE FALSE GUINEVERE (*Ginifer again*)
VOICES OF ELVES
THE FALSE GALAHAD (*Ginifer yet again*)
GAWAIN, *A Knight*

This translation was first performed on the British Broadcasting Corporation's Third Programme on May 22, 1951.

In his impersonations of Gawain, Guinevere and Launcelot, the young demon Ginifer gives himself away from time
to time by slipping back into pronouncing words in an 'uncourtly' accent.

This presents the translator with a difficult problem. This
translation was made for the British Broadcasting Corporation: under the circumstances, cockney seemed the appropriate uncourtly accent, but in other English-speaking com-
munities, in the United States, for example, something analogous but different should be used in peformance. What
particular linguistic error of accent or syntax is appropriate
must be left to the director's choice.

When she gets drunk in Act II, the actress who is playing the False Guinevere should let her accent deteriorate
steadily as the scene proceeds until by the end all trace
of 'courtly' speech has vanished.

W.H.A.

ACT ONE

The Great Hall of the Round Table in the Castle of King Arthur at Camelot. It is Whitsunday, Merlin is on stage.

ARTHUR, *offstage.* Where can the dear boy have got to? Gawain! Gawain!

Arthur enters.

Gawain! Are you there? Gawain! Ga - wain!

MERLIN. Is Your Majesty looking for his nephew?

ARTHUR. Do you know where he is?

MERLIN. I've no idea, I'm afraid.

ARTHUR. He must be outside somewhere. I'm going to look for him. If he should come in without my seeing him, tell him I've been hunting for him everywhere.

MERLIN. I will, indeed.

ARTHUR. The little devil is as slippery as an eel. I can never learn how to catch him.

Exit Arthur left. He can be heard calling.

Gawain! Gawain! Gawain!

The moment he leaves, Gawain pokes his head out from the tablecloth which covers the Round Table. He is crouched on all fours. He imitates the King's voice and makes faces.

FALSE GAWAIN. Gawain! Gawain! Gawain!

MERLIN. This is too much. What are you hiding like that for?

FALSE GAWAIN. Why am I hiding? Because he bores me.

MERLIN. Ginifer!

FALSE GAWAIN. Who's being imprudent now? That is a name which it is wiser never to say out loud in this castle.

MERLIN. Are you daring to give me orders?

FALSE GAWAIN. Just advice, master, just advice.

MERLIN. My weakness for you will be my ruin. I should work alone.

FALSE GAWAIN. But you don't work alone and you've given me a tough job to do.

MERLIN. Have you any complaints?

FALSE GAWAIN. Do you think it's fun never being oneself, never living inside one's own skin. I used to be such a nice young demon, so young, so quiet.

MERLIN. Go on.

FALSE GAWAIN. Oh, yes, I know. You rescued me from the claws of an old sorcerer who had me in his power. And then what? From that day to this I have been the servant of another one; your page, your factotum, your accomplice.

MERLIN. If it hadn't been for me, Klingsor would have left you to rot in his cellars at Roche Sabine.

FALSE GAWAIN. In a bottle in the caves of Roche Sabine. The idea of putting a nice boy like me in a bottle.

MERLIN. Perhaps he was wise. The day you got round me by making funny faces, I made a mistake in judgment for which I am going to have to pay heavily.

FALSE GAWAIN. Have I played my latest role badly? Can you complain about the results?

MERLIN. When the King calls you, you hide.

FALSE GAWAIN. It's a little game.

He pronounces it "gyme."

MERLIN. Game.

FALSE GAWAIN. What?

MERLIN. Game, not gyme. You're going to sink us one of these days with your ridiculous mistakes.

FALSE GAWAIN. Oh — game. Game. Gyme. Game. Gyme.

MERLIN. Don't you realize, you little wretch, the danger of our situation? The whole castle is already bewildered by this Gawain of yours who is as like Gawain as the moon is like the sun.

FALSE GAWAIN. As the sun is like the moon, you mean. The real Gawain went about with a long face. Do you think his dear uncle looked at the chaste fiancé of his daughter Blandine in the way that he looks at me since you made me assume his form? You should congratulate me for being so jolly and cheering the King up.

MERLIN. I must admit that you have turned his head.

FALSE GAWAIN. Well, then.

MERLIN. But in my opinion, you're going too far.

FALSE GAWAIN. First you're cross with me for hiding and then you scold me for showing myself too much.

MERLIN. I'm cross with you for hiding under the Round Table and I'm cross with you for playing monkey tricks behind the King's back when he's looking for you everywhere.

FALSE GAWAIN. I was just going to explain.

He says "explyne."

MERLIN. Oh!

FALSE GAWAIN. I was just going to *explain* to you. It's a gyme, game. The more I hide, the more he looks for me. I have my fun and you have yours. What did you tell me to do? To bewitch Arthur, to distract him, to become his favorite, his bad angel, to lead him by the nose wherever I like — wherever you want him to be led.

MERLIN. The Queen asked me to distract him.

FALSE GAWAIN. Wasn't that kind of you? So in order to protect the affair between Queen Guinevere and Sir Launcelot, you made Arthur's nephew disappear and produced me in his place.

MERLIN. Your behavior is becoming more and more shameless. You revel in idleness and vice. Thanks to you, the whole place is full of disorder, dishonesty, and debauchery. The kennelboys are your only company, poor Blandine is in tears, Segramor avoids you, and if things go on this way much longer, we shall be lost, I assure you. Arthur is fast asleep under the influence of a charm.

FALSE GAWAIN. My charm.

MERLIN. One day he's going to wake up and expel you.

FALSE GAWAIN. Fancy you becoming so virtuous and so pessimistic all of a sudden. Do you seriously imagine that these simple people are going to guess, one, that an extremely ugly magician, disguised as an honest steward, has made a country barren merely by his presence because in order to live he needs all the forces which before he came were distributed among the grasses, the trees, the vines; two, that this magician has the power to change his poor servant into Gawain while the real Gawain is miles away, shut up in a ruined tower biting his nails? Are you going to tell me —

MERLIN. Ssh!

He listens.

FALSE GAWAIN. What is it?

MERLIN. I thought I heard the King returning.

Merlin leads the False Gawain downstage.

Listen, I need your help.

FALSE GAWAIN. Go on, I'm listening.

MERLIN. Today is Whitsunday. An unknown knight is expected to arrive and take a seat at the Round Table. He has just been deposited on the coast in a stone trough.

FALSE GAWAIN. Between you and me, that sort of thing smells of sorcery.

MERLIN. Or miracle. At present I'm not sure which. All I know is that this person gives himself out to be The Pure-in-Heart One and that he intends to submit to the ordeal of the *Siege Perilous.*

FALSE GAWAIN. But nobody in the world can sit in that without receiving a nice little wound in his chest which never heals.

MERLIN. Nobody except one person, and that person could expose us and ruin all our plans.

FALSE GAWAIN. How can you get the wind up over some adventurer or other? Look how many people we've seen come to Camelot who all thought they were the Savior of the world.

MERLIN. Perhaps this time you will have the privilege of seeing that sad spectacle. But I haven't a moment to lose. Listen carefully and don't forget a single word.

Merlin puts the False Gawain to sleep.

FALSE GAWAIN. You can trust me.

MERLIN. If by any chance this knight should come through the ordeal successfully, I have prepared my attack. The moment the ordeal has been passed, the hall will go dark, a glimmer of light will circulate from this door to this window and you will hear an unearthly voice crying: "The Grail is leaving you. The Grail is forsaking you. If you do not want to lose it, follow the Grail."

FALSE GAWAIN. The Grail can certainly take it.

MERLIN. Exactly. All the misfortunes that my presence unleashes are put down to it. Our motto: "The deadly spell of the Grail hangs over Britain." Well then, the moment you hear the False Grail, you jump up.

FALSE GAWAIN. The False Gawain jumps up.

MERLIN. And cries: "Dear Uncle, fellow knights. Are we going to let the Grail leave us? Are we just going to sit here like stuffed owls without following and clearing up this mystery? I for one would like to pursue it and come face to face with it. I propose that we all go after it. I propose the quest of the Grail."

FALSE GAWAIN. Confusion and then more confusion.

MERLIN. The Table is nearly empty. The best knights are miles away fighting phantoms and mirages. Launcelot remains because of the Queen and Segramor so as not to leave Blandine alone. But they're already a bit ashamed of themselves. They will jump at your suggestion. If the King tries to hold you back, talk at the top of your voice, and if he tries to prevent the quest, bang on the Table and say, "Really, Uncle. Are you trying to teach us to be disloyal?" Carry on, in short, until the quest has been organized, the knights have put on their armor and the courtyard is echoing with the jangling of harness, the neighing of horses, the barking of hounds. The knights must have set off by this evening.

FALSE GAWAIN, *waking up with a start from his hypnotic trance.* This evening.

MERLIN. This evening.

FALSE GAWAIN. What about the unknown knight? If he really is the Knight of the Grail he won't fall into the trap and will warn the others.

MERLIN. Don't worry. I shall create so much confusion that whatever happens we shall profit from it.

FALSE GAWAIN. So my job, then, is to get the quest started. If they hesitate ... ('esilyte)

MERLIN. You're incorrigible. And now, hurry. It's nearly time for the ceremony. Go and get dressed.

FALSE GAWAIN. Get dressed?

MERLIN. Put your armor on. You can hardly be expecting to appear in a kennelboy's uniform.

FALSE GAWAIN. As a matter of fact, I am.

MERLIN. The King will insist that you dress.

FALSE GAWAIN. The King will like what I like.

MERLIN. Do you want to create a scandal?

FALSE GAWAIN. Where does the scandal come in? It's no cushy job, I assure you, never to be living in one's own skin. For once you've made me take a form which I like and it's only natural that I should take advantage of it. I like being Gawain very much.

MERLIN. What are we coming to? This business is serious, Ginifer. Stop admiring that costume with such revolting frivolity.

FALSE GAWAIN. So now I'm admiring my costume. I thought you were scolding me for not having one.

MERLIN. By costume I mean an appearance which is not your own and which I have the power to take away from you.

FALSE GAWAIN. Please don't get angry. I'll be attentive and sensible. I promise I will.

MERLIN. Then remember, if the stranger is successful, the knights are to set off this evening. I rely on you.

FALSE GAWAIN. O. K.

ARTHUR, *offstage*. Gawain, dear boy. Where the devil is he?

FALSE GAWAIN. Not again.

MERLIN. Shut up.

FALSE GAWAIN. There, you see! If it's a question whether he loves me or not, he does.

MERLIN. We shall see if he feels the same about admitting you to the Round Table in that get-up.

FALSE GAWAIN. How much will you bet?

MERLIN. Here he is.

Enter Arthur.

Your Majesty, Gawain has been looking for you.

ARTHUR. What on earth is this get-up, Gawain? Time's getting on and the knight is about to arrive. Go and get dressed.

MERLIN, *aside*. I told you so.

FALSE GAWAIN. You surprise me, Your Majesty. Why should youth hide its body as if it were old and decrepit? Do young colts cover themselves up with brocade and velvet? Am I deformed? Have I a hump or a clubfoot? Why should I rig myself up in uncomfortable clothes?

ARTHUR. By Jove, I believe you're right.

FALSE GAWAIN, *to Merlin aside.* You lose.

Aloud.

Thank you, Uncle dear. I knew you would appreciate the new fashion.

ARTHUR. I'm only wondering what our prudes and our poet are going to say about it. They're always hanging about to keep an eye on me. Of course they are all devoted to me, Merlin, but they don't want me to laugh and have a good time. To tell you the honest truth, my son and my daughter are too earnest, and my wife intimidates me.

MERLIN. The Queen is a saint.

ARTHUR. I know, I know. The Queen is a saint and I am not a saint and my innovations displease her.

He calls.

Blandine! Guinevere!

BLANDINE, *offstage.* Yes, Father.

ARTHUR, *to Merlin.* What did I tell you?

Aloud.

Ask your mother and your brother to come downstairs and come down yourself, will you?

BLANDINE. Very well, Father.

FALSE GAWAIN. Perhaps I'd better go.

ARTHUR. No, you stay here.

The door backstage opens. Enter the Queen, with her son and daughter. They come downstage right and stand there with eyes lowered. Segramor carries on his tunic in the middle of his chest the red stain caused by his incurable wound. Merlin makes a deep bow. The group remains motionless.

GUINEVERE. You sent for me.

ARTHUR. Guinevere, Blandine, Segramor. I want your opinion on a fashion which our dear nephew has started. Come here, Gawain! Now, what do you all think of his court dress?

All look, then look away. Silence.

Just as I thought. Our saints and our poet disapprove.

GUINEVERE. Did Your Majesty bring us downstairs just to see Gawain with bare legs?

ARTHUR. Our Majesty finds your annoyance very funny.

FALSE GAWAIN, *furious.* Don't turn away in disgust like that, Blandine. Am I so repulsive to look at?

SEGRAMOR. No doubt you've given my father some plausible reasons, but your costume remains incorrect, all the same.

FALSE GAWAIN. Oh, it's incorrect, is it? Well, let me tell you, Segramor, that you will soon be imitating me and letting your legs move unhampered just when I start covering mine with rich materials. That's the way fashion changes and the fools who follow it.

ARTHUR. Our little friend is a great hunter, so he adopts the clothes of our kennelboys.

FALSE GAWAIN, *aggressively.* Who are a damned sight more decent to look at than the gentlemen who flatter you and have guilty secrets to hide.

BLANDINE. I'm not in the habit of looking at servants.

FALSE GAWAIN. No, you'll look at the animals but in your detestable pride you won't raise your eyes to look at the boy who serves you and works himself to death for your pleasures.

BLANDINE. Gawain, really.

SEGRAMOR. This is too much.

ARTHUR. Now now now. Control yourself, you little monkey. There're some things kings shouldn't hear and you will make us very angry if you say them.

MERLIN, *pinching False Gawain*. He was joking.

FALSE GAWAIN, *in rage*. I wasn't.

ARTHUR. My harmless little joke has degenerated into a quarrel. Gently, gently. Shut up, Gawain. On a day like this I won't have any arguing.

FALSE GAWAIN. In any case, I was going out.

ARTHUR. No sooner do I catch him than he slips away again.

SEGRAMOR. Blandine and I were counting on him to decorate the porch for the holiday.

FALSE GAWAIN. That's the servants' job. You can see to it yourselves. The birds are being blinded for hunting and I wouldn't miss that operation for the world.

BLANDINE. How horrid!

ARTHUR. This operation on the birds sound interesting. I'll come with you.

FALSE GAWAIN, *annoyed*. But, er, it's hardly . . .

MERLIN, *quickly*. What Gawain wants to say, Your Majesty, but is afraid to, is that perhaps the kennels are not the place for you to visit.

ARTHUR. Nobody wants me to have any fun. Everybody tries to prevent me having any.

FALSE GAWAIN. Uncle.

ARTHUR. Very well. Very well. I'll just go part way with you.

To Merlin.

Come, my dear minister, drag me away and compel me to occupy myself with the most boring business of my kingdom.

He bows to the Queen, Blandine, and Segramor.

Make a nice triumphal arch before the unknown knight arrives and dress it with lots of garlands of flowers.

BLANDINE. But . . . Father . . . Flowers don't grow in Camelot any more.

ARTHUR. Oh dear, no, they don't. I forgot. Then you must cut some out of wastepaper instead. I know you have good taste, so I needn't worry.

Exeunt Arthur, Gawain, and Merlin, left. Merlin bows to the Queen before leaving. The door closes.

BLANDINE. Oh, Mother, Mother! It's so awful!

GUINEVERE. Please, Blandine, please don't be upset.

SEGRAMOR. She has the right to be upset. I was itching to knock him down.

GUINEVERE. Control yourself, Segramor. You mustn't strike a friend of the King.

SEGRAMOR. There are limits.

BLANDINE. You saw how he behaved. How cruel and insolent and pretentious he was!

GUINEVERE. I simply can't understand it.

BLANDINE. He doesn't seem the same person. It's as if some monster had taken his place and was making fun of us.

SEGRAMOR. I questioned Merlin in private, as you asked me to: he is convinced that Gawain is putting it on to test you.

BLANDINE. To test me?

SEGRAMOR. You've been engaged since you were small children. Perhaps he wants to find out if your love is only a habit, or whether you would love him in spite of everything.

BLANDINE. Everything he says hurts me. All his gestures annoy me. He has taken on the ways of those brutes with whom he prefers to spend his days and nights. He doesn't even speak correctly any more.

SEGRAMOR. He stinks of liquor.

GUINEVERE. And he used to be so sober and sensible and nice mannered. Is he ill? Or mad? Do think he should be exorcised? Perhaps he is possessed by a devil who wants to do him harm.

BLANDINE. The way he looks at me makes me shiver. There's no tenderness in it at all.

SEGRAMOR. But we must remember what Merlin says.

BLANDINE. Oh! Merlin. I hate him.

GUINEVERE. But Blandine, he's never done anything to you.

BLANDINE. No, Mother, but instinctively I hate him. I get goose flesh whenever he comes near me. Since he came into our lives two years ago, nothing has been the same. For instance, Gawain hasn't been himself for almost a year now.

GUINEVERE. Now really, Blandine, you can't hold our steward responsible for the change in Gawain.

BLANDINE. There are times when I think he's responsible for every bad thing that has happened to us.

GUINEVERE. But your father has the highest opinion of him.

BLANDINE. Oh, Father..... Father's changed too. Haven't you noticed? He used to be fond of Gawain, I grant you, just as he was fond of all his other knights and, besides, he was his nephew and his future son-in-law. But now, when Gawain is degrading himself and estranged from us, he can't bear to let him out of his sight. It's not natural.

Seriously, Mother, don't you think that Gawain and he must be the victims of magic? Every time Gawain behaves outrageously, the King seems to like it. This absurd caprice of attending the Round Table Council dressed as a kennel-boy is only one example. There have been dozens of others. I adore my father but where Gawain is concerned he seems to be blind and allows himself to be led by the nose.

GUINEVERE. Try to be a bit more tolerant, Blandine. Your father is infatuated with the idea of youth. His own boyhood was quite incredible and both you and Segramor are serious by nature. Gawain, since his mysterious crisis, has led him a dance which prevents him seeing things clearly. But one day Gawain will become his old self again and then your father will get over his infatuation and feel ashamed of himself for having been so silly.

BLANDINE. I only know one thing. Gawain doesn't love me any more.

GUINEVERE. He'll come back to you. He's just sowing his wild oats. The wisest thing for you to do is to shut your eyes and let him have his fling.

BLANDINE. I don't think I'm brave enough to do that.

GUINEVERE. Nonsense, Blandine, of course you are. This crisis won't last much longer.

She embraces her daughter.

You run along and decorate the porch.

The door, right, opens. Enter Launcelot.

I shall stay here and talk to Launcelot.

SEGRAMOR. Get Mother to tell you about the latest fashion.

LAUNCELOT, *to Guinevere.* What sort of fashion is he referring to?

GUINEVERE. Gawain's latest little idea. He is going to attend the Council dressed as a kennelboy.

LAUNCELOT, *laughing.* Oh, is that all? Come, come, Blandine, you mustn't let it upset you. I've done lots of similar things in my time and am none the worse a knight for that.

SEGRAMOR, *as he and Blandine go out.* You're the noblest of them all.

The door shuts.

GUINEVERE, *in a low voice.* Launcelot, my dear, I never see you alone now.

LAUNCELOT. Be careful.

GUINEVERE. I never thought I should hear you talk about being careful.

LAUNCELOT. I'm always afraid that someone may be eavesdropping.

GUINEVERE. It isn't that. You've never been afraid of anything. Launcelot, you don't love me any more.

LAUNCELOT. Darling, you're crazy.

GUINEVERE. Yesterday, neither of us would have talked about being careful.

LAUNCELOT. Yesterday was yesterday. I'm thinking of eighteen years of faithful love. Our love has survived all tests. For that very reason we cannot go on living in this state of uneasiness and insecurity.

GUINEVERE. When love starts being reasonable, it's no longer the same thing. You don't love me as much as you used to.

LAUNCELOT. I love you more. We were crazy.

GUINEVERE. Crazy about each other. Now you've become sensible and I am still crazy. That's all.

LAUNCELOT. Nonsense. I adore you, but I get exasperated by your passionate refusal to look at facts. It's a real madness, I tell you, a madness which turns you against yourself, against me, against the two of us, and now begins to accuse me of not loving you.

GUINEVERE. Our lives were so happy.

LAUNCELOT. We tried to force them to be happy. We succeeded, and our guilty life became the life of this castle. But don't you realize that everything has subtly changed. This castle is no longer awake, but asleep, and we are its dreams. Life is dead, dead, dead, I tell you. It's no good your thinking that the sun of our love can alter that. It can't. Life is dead all around us and perhaps because of us.

GUINEVERE. I see it all now. These past two years, which for me seemed so wonderful, you have been chafing because you were kept at home instead of seeking adventure. You want to break a tie which has become irksome to you, and go out into the world.

LAUNCELOT. Our love would be better for it. It's true, I admit. I *would* like to follow the example of my comrades if only they didn't run into ladies who change into hyenas, invisible knights in armor, and battlements which vanish at dawn.

GUINEVERE. It's the Grail's fault.

LAUNCELOT. Oh, the Grail. The Grail. It's always the Grail. I refuse to put down every incomprehensible thing that happens to the Grail. It's too easy. Its mysteries provide an opportunity for other mysteries of a much less supernatural character which in time I'm going to clear up.

GUINEVERE. Don't be blasphemous.

She crosses herself.

LAUNCELOT. I'm not being blasphemous. The Castle of Carbonek contains the cup in which Joseph of Arimathea preserved the blood of Christ, and this cup has the power to work miracles or bring down disasters. That's what the Grail is. Any enemy who wants to mix up the cards has the game in his handes. Two years ago the Grail stopped giving its blessings to Britain. Why? Why has it become a synonym for dread? Has a single one of us asked himself if his own deeds were not the real reason for this change? Has a single one of us reformed his life? Has a single one of us cared to consider the possibility that he might be responsible for this disaster?

GUINEVERE. Love has never been caused by the devil, that I know of.

LAUNCELOT. I'm certain, too, that our love is from God. But it lies and deceives. Segramor is the son of our sin. He thought he was pure in heart and he had good reason to think so. The lance which struck him in the *Siege Perilous* was our doing; it was striking at adultery. You know that as well as I do.

GUINEVERE. Stop, Launcelot, stop. I won't think about it.

LAUNCELOT. That's exactly what I complain about.

GUINEVERE. I adore you.

LAUNCELOT. It's because I adore *you* that I insist on your facing facts. We are deceiving the simplest of men, my host, my friend, my King. It's come to the point where I ask myself whether the only decent thing to do wouldn't be to kneel at his feet, confess our unhappiness, and beg for advice and forgiveness.

GUINEVERE. It would be madness.

LAUNCELOT. Not so mad as the state we're in now. I haven't got that facility which women seem to have of inventing happiness whenever they want it. I want a real happiness, a real love, a real castle, a real earth where the sun alternates with the moon, real seasons follow each other in the proper order, real fish live in the rivers and real birds fly in the sky, real snow melts, revealing real flowers, and everything is real, real, real and genuine. I'm fed up with a sad twilight which is neither day nor night, a barren landscape in which only the most ferocious and greedy creatures can survive and the laws of nature no longer function.

GUINEVERE. I carry a real sun in my heart.

LAUNCELOT. I don't know yet whom I'm fighting against, but I'm in the fight. I lodge a protest against a person or persons unknown.

GUINEVERE. There's nothing I can say. I only know that when you are with me, I cannot be sad.

LAUNCELOT. But look at the faces of Blandine and Segramor. They've forgotten how to smile.

GUINEVERE. Segramor is wretched over his defeat and his wound, Blandine on Gawain's account.

LAUNCELOT. Now, Guinevere, wait a moment. Hasn't this wonderful love of yours made you a little selfish? Think! First Segramor, then Blandine. Two victims already. And then, haven't you, yourself, at Merlin's suggestion, encouraged this infatuation of Arthur's which makes him look ridiculous and is the gossip of the servants' hall?

GUINEVERE. I wanted to keep Arthur occupied . . . to distract his attention from us.

LAUNCELOT. With the result that Blandine is in despair. I suspect that if a nephew hadn't done the trick, you would have got hold of a mistress for him.

GUINEVERE, *laughing*. I would much rather it were our nice-looking nephew, I asssure you.

LAUNCELOT. I share Blandine's fears. I'm inclined to believe that Gawain is a pawn in the hands of some evil power which is being remorselessly directed against us.

GUINEVERE. You're exaggerating and being overdramatic. Your mood makes you see everything in dark colors.

LAUNCELOT. You think so, do you? Then look about you. In the old days one met honest faces which smiled and greeted one when they passed. But ever since Merlin came to live here and got in with Gawain, I only come across sinister faces that keep their hats on and give me impudent stares.

GUINEVERE. Have the courage to stand by what you have done and stop looking for scapegoats. When the King married me, he knew that I was not in love with him. He was willing to marry me all the same and to leave my heart free. The love I feel for you and have always felt since we first met is from Heaven. Circumstances, alas, have involved us in deceit, but I warn you, Launcelot, that if you once start thinking that this love comes from the devil, you will never surrender to it or taste its sweetness again.

LAUNCELOT, *passionately*. Guinevere.

GUINEVERE. Let me go. I know that you do love me. But we don't love each other in the same way. I dare say that your love is a better kind than mine. I love you, nevertheless. You accuse me of being blind. I see one thing, alas, only too clearly. You're bored.

LAUNCELOT. My dear child, what are you making up now?

GUINEVERE. You're bored, Launcelot of the Lake, you miss the lake and you're bored.

LAUNCELOT. You don't know what you're saying.

GUINEVERE. Elfin blood runs in your veins and, because of our sin, in Segramor's too. A son of the elves, brought up by elves in the enchanted lake, the husband of Melusine. You miss them all and you miss the son of your elfin marriage. In comparison, everything here seem dull. Aren't I right?

LAUNCELOT. I swear by the Grail that you're wrong. Elfin blood cannot overcome my dislike of elfin tricks. I shall always avoid them. I left Melusine with my eyes open. When I broke the pact, I was warned that the break would be final. Now and then I think of my son, I admit, but I can't imagine that shocks you.

GUINEVERE. No child ever had so many godparents round his cradle. You needn't worry about him.

LAUNCELOT. I didn't say I worried, I said I thought about him. Since we are talking of the lake — you promised me you would never mention it again — there is one thing I ought to tell you. I was often warned in those days against a certain old magician. When he takes a place over, he puts it to sleep and lays it waste by sucking the juices from all the living creatures in it. He lives there like a spider at the center of its web. His name is a rather curious one . . . Merlin.

GUINEVERE. Poor old Merlin. Why not accuse Arthur of sorcery?

LAUNCELOT. I'm not accusing anyone in particular, but until further notice I accuse everyone. Everyone is suspect.

GUINEVERE. What do you hope will happen?

LAUNCELOT. I put my hope on the knight we are expecting, and whatever happens I ask you to have faith in me and not become mistrustful.

GUINEVERE. I shall never mistrust you. I only know of one charm: that which binds us together. One spell: the spell you have cast over me. One magic: yours.

LAUNCELOT. Kiss me.

Their faces come close. Suddenly the Queen draws back.

GUINEVERE, *in a low voice.* Arthur.

LAUNCELOT, *in a low voice.* Keep your head.

They draw apart. The door left opens: Arthur enters, backward, speaking into the wings.

ARTHUR. I'm not going to say a thing. It's a surprise.

LAUNCELOT. Your Majesty.

ARTHUR, *turning.* I'm sorry, Launcelot. I didn't know you were here.

Merlin enters.

GUINEVERE. Am I allowed to ask, Arthur, what this surprise of yours is?

ARTHUR. A big surprise. Our steward friend would dearly like to know, but I've kept my secret since yesterday. Admit, Merlin, my surprise has you guessing?

MERLIN. I'm not very fond of surprises. Experience has taught me to distrust them.

ARTHUR. He's jealous! He's jealous. Our alchemist is jealous.

LAUNCELOT. Will you tell us, all the same?

ARTHUR. The surprise has been sent me by King Bagdemagus. The Round Table has so many empty chairs. The old magician King cannot come, but he has sent me in his place a kind of box. That's all I'm going to tell you now. This box will enhance the prestige of our ceremony.

GUINEVERE. A box?

ARTHUR. Yes, madam, a box, just a box. A box which I shall open in due time.

He goes to the window.

Where is Gawain?

Through the window.

Gawain! Gawain!

He comes back.

Is he in the house?

Silence.

Oh dear oh dear, of course. I forgot that he went out with bare legs and that our prudish friends refuse to look at him.

GUINEVERE. Arthur, couldn't we talk of something else besides Gawain's bare legs?

ARTHUR, *jovially.* Now it's the Queen who's jealous! First my alchemist, then my Queen. Everybody in the castle seems to be jealous today.

MERLIN. Sir, shall I go and look for your nephew?

ARTHUR. Do, and tell him first of all to carry up our magician's box; no one else is to touch it. Tell him to be careful as it is fragile. Thank you.

Exit Merlin left. Trumpets are heard.

LAUNCELOT. At last.

ARTHUR. The knight is arriving. Segramor! Segramor!

To the Queen.

I'm sorry, Guinevere, but I must ask you to leave the room. By custom no women may be present at our Council.

GUINEVERE. I know. I was just getting ready to go back to my room.

In a quick whisper to Launcelot.

I shall be there watching from the turret.

Aloud.

Good luck and God be with us.

She gives her hand to Launcelot who kisses it, curtsies to the King, and exits right.

ARTHUR. She looks poorly.

LAUNCELOT. We're all a bit pale, Arthur. And with reason. Still, this time I am very hopeful.

ARTHUR. Launcelot, my good friend. We've seen too many who fancied themselves worthy but were struck by the lance.

LAUNCELOT. Ssh! Segramor.

Enter Segramor right. Merlin and Gawain left. Gawain carries in front of him with stretched arms a large square box.

FALSE GAWAIN. Pouf. It's heavy.

ARTHUR. Here you are at last, you little monkey. Wouldn't you like to know what's inside it.

FALSE GAWAIN. Where am I to put it?

ARTHUR. On the table facing Bagdemagus' chair.

Gawain puts the box on the table facing the last chair on the left. Trumpets.

Take your places now, my friends.

Tableau. The chair in the center is empty. On the right, Arthur, on the left, Launcelot. Next to the King, Gawain, next to Launcelot, Segramor. Standing behind the King, Merlin. Except for Gawain, who has, however, put on a helmet, all are wearing armor and magnificent helmets. Merlin places documents in front of the King. Besides the Siege Perilous, there are seven empty chairs. A blast of trumpets, followed by a triumphal march. The door at the

*back opens on two hinges and Galahad appears, wearing
white armor. He advances to the middle of the hall, facing
the Round Table, bows and waits.*

ARTHUR. Sir Knight, a miracle has landed you on our
shores. A stone trough carried you over the waters. If this
place is yours, peace be with you. Unfortunately, our table
is rather empty, for the knights who used to sit in these
chairs are galloping along far-off roads, seeking adventure.
Shall I give you their names?

GALAHAD. What knight, seeking adventure, has not heard
of Bohort, Perceval, Clamadien, Florent d'Iloac, King Bagdemagus, Seneschal Kay, Gamuret of Anjou, and Patrick
of the Golden Ring?

Murmurs.

ARTHUR. What you say surprises and delights us. Allow
me to present those who are sitting at this table. Launcelot
of the Lake, son of the elves and brought up by them, the
best knight in the world; Gawain, our nephew, who has a
foolish head but a heart of gold; our son, Segramor, the
poet, who since his birth has possessed the strange privilege
of understanding the language of the birds. And this is Merlin, our steward and astrologer. And now, my friends, I have
a nice big surprise for you all. King Bagdemagus, who is
too old to leave his kingdom from which no man can return,
has sent us in his place a talking flower.

*The King rises, lifts the lid of the box, and shows a
plant. It is a kind of cactus with a thick stem and yellow
petals.*

This unique flower has the property of retaining any words
which are spoken to it. To make it repeat them later, one
has only to press the stem. If one tears off one of the leaves,
the words are effaced and the flower is ready to take a new
message.

There is intense curiosity among all.

FALSE GAWAIN. A plant like this, Uncle, should teach one to keep his mouth shut.

ARTHUR. Quiet! First the flower will speak to the knight. Then he will approach it and reply. After that it will record our meeting for its master.

He pinches stem.

THE FLOWER, *Bagdemagus' voice*: Sir Knight, I send you my greetings and my regrets that my infirmities prevent me from attending the Round Table and meeting you in person.

The King tears off a leaf. Galahad advances and speaks to the flower.

GALAHAD. Your Majesty, I pay you my homage. If I am victorious, I will cross your kingdom as the salamander passes through the fire and bring you my thanks.

The King turns to Merlin.

ARTHUR. Well, Merlin, what do you think of my surprise?

MERLIN, *icily*. That I was right in finding this box suspicious.

ARTHUR. And what do you think, Sir Knight?

GALAHAD. As I said, Your Majesty, if I am the person I claim to be, no sorcerers can harm me, and tomorrow I shall personally return the talking flower to King Bagdemagus.

ARTHUR. I accept your offer. And now, sir, that you know the names of your hosts, it is your turn to introduce yourself to us.

He takes off the cover which he had put back when he turned to Merlin, and lays it beside the box.

GALAHAD. Galahad of the White Armor. My birth is shrouded in mystery. One evening, in a forest, I saw your knights passing and took them for angels. I wanted to follow them. For a long time I wandered seeking your kingdom. At last a stone trough landed me on your shores. Now I wish to submit to the ordeal of the *Siege Perilous* and to undertake the quest for Carbonek, the undiscoverable, the Castle of the Grail.

MERLIN. Sir Knight, before submitting to the ordeal, the King will instruct you in the ritual.

ARTHUR, *stands up and reads*. Visible to some, invisible to others, the cup of the Holy Supper in which Joseph of Arimathea preserved the Divine Blood, waits in Carbonek, a castle the location of which is unknown, for the coming of the Pure Knight.

Galahad kneels.

The knight who, thanks to his chivalry and wisdom manages to discover the Grail, to break through the obstacles which isolate it, to overcome mirages and phantoms and instead of asking many stupid questions, asks only one, will hear this answer:
"Welcome! We have waited for so long!"
And then what is heavy will become light, what is light will become heavy, what was dark will become clear, the Grail will cease to be an enigma, the Spirit shall rule over Matter. The Dragons of the Desert will die and reality will emerge from the enchantments in which it was swaddled.
Galahad of the White Armor, are you that knight?

GALAHAD. I am.

ARTHUR. Will you prove it?

GALAHAD. I will.

He walks around the Table, sits in the Siege *Perilous. Trumpets. He opens his tunic and shows his chest.*

LAUNCELOT. Look! He is unharmed! There's not a mark on him?

ARTHUR, *kneeling before Galahad who has arisen.* Allow me to embrace you. You are the one we have been waiting for.

At this moment the stage darkens, a phosphorescent light floats above the heads of the knights, moving from the rear door toward the window.

VOICE OF THE FALSE GRAIL. The Grail is leaving you. The Grail is forsaking you. Beware! If you do not wish to lose it, follow the Grail.

FALSE GAWAIN. Uncle and all of you, my lords. Are we going to let the Grail go? Are we going to sit here like stuffed owls instead of following it and clearing up the mystery? I, for one, am determined to follow and confront it face to face. Gentlemen, I propose that we set out on a quest. I propose the Quest of the Grail.

LAUNCELOT. Bravo! Gawain. I agree with you. Segramor, are you on our side? On with the Quest of the Grail.

SEGRAMOR. I shall follow the Grail and it will heal me. Victory. On with the Quest of the Grail.

MERLIN, *patting the False Gawain on the back.* Sir Gawain, I congratulate you.

To the King.

Your Majesty should be proud of his nephew.

ARTHUR. Just a moment, please. Everyone is so excited that no one will let me get a word in edgewise. We were expecting the Knight of the Grail, and the Knight of the Grail has arrived. None of us has the right to infringe on his perogatives. I am against this idea.

FALSE GAWAIN. Really, Uncle, would you preach disloyalty to us?

ARTHUR. Now, listen.

FALSE GAWAIN. The Knight will think us contemptible if we waste time palavering. Till this moment the Grail has been silent and in hiding; now everything's changed; it has spoken. I shan't rest till the Quest is arranged.

LAUNCELOT. There spoke the old Gawain.

SEGRAMOR. Gawain, my brother, my friend. Forgive me for having misjudged you.

ARTHUR. They've all lost their heads. Steady. Steady. You can't decide a matter like this in a second.

LAUNCELOT. Why not?

FALSE GAWAIN. All important matters are decided in a second, Uncle. In trying to prevent us from doing our duty, you are being disloyal to the Round Table.

ARTHUR. They've gone mad.

SEGRAMOR. I shall be healed, Father; Gawain will become himself again and Launcelot will set us his example.

FALSE GAWAIN. On with the Quest of Grail.

ALL. On with the Quest of the Grail. On with Quest of the Grail.

ARTHUR, *taking Galahad aside.* Galahad, you're the only sensible man here. What do you think?

GALAHAD, *in a rapid whisper.* Arthur, all this is very odd and most instructive. I hardly expected it myself, I must confess. But this dramatic development may well throw light on many things. Let them go and don't try to interfere.

ARTHUR. But . . .

GALAHAD. Let them go, I tell you. The sooner the better.

ARTHUR, *turning to the Table.* My friends, Sir Galahad is on your side; since he approves of the quest I can only give way and let you set off on your adventure.

FALSE GAWAIN. Long live Sir Galahad!

ARTHUR. Long live the Quest of the Grail!

FALSE GAWAIN. Long live Uncle Arthur! Long live the Quest of the Grail! Long live Uncle Arthy-warthy!

He skips about.

Ow.

MERLIN, *pinching him.* You idiot. You're overdoing it.

GALAHAD. I shall take the flower back to King Bagdemagus and then rejoin you all on the road.

ARTHUR. You have plenty of time, Galahad. My wife and daughter are looking forward to entertaining you. Put on the silver coat of mail which has been kept ready for the Pure Knight, we'll have dinner and tomorrow —

FALSE GAWAIN. Tomorrow! Tomorrow! And let the Grail escape? Uncle, you're mad. Segramor and I will hurry to get things moving. Have the horses saddled immediately; let the knight go up to my room and change into the silver coat of mail, and then, forward. Quick march.

ARTHUR. Listen, you wretched little monkey, listen —

FALSE GAWAIN. I won't listen. I won't. I won't. I won't.

He dashes out at the back followed by Launcelot, Segramor, and Galahad. Outside, is heard an ever growing noise — cries, hunting horns, oaths, neighing, barking, etc.

ARTHUR. What dear children they are. They make me cross sometimes but I adore them. Yes, Merlin, what a gallant bunch of fellows I have.

MERLIN. Their arms were getting rustier and their mood bluer day by day. Now the knight has arrived and saved everything.

ARTHUR. Merlin, between you and me, this sudden intervention of the Grail astonishes me. To tell you the truth, I find it suspicious. Don't you think it possible that the devil is behind it, trying to lay a false trail to put Galahad off the scent?

The Queen enters right, without being seen. She is very pale. She listens.

MERLIN. Galahad would never follow a false trail. If he approves of the Quest, you should. Our heroes have simply got to stretch their legs a bit. You heard what Launcelot and Segramor said. Gawain has covered himself with glory.

ARTHUR. I'm so happy about that.

GUINEVERE. Why not?

Arthur and Merlin turn around. The Queen comes forward and stands between them.

ARTHUR. Guinevere!

GUINEVERE. Why not be happy at sending Gawain to his doom?

ARTHUR. What do you mean?

GUINEVERE. Are you so happy at allowing Gawain, Blandine's fiancé, and Segramor your son to run blindly into the most terrible trap that the powers of evil have ever set for young men?

ARTHUR. But since Galahad —

GUINEVERE. Galahad has been ordained by Providence to escape from all snares. He has given proof of his powers. Our knights have not. Where did that ghostly voice come from, I should like to know. What if it should be the cheese in the mousetrap?

ARTHUR. Why do you only mention Gawain and Segramor? What about Launcelot? He's old enough to know what he's doing. You heard him, Merlin. Wasn't he the most excited of the lot?

The Queen seizes Merlin's arm.

GUINEVERE. Say something, Merlin. Don't remain neutral. You know perfectly well, don't you, that this Quest can only end in sorrow and disaster. If they leave this evening, we shall never see them again.

MERLIN. What can I do, Madam? I should have thought that your influence could have restrained Launcelot. Now it's too late. He would think it dishonorable to go back on his word.

ARTHUR. Guinevere! Merlin! You've shown me things in a new and terrifying light. Yes, you are absolutely right. Their enthusiasm carried me away. The jolly bustle of their departure prevented me from hearing the deadly silence of the empty castle. It's only now that I begin to see matters as they really are. Guinevere! Guinevere — you've made me feel miserable.

GUINEVERE. It's no use being sorry, we must do something.

MERLIN, *to Arthur.* To begin with, Your Majesty, you could forbid your son to go on the Quest.

GUINEVERE. He would disobey you, and then there's Gawain . . .

MERLIN. And Launcelot . . .

GUINEVERE, *quickly.* And Launcelot.

ARTHUR. Launcelot is a different case. He's bored with staying at home.

GUINEVERE. Are you crazy? Launcelot was made for honest tournaments and noble adventure. Can you picture him caught in this unwholesome labyrinth tempted by beautiful sorceresses and engaged in futile combats? No, it is quite impossible. You must stop the Quest at all costs.

ARTHUR. My poor head is spinning. What do you suggest?

GUINEVERE, *to Merlin.* You must know.

MERLIN. I believe I do see a way.

GUINEVERE. Thank God.

ARTHUR. The problem is how to stop them without their realizing it.

GUINEVERE. Save us, Merlin. Save him.

She catches herself.

Save us.

MERLIN. We haven't a second to lose and you must give me an absolutely free hand.

ARTHUR. An absolutely free hand.

GUINEVERE. Do be quick.

MERLIN. I shall break off the Quest.

GUINEVERE. But if they once leave . . .

MERLIN. Let them.

To Arthur.

Your Majesty, do you want me to take charge, or don't you?

GUINEVERE. I'm sorry.

MERLIN. Very well, then. Let them leave, but insist that I follow them as far as the first halting place, which the Queen will designate. Her choice will be the Dark Tower.

ARTHUR. The Dark Tower? Klingsor's old castle? But that's a ruin inhabited only by bats.

MERLIN. Am I to have a free hand?

GUINEVERE. Arthur, you're unbearable. Leave him alone. The first halting place shall be the Dark Tower.

MERLIN, *bowing.* I'll manage the rest. One thing more. Your Majesty must put Gawain in my charge. He will leave with me.

ARTHUR. Thank you. Now I can breathe freely.

MERLIN. You and the Queen must go up to the highest room in the keep and wave scarfs out of the window. Under no circumstances whatever are you to come downstairs again.

ARTHUR. I'm dying to know what your plans are, Merlin.

GUINEVERE. Arthur, Arthur, don't upset him. You must trust him.

MERLIN. No tears, or at least no more than are necessary. Pretend that you share in the general enthusiasm. Now, Madam, you go and help Blandine receive your guest, get Segramor ready, and enliven the final preparations for the Quest with your presence.

In a whisper to the Queen.

Go and pin your right glove to Sir Launcelot's armor.

GUINEVERE, *also in a whisper.* I'll give you anything you ask for.

Aloud.

I shall expect you.

Exit Guinevere.

ARTHUR. We've had a lucky escape. Thanks to a mother's heart, the scales have fallen from my eyes. Out of vanity, Merlin, sheer vanity, I was willing to sacrifice my little monkey and my son.

MERLIN. Your Majesty can thank me later.

ARTHUR. You mean, a sensible man doesn't count his chickens before they've hatched.

MERLIN. Precisely. Wait until they are back in the castle safe and sound. In the meantime, each to his post. I shall stay here. Say good-by to Gawain and then send him to me. Don't let the others keep you long. Tell them that you and the Queen would rather painful parting scenes were cut short. Take Blandine and go upstairs. Lock yourselves in. Wave your scarfs out of the window. And above all — this is essential to my plan — don't come down again before they have all left. Will you promise to carry out my program point by point?

ARTHUR. I promise whatever you wish.

He opens the door backstage.

What a Whitsunday!

MERLIN, *calling him back.* Your Majesty.

ARTHUR. Did you call me?

MERLIN. I forgot to tell you. Should the occasion arise when I want to communicate with you from the Dark Tower, I shall dispatch a bat. Keep a sharp lookout. If a bat flies in through the window and flutters round the room, you will find a message in its claws.

ARTHUR. A bat! Ugh!

MERLIN. You must get over your disgust. I have a certain power over those charming little creatures.

ARTHUR. I will do whatever you say. I deserve to be taught a good lesson.

Exit Arthur. Merlin goes to the window and looks out at the noisy preparations. Enter Galahad in silver armor. He does not see Merlin and walks toward the Table intend-

ing to cover up the flower. But catching sight of Merlin's back, he changes his mind and places the cover back on the table.

GALAHAD. Well, Merlin.

MERLIN, *jumping.* Goodness, you gave me a fright. I, I thought it was a ghost.

GALAHAD. I should never have thought that ghosts or any creatures from the other world could give you a fright.

MERLIN. I'm only an old alchemist.

GALAHAD. Oh no, you're not.

MERLIN. Really? Then what am I? I should be curious to hear from the lips of the Knight of the Grail, the hero of the hour.

GALAHAD. Between us two, pretense is pointless. We haven't the time. I know who you are. You are Merlin, the sorcerer, a cruel and wicked old man whose designs I'm determined to defeat.

Merlin bows.

You would rather that I were frank, I'm sure, and I shall be. Your one desire is to destroy, to turn life into death. Your power is the power of negation. Truth is hateful to you. You are a vampire, feeding on blood and sap, who never will leave a place till you have drained it dry. This time, however, beware. I have elfin blood in my veins and for once you are playing your game against an adversary who is worthy of you. Don't be alarmed; I'm not going to expose you. I shall compel you to expose yourself.

Merlin bows.

One last piece of information — about myself. I am the son of Melusine and Launcelot. *Au revoir.*

MERLIN. You!

He rushes toward the door but Galahad has already left. He runs to the window and calls.

Sir Gawain! Sir Gawain!

He goes to the rear door.

Sir Gawain! Where are you? Come here! Come here as quick as you can.

As he hastens to the door, right, he bumps into Gawain as he enters.

What have you been up to, you little swine?

FALSE GAWAIN. What have I been up to, indeed! I thought I should never get away. It was Gawain here and Gawain there. Everyone shaking my hand, the King kissing me on both cheeks, the Queen blowing her nose, Blandine forgiving me, and the Knight using my room to change in. Phew! Here I am, but it was a job.

MERLIN. All is lost.

FALSE GAWAIN. What is lost?

MERLIN. Galahad knows who I am. Who we both are. He has elfin blood and is Launcelot's son. He has challenged me.

FALSE GAWAIN. Launcelot's son. Does Launcelot know this?

MERLIN. Not yet.

FALSE GAWAIN. In your expert hands a son like that can be made to give no end of trouble in a certain quarter. Does he know your plans?

MERLIN. Idiot! What plans? The only thing left is to try and get out of the mess with a whole skin, to set them all at each other's throats, ruin Launcelot's image of the Queen and the King's of Galahad.

FALSE GAWAIN. Look who's playing (*he pronounces it "plying"*) with fire now.

MERLIN. When I want your advice, I'll ask for it.

He goes to the window.

The whole lot are in the courtyard. Have the King, the Queen, and Blandine finished saying good-by to them?

FALSE GAWAIN. What good-bys they were! I'm positively drenched in tears.

MERLIN. Excellent. They won't come down again. We shan't be disturbed. The King has no idea that the Dark Tower belongs to me. We must get there a day ahead of them to get the place ready. Have you got the chalk?

He taps his foot.

Goodness. I nearly forgot that damned flower which is listening to us. Galahad came to fetch it but he left it behind and, as I noticed, left it uncovered, hoping to learn as much as possible.

FALSE GAWAIN. Pretty good for a Pure in Heart.

MERLIN. He'll learn nothing. Tear off a leaf and shut the box.

False Gawain does so.

We must hurry. Quick, where's the chalk?

FALSE GAWAIN. Here it is.

MERLIN. Draw the circle.

The False Gawain draws a magic circle on the floor around the Round Table.

Blindfold me.

Merlin takes a black bandage from his robe and gives it to Gawain who blindfolds him.

Clumsy idiot!

He sets it right. Gawain hastily takes the cover off the flower and then pretends to be fastening the window.

What are you up to?

FALSE GAWAIN, *nervously*. Just shutting the window to keep out the noise. I assume that the window doesn't have to be open, as we shan't be going out that way.

MERLIN. We go by a quicker route than the window. Hurry, for God's sake, hurry!

Gawain, humming to himself, moves the flower to the edge of the Table.

What are you doing now?

FALSE GAWAIN. I'm blindfolding myself.

MERLIN. Don't play the fool with me and stop humming. Take my arm and put me in the proper position.

FALSE GAWAIN. You're making me mervous.

Gawain leads him to the edge of the circle and places him facing the flower.

MERLIN. Where am I?

FALSE GAWAIN, *in a coaxing voice*. On the edge of the circle with your back to the window and the Table. Is that all right?

MERLIN. Good. Take the chalk with you. Blindfold yourself.

Gawain sticks out his tongue at Merlin and blindfolds himself with another black bandeau which Merlin draws from his pocket and hands to him.

FALSE GAWAIN. Now, I can't see a thing.

MERLIN. Hop onto my shoulders pickaback, and hold on.

FALSE GAWAIN. Hold me tight, won't you? I've the impression that we're going to cross places where a fall would be most uncomfortable.

MERLIN. Shut up and grip with your legs. Don't strangle me. Keep your balance.

FALSE GAWAIN. I can feel an icy wind tickling the hairs on my legs already.

MERLIN. You should have put on stockings.

FALSE GAWAIN. Dear oh dear, I would give anything to be standing on solid ground. I find these journeys of yours most disagreeable. Do we go through the walls or up the chimney?

MERLIN. We've wasted too much time already. I'm going to begin. Are you there?

FALSE GAWAIN. Alas, yes.

MERLIN. If you play any tricks, I shall throw you off. You know the formula?

FALSE GAWAIN. Yes. Yes. Yes.

MERLIN. Well then, grip tightly, off we go.

FALSE GAWAIN. Mother!

Merlin spreads his knees apart and stretches his head forward. The False Gawain perches on his shoulders like a monkey. Their recitation of the formula begins slowly but gets steadily faster and faster.

MERLIN.
Minus times minus is equal to plus
Denominate, zero, all things and bear us
Not over nor under nor round but straight through
1. 2. 7. 5. 6. 3. 7. 2.
For up shall be down and left shall be right
As we gallop — pell-mell — down the sorcerer's road.

FALSE GAWAIN.

By the rat and the bat and the owl of the night,
By he-goat, by she-goat, by weasel, by toad.

The light changes. A gale ruffles Merlin's robe and Gini-fer's hair.

MERLIN.

Minus times minus is equal to plus
Denominate, zero, all things and bear us
Not over nor under nor round but straight through
3. 6. Point 1. 9. 8. carry 2.
For up shall be down and left shall be right
As we gallop — pell-mell — down the sorcerer's road.

FALSE GAWAIN.

By the rat and the bat and the owl of the night,
By he-goat, by she-goat, by weasel, by toad.

MERLIN.

Minus times minus is equal to plus
Denominate, zero, all things and bear us
Not over nor under nor round but straight through
Point 4. 8. 9. Square 3. minus 2.
For up shall be down and left shall be right . . .

They disappear in the tempest.

CURTAIN

The scene shows the hall of a ruined castle. When the curtain rises the stage is empty. Suddenly a chair standing against the wall slides slowly across the room and stops behind a table downstage. Chessmen which are lying on the table in a heap take up positions as if a match were in progress. The door, center, opens of itself. Launcelot and Segramor appear. They walk around gingerly inspecting the décor. The door shuts.

LAUNCELOT. Another door.

SEGRAMOR. That makes five, not counting the front gates. And every one of them opened by itself.

LAUNCELOT. Apart from a few squeaking hinges, the magic machinery still works pretty well.

SEGRAMOR. Both its old name, the Tower of Wonders, and its present one, The Dark Tower, seem apt enough. I suppose Mother has some feminine superstition about it, but it's a funny sort of place to stop at. After riding for twenty-four hours, a ruin full of disgusting creatures and ghosts is not exactly where I would choose to dismount. Whether it's fatigue or sleepiness which has got me down, I don't know, but I hate these doors. I've the feeling that invisible servants are opening and shutting them and following us about.

LAUNCELOT. The doors must date from Klingsor's time. I agree with you, I wouldn't care to live here but I don't mind just having a look at it.

Segramor jumps.

SEGRAMOR. What was that?

LAUNCELOT. Only a rat. Keep cool. We must be the first arrivals.

SEGRAMOR. I may be a coward but I do wish that Galahad would hurry up with returning the flower and join us again. I wish, too, that Merlin and Gawain would arrive and that we weren't going to stay here at all.

LAUNCELOT. There's never been any question of our staying. It's only a rendezvous where we can work out exactly what to do.

SEGRAMOR. All the same, everything about this place is sinister. If Mother could just see what sort of meeting place she picked for us, she'd have a fit. And I would bet, Launcelot, that, in your heart of hearts, you agree with me and are only putting up a bold front.

LAUNCELOT. Well, Segramor, your mother's choice does rather surprise me, I must admit, but, ghosts or no ghosts, the one thing I can think of just now is sleep.

SEGRAMOR. Sleep! Here!

LAUNCELOT. Why not? The sort of ghost who politely opens doors isn't going to disturb a visitor's sleep. Take my hand and we'll make a tour of inspection. I'll prove to you that this ruin is uninhabited. The machinery may still function but its old owner is not still here to work it.

He takes Segramor's hand. They walk around the room and suddenly come across the chessboard.

SEGRAMOR. Chessmen.

LAUNCELOT. That's odd.

SEGRAMOR. And what chessmen! Here, Launcelot, just look at this piece. I've never seen such beautiful figures, or such big ones.

He picks up a queen and shows it to Launcelot.

LAUNCELOT. Neither have I. But put back that queen or you'll ruin the game. It looks as if we'd interrupted some players or other in a match.

SEGRAMOR, *noticing the writing desk.* A writing desk and ink, even.

LAUNCELOT. I was wrong. Evidently this ruin is a fake. If I wasn't ready to drop with sleep, I'd call on our invisible host to introduce himself and challenge him to a game.

SEGRAMOR. The Quest is starting already. I wonder. Mightn't the chessboard have been set here on purpose to tempt a passionate chess player like yourself? Please don't touch them.

He crosses himself.

LAUNCELOT. Wouldn't you like to watch me play a match with the devil?

SEGRAMOR. It's no joke. Everyone knows that the devil loves empty castles, that he is a gambler and that on occasion he can even be beaten.

LAUNCELOT. Cheer up. To beat the devil would be the crown of a knight's career. Unfortunately, there's a simpler natural explanation for these chessmen. Probably, Merlin and Gawain got here before we did and have gone out for a walk.

SEGRAMOR. That won't hold water, Launcelot. You've heard me complain dozens of times that Gawain's childish tastes and the wild games he invents have made Father give up chess. Gawain hates the game.

LAUNCELOT. Wait and see. It won't be long before we know the answer to this riddle.

He puts one elbow on the table and his chin in his hand, and rests the top half of his body against the table, like a schoolboy at his desk.

Yawning.

Oh. I'm awfully sleepy. Am I awake or am I dreaming?

He becomes motionless.

SEGRAMOR, *walking toward the armchair.* We're not dreaming really but we're living in a dream. You must think I'm behaving like a baby but I have an excuse. Something happened I didn't dare tell you before which has thrown me for a loop.

He sits down in the chair.

When you went ahead to reconnoiter — we'd not caught sight of the Tower yet — I let go of the reins and dozed off. My falcon, Orilus, was perched on my right shoulder. Suddenly I heard him say in my ear: "Segramor . . . Segramor . . . let me go . . . let me go, Segramor. Take my hood off, Segramor." So I did. He rose and flew straight as an arrow toward the Tower. He'd barely alighted on one of the highest window sills when he opened his wings and flew back to his old perch. "Well, Orilus," I said, "What have you brought back with you?" He didn't answer so I turned to look at him. Blood was running from his beak, his little head drooped and he tumbled off my shoulder. He was dead. Orilus was my lucky mascot, Launcelot, so you can see why I behaved as I did when we got to the Tower.

He falls asleep.

LAUNCELOT, *awakening. Yawning.* Where am I?

He stretches.

I'm sorry, Segramor. Funnily enough, I was just dreaming about you. I dreamed that an evil hand in a white glove strangled your falcon as it sat on your shoulder. Poor little Orilus! His beak was bleeding, he was tumbling, tumbling, tumbling — then I woke up.

He realizes that Segramor is asleep.

Each in turn.

In a low voice.

Sleep well, my dearest son, sleep well, and forget the horrid surroundings.

He looks at the table.

Let's have another look at these lovely chessmen. I wonder what would happen if I went on with the match.

He moves a pawn. An opposing pawn moves by itself. Launcelot jumps.

I must be still dreaming.

He pinches himself.

But I'm not. What is this new trick? I'm wide awake and I saw the pawn move itself.

He draws up a chair.

Very well then. Whoever my invisible opponent may be, I challenge him or her to a match. May my elfin blood stand me in good stead.

He plays.

Your move.

A piece moves itself. This continues until the end of the game. Music.

This chap doesn't play so badly . . . For that matter, I don't play so badly myself when I choose and I do choose. Check! . . . Check! . . . Check! . . . Check! . . . Check!

A piece bangs the board violently

No, you're not so good after all . . . Check! . . . Check! . . . Check! . . . Check! . . . Check! . . . Check! . . . Check! . . . Check! . . . Check! . . . Check!

At this point all the chessmen are knocked over on the board. The empty chair is upset, the door opens and shuts.

The noise wakens Segramor with a start. He stretches and yawns.

SEGRAMOR. What was that?

LAUNCELOT, *rising dumfounded.* That was a ghost who hates losing and, incidentally, plays chess damn badly.

SEGRAMOR. Is that you, Launcelot? Goodness, I must have fallen asleep in the middle of a sentence. I was telling you — now, what was I telling you, actually? Sleep has made my mind fuzzy. I was dreaming about you. You were sitting at that table where you're sitting now, playing chess on that chessboard. Facing you there was a young gentleman, dressed from head to foot in scarlet. He was the handsomest young man I've ever seen. You won every move, and every time you said, "Check!" his face was so convulsed with rage that it became almost ugly. Then, the player suddenly got up and knocked all the chessmen over with his right hand.

LAUNCELOT. It's impossible.

SEGRAMOR. I can only tell you what I dreamed. Then he left the room and banged the door. But the most extraordinary part was that when he knocked the chessmen over, I noticed he was wearing white gloves and the glove on his right hand had a red stain and I was positive, in my dream, that is, I was positive that it was made by the blood of my poor little falcon.

LAUNCELOT. And at that point you woke up.

SEGRAMOR. I was waked by the banging of the door; at least, that's what I thought. What do you think my dream meant?

LAUNCELOT, *pacing back and forth.* Segramor . . . you know, Segramor, I think . . . I think it's becoming difficult here to know what is real and what is a dream. I think your handsome player looked like the devil. I notice that our friends have been delayed. I don't like to see this tower making you jumpy.

SEGRAMOR. It was only a dream, Launcelot. Now that I've had a nap, I feel fine. In your company, I should be ashamed to be afraid of anything that might happen. Naturally, I'm upset by my falcon's death, but I keep telling myself that he must have had a fit and these chessmen . . . .

He looks at them and notices the disorder.

Well!

LAUNCELOT. That was my clumsy doing. I dozed off. When I woke up and jumped up to wake you, I must have knocked them over.

SEGRAMOR. What a pity . . . .

He cocks his head.

Listen! Don't you hear a horse galloping? It must be one of our friends.

He runs to the window and leans out.

LAUNCELOT. Galahad?

SEGRAMOR. This time I'm not dreaming, which means that I must have gone mad.

LAUNCELOT. Why?

SEGRAMOR. Look for yourself.

LAUNCELOT, *leaning out and looking.* The Queen!

SEGRAMOR. Mother on her white Arab, in full gallop. But she wouldn't have had the time to follow us. To be here she would have had to . . . No. No. It's impossible. This place is playing another of its ridiculous practical jokes.

LAUNCELOT. I'm beginning to think so, too.

SEGRAMOR. Mother is at Camelot with Father and Blandine, not racing after us.

He stamps his foot.

This ruin is not going to make a fool of me. I refuse to believe the witness of my own eyes.

LAUNCELOT. The Queen! In that case, it must be something so serious that —

SEGRAMOR. It can't be her.

LAUNCELOT, *at the window*. It is, Segramor. It's incredible, but it is her.

SEGRAMOR. What can have happened?

LAUNCELOT. Listen, my child. She's tying up her horse next to ours. The doors will open of their own accord and lead her here. Now I want you to do me a great favor and let me receive your mother alone. She may have some private matter to tell me, in which case your presence would embarrass her. You're not angry wth me, are you?

SEGRAMOR. Dear Launcelot, of course not.

LAUNCELOT, *embracing him*. I'm alarmed and bewildered. Now, you must go, quickly, there's a good boy.

He leads him to the door, left, which opens of itself.

Take a stroll around the Tower. If you need help, sound your horn. There's your mother coming . . . . I hope that I'm not going to hear bad news.

Exit Segramor. The door shuts itself.

FALSE QUEEN, *offstage*. Hullo! Hullo! What sort of house is this where the doors act as guides? Launcelot! Launcelot! Where are you, love?

The door at the back opens by itself. The False Queen appears, rather disheveled, in riding habit, riding boots, whip, etc.

LAUNCELOT, *recoiling*. Guinevere! It can't be. Is it really you?

FALSE QUEEN. What a face (*fyce*) you're making (*myking*). I might have dropped from the moon. What do you find so strange (*strynge*)? Stop staring at me as if I were a ghost. Yes, it's me, it's me all right.

LAUNCELOT. What's happening is so far beyond the bounds of possibility that I have a right to doubt my eyes and ears. If you were a ghost, if you had dropped from the moon, I should be no more bewildered than I am at seeing you in this place and at hearing you imitate Gawain's mistakes in speech. You say: "It's me, all right!" I can hardly believe it. Fatigue and this tower have played me several tricks already.

FALSE QUEEN. What mistakes? Why Gawain? What has Gawain to do with it?

LAUNCELOT. His pernicious influence is leading you down a path of which I disapprove. You have just pronounced several words, in a way which is totally unlike you and which proves that you have picked up more from him than you dare admit to yourself. And then, this escapade of yours! Did Gawain have a hand in that, too? It's just the sort of thing he would think of.

FALSE QUEEN. You're petty. I arrive in this room after galloping like mad all the way. I climb the stairs four at a time, and what do I find? A judge. My poor nephew! And just when I thought he had risen again in your esteem. May I say that the thing *I* find *strange* (*she underlines the a*) is the manner in which you receive your Queen and your mistress. May I sit down?

She falls into an armchair.

LAUNCELOT. Guinevere! Guinevere! What is going on? What is the point of this joke? I don't get it. Perhaps I am asleep standing up. Is it you? Is it really you? Or are we both the puppets of a bad dream.

FALSE QUEEN. If you'd embraced me, instead of scolding me and demanding explanations before I could get my breath, you might at least have discovered that I'm not a ghost.

Launcelot tries to embrace her.

Stop it. Leave me alone.

LAUNCELOT. Is it possible?

FALSE QUEEN, *rising and walking about.* Am I at your beck and call? Really, men are astonishing. You start off by making a family row and then make a pass.

LAUNCELOT, *with closed eyes.* Stop. Please, please stop talking. Please please stop talking.

FALSE QUEEN. I —

LAUNCELOT. *Stop talking!* You are the victim of someone or something dreadful that means us harm, and I'm afraid of the consequences. I still don't know the reason for your escapade, but whatever it is, I shan't blame you. The words you have uttered since you entered this room may have passed your lips but they did not come from your heart; it wasn't you who spoke them. I'm not accusing you of anything: nothing is your fault. Refuse me your lips, if you like, but let me hold your hands.

He takes her hands.

There, now. I'm holding your hands in my hands. I'm squeezing your hands. I'm squeezing a shape that is warm, human, real, and part of you. I'm squeezing your hands which belong to you, your hands which belong to me, your hands which belong to us both and which I adore and respect. And now, Guinevere, it's over. The terror is over .... There, there, it's all over. Let the poison escape through my hands, the ice melt, the nightmare vanish. You are my little queen, my Guinevere, the mother of my son, the faithfullest, lovingest, noblest, sweetest, person in the world. It's over, over, over. Lay your head on my shoulder and tell me everything.

FALSE QUEEN, *disengaging herself with an effort*. Naughty, naughty. I see through your little game, Launcelot. You're devoured by curiosity. You can't take me in as if I were a silly little girl from the country, you know. Tell me everything, eh? One thing at a time, my dear. Perhaps you'll come to regret having wanted to know everything. Who knows? In the meantime, a little more patience, *if* you please. You seem to forget that I am a woman, that I have just done a man's ride, and it's already a great deal that I am talking and walking about instead of fainting into that armchair.

LAUNCELOT, *kneeling on the chair with his head in his hands*. King of Heaven, Queen of the Angels, she whom I left with Arthur and Blandine, waving her scarf from the highest window, was a model of modesty and love. Who is this Guinevere, who, having lost on her gallop both love and modesty, now answers me back and makes me suffer so?

FALSE QUEEN. Encore! Encore! And what does Heaven have to say? Nothing? Well then, I will answer instead. There is only one Guinevere, Queen of Britain. It's quite true that she *was* waving her scarf in the company of her daughter and her royal husband, but there are times when waving a scarf becomes boring. The Queen made some excuse or other and left her post; instead of shutting herself in her room, she put on her riding boots, saddled her horse, and galloped off.

LAUNCELOT. And Arthur? And Blandine?

FALSE QUEEN. Are hunting everywhere for me and getting in a state. Hop. Hop. Hop. My dear little horse knew all the short cuts. How he galloped! It was as if the world split in two and I rode through the gap. Perhaps you are right. Perhaps she did lose her hat and her veil, her shame on the way, and her love too. Hop. Hop. How well he knew the road. I must be the first to have arrived.

LAUNCELOT. Guinevere, either you're mad or I am.

FALSE QUEEN. Who isn't, Launcelot? Of course I'm mad, and presently I'm going to tell you what about.

LAUNCELOT, *clenching his fists and his teeth.* Let me sleep, sleep, sleep and know nothing, hear nothing more. Sleep, sleep.

FALSE QUEEN. A sensible remark, at last. I patted your horses as I was tying up mine. They were asleep, covered in foam and dust. My Arab was in much better condition. However, even if Arab horses and women do have exceptional powers of endurance, it might have occurred to you that my horse could do with some fodder and that I myself am dying of hunger and fatigue.

LAUNCELOT. I'm afraid that you will have to put up with the consequences of your caprice. Ask Segramor what he thinks of this tower as a stopping place. Would you like a rat or some stagnant water? We'd finished all the provisions we carried by the time we got here and I have no other menu to offer you.

FALSE QUEEN. Oh, men, men, you always know how to leave the hard work to others. Your lack of initiative is the limit. I repeat: I'm hungry; I'm thirsty; I won't touch your stagnant water or your rats.

LAUNCELOT. With the best will in the world, Madam.

FALSE QUEEN. Your good will isn't going to feed me. I shall try a better method. Let me see ... in the old old days this tower was called the Tower of Wonders ... and wasn't it also one of Klingsor's residences? Now Klingsor. . . . Hm, judging by the doors, the walls should also possess some magical resources.

LAUNCELOT. Neither I nor you, Madam, have any means of making these resources work. Besides, a certain experience I have just had with those chessmen over there, gives me little hope so far as the hospitality of this tower is concerned.

FALSE QUEEN. Go on. Grumble, sulk. I'm going to try my luck.

On the wall to the left of the rear door she traces a star of David with her finger while slowly reciting the following.

> Ann is Dick and Tom is Mable,
> Ifs are Buts and Theirs are Mine;
> Table, Table, Table, Table,
> Serve us dishes, pour us wine.

She strikes the wall with her riding whip. The wall opens immediately and a table comes out. Tablecloth. Biscuits. Cheese, fruit, wine. Launcelot draws back.

How's that?

LAUNCELOT, *in terror.* Guinevere.

FALSE QUEEN. My, how you jumped. I didn't know knights were so easily scared. Now, don't be silly, help me shove this table in front of the chair.

Launcelot doesn't move.

All right. I'll shove it myself. Women are made for jobs like this.

She pushes the table across and sits down.

What have we got today? Apples, biscuits, and cheese. Have some!

She pours out a glass of wine and drinks.

The wine is excellent.

LAUNCELOT. Guinevere, you've never drunk wine in your life.

FALSE QUEEN. Once is not a habit.

LAUNCELOT. If you still have an atom of tenderness for me, don't touch this stuff. Please, please, please.

FALSE QUEEN. When I'm thirsty, I drink; when I'm hungry, I eat. That's my motto.

LAUNCELOT. This is devil's food.

FALSE QUEEN. Oh, to hell with your scruples. It's idiotic to deprive yourself and deprive your son of —

LAUNCELOT, *looking out of the window.* Segramor is wandering round the moat like a lost soul and keeps looking up at this window in fear.

FALSE QUEEN, *speaking with her mouth full.* When I've eaten and not before, I'll talk to you, and when I've talked to you, I'll see Segramor.

She drinks.

Chin-chin, dearie!

She winks. Launcelot's stupefaction and uneasiness increase as the False Queen lets herself go. As the scene proceeds the Cockney in her accent becomes more and more pronounced.

LAUNCELOT. Guinevere! Not you. Not you.

FALSE QUEEN, *giggling.* Yes, me! Yes, me!

LAUNCELOT. One glass of wine has gone to your head.

FALSE QUEEN. Ha! Ha! That'll help me to say something I have to tell you. It's a rather delicate matter . . . a very delicate matter indeed.

LAUNCELOT, *speaking while the False Queen goes on eating and drinking*. For pity's sake, don't prolong this nightmare. Little is left of our beautiful dream as it is. Harm enough has been done already.

FALSE QUEEN. Harm! What harm?

A pause. She drinks.

You know, my dear, it's really rather amusing.

LAUNCELOT, *to himself*. Oh God, what shall I do?

FALSE QUEEN, *making little signals*. Launcelot! Launcelot!

Angrily.

Launcelot!

LAUNCELOT. What did you say?

FALSE QUEEN. Do you really want to know why the Queen left that upper window, why she secretly saddled her horse and galloped and galloped?

Silence.

The Queen is in love, my dear. Madly in love. And when her love left her she couldn't stay behind. Launcelot, my dear, Guinevere only wanted to rejoin her love. That was the only reason she behaved as she did.

She gets up and leans her back against the table.

LAUNCELOT, *rapturously*. Guinevere, darling, do you really mean that? Was it really for me that you were willing to give up everything? In that case, I shall throw up my knightly career. I'll take you away with me and look after you. That will be disloyal, I know, but I don't care. I love you and I shall help you to get well. I shall devote my whole life, if necessary, to freeing you from the black magic which is trying to destroy you. I love you. I adore you. Forgive me, my darling, for having ever misunderstood you.

He falls on his knees and kisses her hands. The False Queen gives a Bronx cheer.

Uh?

FALSE QUEEN. Do you imagine that after eighteen years, adultery still keeps its charm? After eighteen years, dearie, adultery becomes a menage like any other and deception a boring nuisance. The Queen drinks. The Queen is in love. With whom? With whom? With a Launcelot as new and young and brave and charming as ever? I don't think. That is one habit she's got over since . . .

She drinks.

. . . since she has drunk the philter of fire and ice, the philter which brings sorrow. Then who is the Queen in love with? Guess, my dear, guess. Eighteen years. Eighteen years of being a faithful Queen. Here's to the faithful Queen of Britain, God help her, and to her loves!

LAUNCELOT. Madam!

FALSE QUEEN. So you thought to yourself did you, "Shall I go? No, I'll stay. Shall I stay? No, I'll go. The poor Queen is in love with me." Gadabout's place is soon filled, my dear. He's nicer and younger than you and a great deal better-looking. Can you guess who I mean?

LAUNCELOT. Guinevere.

FALSE QUEEN. Take your paws off me. There is no contract between us that I know of. Nothing lasts forever. I love Launcelot of the Laky-Waky, and I love . . .

She drinks and gives him a wink.

I love . . . I love . . .

LAUNCELOT. Galahad!

FALSE QUEEN. Laky-Waky has said it.

LAUNCELOT. How horrible. If he ever knew —

FALSE QUEEN. And what makes you think he doesn't?

LAUNCELOT. I'm going mad.

FALSE QUEEN. Naturally. Laky-Waky's mad. I'm mad. Madness is now the fashion in Britain and in royal households. Even steady old Arthur cannot do without Gawain and his mad tricks.

LAUNCELOT. Gawain! I'll swear that he's behind this intrigue of yours somehow. I've been aware for some time of his increasing influence over you, goading you into mischief.

FALSE QUEEN, *who is beginning to get really drunk.* Arthur is a wise man and Gawain a naughty boy. Well, I can only say that Gawain . . . that Gawain . . .

She hiccups.

Klingsor, Klingsor, your tower is swaying. Where was I? Oh yes . . . that Gawain has done me a favor, a favor I shall —

LAUNCELOT, *brutally.* Sit down!

FALSE QUEEN. I shall sit down when I like. At this moment I like standing up. Just to annoy Klingsor, the old beast. Did you know that it was in this very castle that they took the knife to him?

She giggles behind her hands.

Poor Klingsor! King Ibert got his revenge. King Ibert made a capon out of him.

LAUNCELOT. What was the favor that Gawain did you?

FALSE QUEEN. Well, well, so Laky-Waky's not mad after all. He can still follow up an idea. What do you think of that? Yes, my dear, Gawain did do me a favor. A very great favor indeed.

LAUNCELOT. What was it?

FALSE QUEEN, *mysteriously*. Picture me in my room. There I am, my dear, mad with love, quite ill, wondering how I can manage to see the knight again when, suddenly, Gawain pops his head round the door: "Auntie," he says, "come quickly, hurry up." So then he leads me . . .

LAUNCELOT, *with a cry*. Where?

FALSE QUEEN. Patience, my dear, patience, or I shan't say another word. I've told you that I'm going to tell you everything. So then he leads me. . . . He leads me to the door of his own room and he says, "Auntie dear, the Knight is undressing in my room, if you want to see something di-vine, put your eye to the keyhole."

LAUNCELOT, *with a jump*. What!

FALSE QUEEN. "Put your eye to the keyhole. Quick. Quick."

LAUNCELOT. This is too much. I won't stay in this room another second. I shall go and hide myself somewhere, I don't care where, and take my son with me. I shall die of shame.

He rushes for the rear door and tries to open it. It remains shut.

Let me out. How dare you!

He shakes the door.

Let go of that door. Let go of that door.

FALSE QUEEN. So I put my eye to the keyhole and, my dear. . . .

A babble of voices is heard, very soft, fresh, and high. The Voices of the Elves.

VOICES OF THE ELVES. Launcelot of the Lake. Launcelot of the Lake. Launcelot of the Lake. Launcelot of the Lake.

LAUNCELOT, *aside*. The Elves!

He lets go of the door and stands motionless beside it.

FALSE QUEEN, *advancing toward Launcelot.* And through the keyhole I saw, my dear . . .

VOICES OF THE ELVES. Launcelot of the Lake, look at the Queen. Launcelot of the Lake! Launcelot of the Lake! It is not the Queen! Look at the Queen. It is not the Queen. Look at the Queen. Launcelot of the Lake.

FALSE QUEEN. Jealous, isn't he? He'd like to know what I saw.

VOICES OF THE ELVES. Slap the Queen! Slap the Queen! Launcelot of the Lake! It is not the Queen. Slap the Queen! It is not the Queen! Launcelot of the Lake!

FALSE QUEEN, *holding herself up with difficulty.* Either you listen to me, ducky, or you'll never know what I saw.

Launcelot makes up his mind and gives the Queen a violent slap in the face.

Help. Help! He hit me. He slapped me! Help.

She rolls on the ground in a paroxysm of rage.

Master, master, I've had enough. Help! Call out the guard. The Queen has been struck and insulted. Ho. The swine. He hurt me. Help!

Launcelot watches the spectacle in a stupefied silence. The rear door opens. Noise. Enter Merlin and Galahad.

LAUNCELOT. Galahad. Look!

Merlin stands motionless looking first at the table and then at the False Queen.

GALAHAD. I've got here in time.

LAUNCELOT. She's possessed by some devil. She must be exorcised.

GALAHAD. It's simpler than that. You needn't be alarmed, Launcelot. You must have been through a terrible time, I know.

LAUNCELOT. I've seen and heard things which have put ten years on my life. I daren't repeat them.

GALAHAD. You needn't. I can guess. I have unmasked this man.

He points to Merlin.

He is Merlin, the sorcerer. And that . . .

He points to the False Queen who is lying, sobbing on the floor.

. . . is his young servant, Ginifer, a minor demon who has the power to assume any shape he chooses and has been trained for this sort of work.

To the False Queen.

Get up, you worm.

LAUNCELOT. It's not possible.

GALAHAD. It doesn't seem possible, I know, but it's the truth. The Queen isn't here. The Queen is in Camelot with Arthur and Blandine. You are in the presence of a false queen, controlled by this master impostor. Since he can change his shape but not his heart, his impersonation was likely to cause you considerable pain.

LAUNCELOT. My elfin blood had already put me on the right track, but if you hadn't come in, I think I should have died of shame and despair.

He turns toward Merlin.

As for you, Merlin.

GALAHAD. Leave him alone. We'll settle with him later. We've got a more urgent job to do now.

SEGRAMOR, *from the tower.* Launcelot! Launcelot! Sir Galahad. Come up here quick.

LAUNCELOT. Is he in danger?

GALAHAD. Not the least. He's made a discovery. Follow me.

He leads him out leaving Merlin and the False Queen alone.

FALSE QUEEN. He hit me, Master. He slapped my cheek, here.

MERLIN, *giving the False Queen a slap. She yelps.* Here's one for your other cheek. It's lucky for you that time is pressing.

FALSE QUEEN. You're horrid! Is it my fault if you give me roles which are too difficult for me? I warned you. You never listen. I don't forget the lines I've learned by heart, but there are the others. How can you expect me to improvise and at the same time sound completely natural?

MERLIN, *pointing to the table.* Don't lie to me. I can turn even your stupidity to good account. That's not it. You got drunk.

FALSE QUEEN. Who? Me?

MERLIN. The slapping has sobered you up, I dare say. You got drunk. You knew about the secret pantry in the wall. You have eaten the food I keep for emergencies, drunk my wine, stolen from me, spied on me, betrayed me.

FALSE QUEEN. It's not true.

MERLIN. Did you think, dumbbell, you were going to stay and sleep off your hangover?

He imitates False Queen.

"Where are we going?" To Camelot, to stave off disaster. The chalk, quick.

FALSE QUEEN. The chalk? What chalk? All I've got in my bag are feminine doodads. It was your business to think of the chalk.

MERLIN. We're lost!

FALSE QUEEN. Wait a moment! There's just a chance that there's a piece in the real Gawain's pocket. You were in such a hurry to make the substitution that you got me all muddled up. Switching from Gawain to Ginifer and from Ginifer to a vamp.

MERLIN. We must get that piece of chalk at all costs.

FALSE QUEEN. That's easier said than done.

MERLIN. I must have it.

FALSE QUEEN. Segramor and Galahad have found the real Gawain. While you face the row which I see coming, I'll pick his pocket.

MERLIN. As a precaution, I'll send a message first. I'll ruin Launcelot. I'll ruin them all. Catch a bat for me.

FALSE QUEEN, Oh Mary! What a job for the Queen of Britain!

She climbs onto a piece of furniture and catches a bat.

Here you are. The dear little thing was asleep, hanging delicately by one wing.

MERLIN. Hold its foot out while I tie on a message. Gently, you idiot. That's right. And now.

He stands at the window.

Fly pitchfork, fly besom, fly up in the air.
The big one has horns and the little one hair.
As far as a rumor, as quick as bad news
Carry my letter wherever I choose.

FALSE QUEEN. "The big one has horns and the little one hair." What a nice little letter that must be, written, I fancy in your most venomous ink.

There is noise without.

Do you hear that? Your prisoner is free and they're all coming down.

MERLIN. The swine.

FALSE QUEEN. It looks as though we're going to be the swill.

The rear door opens. Enter the real Gawain, pale and feverish, his clothes in rags, Galahad, Segramor, and Launcelot. The False Queen backs away into the front left corner of the stage. Merlin stands on the right.

GAWAIN. Where is that scoundrel?

SEGRAMOR. This is the fellow, Gawain, who left you to starve in the turret. Orilus, who was devoted to you, found you before we did and he paid dearly for his discovery.

GAWAIN. The bandit.

He threatens Merlin with his fist and is restrained by Galahad.

He's going to pay dearly for having kidnaped, imprisoned, and starved the nephew of the King.

MERLIN. Sir Knight, in your absence the King has been enjoying the companionship of a double of yourself; he has become so devoted to him that he may well regret the change.

GAWAIN. Someone has dared to play my role with the King?

SEGRAMOR. And in such a manner that I couldn't stand you, and no one in the castle could make head or tail of your behavior.

GAWAIN. But Blandine. I tremble to think —

LAUNCELOT, *smiling.* In that quarter, Gawain, I fancy you have nothing to fear. You're going to hear some curious stories about yourself.

SEGRAMOR. This person preferred the servant's hall.

The False Queen raises her head. Segramor jumps.

Oh, I didn't see him. No? Mother? Not Mother? To have dared involve Mother in this web of sorcery and mystification, this crime of *lèse-majesté*. Let me go, let me go, Galahad. I'll teach him.

He rushes toward the False Queen.

FALSE QUEEN, *crying out*. Don't hit me.

SEGRAMOR. The coward is in luck. I meant to give him a good thrashing, but I find I simply can't lay a finger on him.

LAUNCELOT. I understand how you feel, Segramor. Even though one knows perfectly well that it is not her, the feeling is stronger than one's knowledge.

GAWAIN. So I was living among you all the time. While I was eating my heart out in the turret, I was being robbed of my happiness and my honor. They shall pay for that.

SEGRAMOR. Calm down, Gawain; it's all over now, thanks to Orilus and Galahad, for without them I should never have discovered that frightful dungeon.

GAWAIN. Order Merlin to remove this odious and embarrassing resemblance. Launcelot, do something.

SEGRAMOR, *to Merlin*. In the name of my father, the King of Britain, I order you.

MERLIN. Order? How do you know, my fine young prince, to what extent the King approves or disapproves of this setup?

SEGRAMOR. How dare you!

GAWAIN. How dare you pretend that the King is your accomplice!

MERLIN. You needn't shout, Sir Gawain.

LAUNCELOT. Why not go further and say the instigator of this masquerade ...

MERLIN. I shall not explain anything now. I shall wait till I'm permitted to speak.

GALAHAD. You would let it be understood that you are carrying out the orders of your master. I, for one, refuse to believe it and I must ask you to return this young demon immediately to his original shape, that is, if he has one.

FALSE QUEEN. Thank you, Galahad. Indeed I have a shape of my own like any of you and I'm sick and tired of never living inside it. Do you hear, Master?

MERLIN. Ginifer!

FALSE QUEEN. Take the advice of these sensible gentlemen instead of glowering at me.

MERLIN, *to the group.* Very well, then, I will restore my servant to his own shape. But for that I need something — it's nothing much, but it's unfortunately indispensable — just a piece of chalk. Sir Gawain, would you mind looking in your pocket?

Gawain searches in his pocket and finds a piece of chalk.

GAWAIN. What on earth is this piece of chalk doing in my pocket?

MERLIN. Give it to me.

GALAHAD. Just one moment, Gawain. The King's steward must excuse me, but this was the one thing I lacked.

THE OTHERS. Why? What's this? Tell us.

GALAHAD. Fellow knights, the Quest is finished. With the help of this chalk you will return to the castle by the same way that these impostors came from it.

MERLIN. You lack the essential thing.

GALAHAD. What?

MERLIN. The formula.

GALAHAD. You're mistaken, Merlin. I haven't yet taken the flower back to its owner. You may recall that I came in to fetch it. But finding your attitude suspicious, I left it on the table uncovered.

MERLIN. I'm not as naive as that. I put the cover back.

GALAHAD. I'm sorry to contradict you. I possess the formula and it will be you yourself who will enable them to leave.

MERLIN. You're lying.

LAUNCELOT. Galahad, aren't you leaving with us?

GALAHAD. I wish I could, but magic is forbidden me. We have no power over each other. That is my destiny. As soon as this flower has enabled you to depart, I shall tear off a leaf, repeat my former message, and then take the box back to Bagdemagus.

LAUNCELOT. Whereabouts in the castle will this formula land us?

FALSE QUEEN, *skipping around.* In the hunting lodge! In the hunting lodge. You leave from the council chamber and you arrive at the hunting lodge.

Merlin represses a gesture of rage. All the chessmen noisily arrange themselves on the board. Silence and a general uneasiness. All eyes turn toward the table. The False Queen falls on her knees at the right of the stage.

MERLIN. Don't forget, Ginifer, that you serve a master who is stronger than you.

GALAHAD. Come, all of you. Good-by, Merlin.

MERLIN. We shall meet again presently, Sir Galahad.

GALAHAD. As you say, presently.

Galahad leads out Launcelot, Gawain, and Segramor. At the threshold Gawain turns and spits at Merlin. Segramor follows suit. Exeunt.

MERLIN, *going to the window, right.* Spit away! My little bat will be there before you.

FALSE QUEEN. You're getting past it, Master. If I were you, I'd drop the whole business. These people have the whip hand over us.

MERLIN. Over both of us.

He advances toward the False Queen when suddenly Galahad's voice is heard behind the door speaking very distinctly.

GALAHAD, *offstage.* Are you ready?

FALSE QUEEN. Listen.

They both put their ears to the door, facing each other, one on each side.

GAWAIN, *offstage.* I've drawn the circle.

LAUNCELOT, *offstage.* Blindfold yourselves.

SEGRAMOR, *offstage.* Do we travel underground or do we fly?

GALAHAD, *offstage.* Neither, I believe. Don't move. I'm going to begin now. You'll hear a rather instructive dialogue.

The voices of Merlin and the False Gawain are heard as in Act One.

VOICE OF MERLIN. Where am I?

VOICE OF FALSE GAWAIN. On the edge of the circle with your back to the window and the Table. Is that all right?

VOICE OF MERLIN. Good. Take the chalk with you. Blindfold yourself.

VOICE OF FALSE GAWAIN. Now, I can't see a thing.

VOICE OF MERLIN. Hop onto my shoulders pickaback, and hold on.

MERLIN, *in a furious whisper to the False Queen.* The box was covered. It was you, you who uncovered it again. Who else could it have been? I know it was you.

FALSE QUEEN, *in a furious whisper.* How can you suggest such a thing!

VOICE OF FALSE GAWAIN. Hold me tight, won't you? I've the impression that we're going to cross places where a fall would be most uncomfortable.

During what follows, the final scene of Act One is repeated offstage.

MERLIN. You know, don't you, what it costs to betray me?

FALSE QUEEN, *avoiding Merlin by jumping this way and that.* Don't hurt me. I can't bear it. When the ship is sinking, it's every man for himself. It's your own good I'm thinking of.

MERLIN. I suppose it was for my own good that you opened the box, for my own good that you forgot the chalk, for my own good that you gave away the whereabouts of their return.

FALSE QUEEN. Yes, it was. It was. It was. To get rid of them and force you to pack up. I wouldn't care to be in your shoes. Let's have a change of air. Take me along with you. Let's go back to my godmother, Morgana. Please, please, don't let's go back to Arthur's castle.

MERLIN. That'll do.

He listens...

VOICE OF MERLIN.

For up shall be down and left shall be right
As we gallop—pell-mell—down the sorcerer's road.

VOICE OF FALSE GAWAIN.

By the rat and the bat and the owl of the night,
By he-goat, by she-goat, by weasel, by toad.

The voices are silent.

MERLIN. They're already far away. You can congratulate yourself on your handiwork. That's what I get for saving you from Klingsor's claws.

FALSE QUEEN, *in a whining voice.* You're so strange (*strynge*). Am I to blame (*blyme*) if you won't listen to my advice, if you're determined to break (*bryke*) your neck?

MERLIN. Go on, go on.

FALSE QUEEN. In the end I couldn't stand it. Didn't I tell you time and time again that it was crazy to rig me out in veils and petticoats when I've never been taught how to manage them?

MERLIN. You got drunk.

FALSE QUEEN. Suppose I did. I got drunk because I lost my head and didn't know what line to take. Launcelot is no fool. You seem to imagine that you're the only person in the world who knows anything.

MERLIN. I shall hand you over to Klingsor, and the two of us will put you back in that bottle.

FALSE QUEEN. First let me out of this disgusting drag.

MERLIN. Get out of it by yourself, my friend, since you think I'm so old and good for nothing.

FALSE QUEEN, *clasping her hands.* Don't be angry. I was only joking. Please be kind and let me out of this drag.

MERLIN. It's only fair that I should let you out of it, or rather, that I should lock you up in Gawain's place. That's what you deserve.

FALSE QUEEN. Lock up your factotum? Your slave? Your son?

MERLIN, *looking through the window.* The horses!

FALSE QUEEN. What do you mean, the horses?

MERLIN. It's Galahad. After taking his own horse, he cut the others loose. They were our one and only means of arriving in time.

FALSE QUEEN. To learn that we have been expelled.

MERLIN. Or that the Queen has been expelled.

FALSE QUEEN. What are we to do now? What about my white Arab?

MERLIN. Your Arab, ours, theirs. Galahad has cut off our retreat.

FALSE QUEEN. There you are, Master. Fate is against us. Why not set up house somewhere else? Haven't you squeezed Camelot like an orange?

MERLIN. I must have my revenge.

FALSE QUEEN. What ugly words to hear from you, who are always so noble and just.

MERLIN. Shut up. Run and catch a couple of horses. We have no option.

FALSE QUEEN. Run and catch horses? If that's what you want, take away my false petticoats and give me back my nimble legs.

MERLIN. I'm sick of hearing about your petticoats. I'll free your limbs on condition that you catch the horses.

FALSE QUEEN. I will, I promise.

MERLIN. I don't know why I bother about you. You don't deserve it.

FALSE QUEEN. Who else can fetch the horses back?

MERLIN. Take care!

FALSE QUEEN. I didn't mean it. I'll be good. As good as gold. Change me back into Ginifer and I'll catch you a couple of horses.

MERLIN, *shrugging his shoulders.* All right. Then we mustn't dawdle. Get two chairs.

The False Queen obeys.

Set one against the other. Not like that, you fool, like this.

He puts them center stage facing the audience, slightly apart.

Lie down on them. No. On your stomach.

FALSE QUEEN. Don't be so rough.

MERLIN. Since I've no rope, these curtains will have to do.

He tears some old curtains off their rods.

You must be tied up.

FALSE QUEEN. It looks as if you were going to put me on a spit and roast me.

MERLIN. Another knot.

FALSE QUEEN. They're cutting into my ankles. Ow. Ow.

MERLIN. Shut up. Do you want to leave here, or don't you?

FALSE QUEEN. God knows what you're capable of. You're not going to turn me into a horse, are you?

MERLIN, *bursting into laughter.* Now, that's an idea!

FALSE QUEEN. Master, Master, I didn't say a word.

MERLIN. On the contrary, that's the first sensible suggestion you've made.

FALSE QUEEN, *struggling.* No, mercy, no, have pity. What use is a horse to you at this stage?

MERLIN. For a sorcerer, there are no stages. But I won't be betrayed.

FALSE QUEEN. I'll never do it again. I'll obey you. I'll do whatever you say. Ow. You're squeezing me to death.

MERLIN. Why didn't I think of this sooner?

He casts a spell over Ginifer.

FALSE QUEEN. You beast! You filthy beast! You old billy goat! You old basilisk! You swine! You swine! You swine!

MERLIN, *sits astride the False Queen, grasping her braids as if they were reins.*

In the name of the monkey, in the name of his son,
Let five be eleven and twenty be one,
Let rivers turn backwards and flow to their source,

And the queen who is no queen,
And the queen who is no queen,

The queen who is no queen become a white horse.

He repeats the last lines without stopping, faster and faster.

And the queen who is no queen,
And the queen who is no queen,

The queen who is no queen become a white horse.

FALSE QUEEN, *at the top of her lungs.* Let me go! Let me go! Help! Have mercy! My bones are breaking! He's tearing my hair out! I'm on fire! I'm dying! Have mercy! Help! Help!

Holding her braids in one hand and whipping his mount with the other, Merlin goes on reciting the last lines of the formula. The wind of the end of the first act rises. Darkness and flashes. The walls disappear.

CURTAIN

ACT THREE

The Queen's chamber in the castle at Camelot. The Queen is seated at a writing table in her dressing gown. The King is pacing up and down. One has the impression that the discussion has already been going on for a very long time.

GUINEVERE. I want to sleep. Have I your permission to retire?

ARTHUR. Not until you've given me an answer. I've absolutely got to have an answer.

GUINEVERE. I've told you already, Arthur, that we're living in a dim twilight where there is no difference between night and day, no natural reason why one should get up or go to bed. Our nerves are all on edge waiting for this inexplicable phenomenon, which is contrary to all our habits, to be over. The Grail has left us. Is it nighttime? It feels like it. The castle is asleep. The servants are asleep. The animals are asleep. I'm dead tired, Arthur. I want to sleep. Have I your permission to retire?

ARTHUR. You're still avoiding the issue. I've asked you certain definite questions. Our honor and happiness depend on your answers, and all you will say is that I am preventing you from sleeping, that it is nighttime — when it isn't, and that we should follow the example of the animals, when this house has just been struck by lightning.

GUINEVERE. This house has only been struck by lightning in the sense that the Grail has scattered our circle and interrupted the pleasant existence we were leading. I sympathize with your distress, but I fail to see why that distress should be turned against me.

ARTHUR. Madam.

GUINEVERE. Is it my fault that Galahad came through the ordeal triumphantly, that the Grail spoke, that your nephew lost his head and made the others, including you, lose theirs? Who was it who brought you to your senses when you were as carried away by excitement as any of them? It is thanks to me that your minister has promised to bring our mad friends back to the castle. If there was any thunderstorm, it was this rushing off. It has struck us so hard that I don't blame you for losing your self-control.

ARTHUR. Madam, Madam.

GUINEVERE. Come now. Are you so superstitious that the mere entry of a bat into the council chamber is enough to alter your whole attitude toward me, after making a scene unworthy of your rank and age? The truth is, Arthur, that this unhappy Whitsuntide has depressed you, and you are taking as a symbol of unhappiness a harmless creature who is only, like us, a victim of the Grail and its mysteries.

ARTHUR. You talk very well, Madam, and you talk a great deal; a great deal for a person who is dying of sleep.

GUINEVERE. Arthur.

ARTHUR. I've had enough of this. I'm not asking for advice. I'm asking for a simple direct answer. It's true that a bat is partly responsible for my change of attitude, but I'm not accusing the Queen without grave reasons.

GUINEVERE. Sir, if it is true that bats can carry messages, would not such nocturnal messages be the ideal vehicle for libel and slander?

ARTHUR. You keep on trying to sidetrack me instead of giving a straight answer. Don't let this doubt take root, this ugly stain grow any bigger. Answer me, I tell you, answer me.

GUINEVERE. You know quite well why I put off answering. I have been hoping that you would come to your senses before being forced to ask my pardon.

ARTHUR. Stop trying to confuse me. I would like to believe that your prevarications are not the wiles of a woman, and that your evasions proceed from a distaste for defending yourself. I would like to believe it. But whatever the consequences of my actions may be, I will accept them rather than suffer as I am suffering, rather than endure a doubt which has poisoned both the past and the future.

GUINEVFRF. Haven't I given you an answer?

ARTHUR. No. What I ask and insist upon hearing from your own lips is the truth about Launcelot and yourself. Are you in love with Launcelot?

GUINEVERE. Suppose I were?

ARTHUR. Ha!

GUINEVERE. Let me say a word, for a change. Suppose I were: would that make me a criminal? You talked me into agreeing to a marriage without love. I felt the greatest friendliness and respect for you. I told you quite frankly why I held back, my aversion to committing myself without knowing what might happen to my heart. You overrode my objections. You told me that my heart remained my own, that love would come by degrees, that if it didn't come through you, you would be content with a chaste friendship, that I was too young to understand such matters. Then Launcelot arrived from the Lake. He was surrounded by an air of daring and magic, a sort of phosphorescence, He was young, handsome, brave, irresistible. No one, least of all yourself, could resist his prestige. You loved him, we all loved him, I loved him. What objection have you to my loving someone whom you and everyone else love, to my admiring someone who is admired by all?

ARTHUR. No, Madam. That won't wash: you're taking advantage of the fact that I recoil from asking the real question which is sticking in my throat and tearing at my heartstrings. I should never dream of objecting to your sharing my own feeling for Launcelot. And even if Launcelot had aroused in you a feeling which was a little ... a little too warm ... a regret, shall I say, at not being free ... your heart was your own and there was nothing I could say to that. No, Madam, the question I am asking is whether this castle has become the home of lies and adultery, whether my wife and my friend have been taking advantage of a blind trust and made a fool of me by their sustained and cunning treachery. I ask you whether you are Launcelot's mistress.

He hides his face in his hands.

GUINEVERE. If you have ceased to believe in me, why should you believe in me this time? If I am guilty, it wouldn't be very hard to add one more lie to all the others, and tell you no.

ARTHUR. I won't accept your evasions any longer. I refuse to follow your twists and turns. I order you to answer.

He grips her arm.

Are you Launcelot's mistress? Is Launcelot your lover? Answer! Answer! Will you answer me?

GUINEVERE. You'd better ask Launcelot. I wonder if you will treat him as you treat a woman.

ARTHUR, *breaking down.* Oh God! I am all alone in the world, confronted by a secret which the executioner could not drag out of her, and if I'm wrong she will punish me by leaving me in doubt, in this vague, sickening, monstrous doubt.

He falls on his knees.

Please, Guinevere, please. I've no pride left. Look, I'm kneeling before you, to beg forgiveness for my violence, I implore you — listen to me — I implore you to give me an answer, to answer yes or no. If it's yes, I'll disappear, I'll go away, I'll fade out of the picture. If it's no, I'll put on a hair shirt, I'll enter a monastery, I'll set you free. But not this doubt... not this torture of doubt... Have pity, Guinevere, have pity.

GUINEVERE, *coldly.* I feel sorry for you.

ARTHUR, *getting up and banging the table.* Your audacity goes too far. Generosity is stupid and only puts a weapon into the hands of those who should be begging for mercy. I won't be made a dupe. I want to know and I will. If you refuse to tell me, I shall challenge Launcelot. And I shan't have long to wait, either. I know he's hiding somewhere nearby, waiting for the right moment, taking advantage of this famous sleepiness of yours and the trusting sleepiness into which he has lulled me for — who knows? — perhaps seventeen years. Are there any clean hearts left? Why shouldn't I find that Blandine . . . that Segramor, that Gawain even. Suppose Gawain has been your accomplice. "Dear Uncle isn't there, come, dear Uncle has gone out. Look out, dear Uncle is coming." No. No. No. I won't have it. It's too much. I can't suffer so much. Monsters. Monsters. Monsters.

GUINEVERE. You've gone mad.

ARTHUR. The traitor. He's going to come. I can feel it. I'm certain. I know he's hiding somewhere waiting for a signal from you.

GUINEVERE. Launcelot is with the others at the Dark Tower. You know that perfectly well. They will all return together. You've gone mad.

ARTHUR. Suppose I countered tricks with a trick, treacheries with treachery. Suppose I dictated a letter from you to Launcelot which said: "Come up to my room. I shall be alone. Approach the bed and say three times, Guinevere, darling." And suppose I made you pin this letter to the door of the porch and suppose I lay down in your place, and suppose I received Launcelot?

GUINEVERE, *smiling*. Try it, then, and see. I'll write this letter and pin it to the door of the porch and give you my room. I'll use yours instead. Launcelot is at the Dark Tower seeking adventure. All I want is sleep. I'm very sleepy.

ARTHUR. You're thinking to yourself: "If I treat the whole thing lightly, he'll find the scheme inept and drop it." Well, you're very mistaken.

He fetches her parchment, pen, and ink.

Write.

GUINEVERE, *shrugging her shoulders*. Just as you please, on condition that the letter is short and the servants don't learn about it in the morning.

ARTHUR. If you are innocent, you need have no fear for your honor. Either Launcelot will find this letter, or I will take it away myself. Take this down. "Come up to my room. I'm in bed alone. Open the door quietly and slip in. Approach the bed and whisper three times: Guinevere, darling."

GUINEVERE. Now I sign, I suppose.

Contemptuously.

What an ingenious trap!

ARTHUR. There's no harm done in setting a trap. If the animal lets itself be caught, the trap is a good one.

GUINEVERE. Poor Launcelot.

ARTHUR. Mock away. I shan't listen. I shall only listen to the voice of my instinct. If Launcelot is a villain, it won't embarrass him much to tangle the threads still further and continue the comedy. It's only by a surprise that I shall learn my woe. And woe to him if he denounces you.

GUINEVERE. He's miles away.

ARTHUR. I hope so, for his sake.

GUINEVERE. Have I your permission to sleep when I've pinned up your parchment?

ARTHUR. Go, Madam. . . . Guinevere!

GUINEVERE. Sir.

ARTHUR. Once more, for the last time, do you refuse to give me a straight answer, an answer which will exonerate you. I will believe you, Guinevere. I'll believe your word, I promise I will.

GUINEVERE, *at the open door.* It's no use now. Things can never be the same between us. You can be proud of your work. I've nothing to say.

ARTHUR, *losing all control.* So much the worse for you, then. I'll break down your resistance. You think I'm old and feeble and that you can outface me, despise me, insult your King. But I shall get the better of your abominable obstinacy, I shall break down your resistance, I shall break you down.

At this moment the Queen turns around, hearing Blandine's voice.

BLANDINE. What's the matter?

She enters, wearing a long chemise.

ARTHUR, *confused.* Blandine, my child.

BLANDINE. What's the matter? I couldn't sleep. I heard comings and goings and then I thought I heard shouting. The voice sounded like Father's. I was frightened.

ARTHUR. It was nothing.

To the Queen.

Go, Guinevere, and then come back to fetch Blandine. Your mother was just going to look for something.

He shuts the door and comes back with his daughter.

BLANDINE. Father, Father. Your eyes look so terrifying.

ARTHUR. This quest has upset us all completely. Your mother has been calming me down and I have been reassuring your mother.

BLANDINE. They haven't really gone, have they, Father? They're going to return to us?

ARTHUR. I've arranged matters behind their backs so that they'll return and leave Galahad to continue the Quest of the Grail by himself.

BLANDINE. But mightn't the Quest be the saving of Gawain? Mightn't it get him out of his bad habits? Segramor says that he behaved so wonderfully. What do you think?

ARTHUR. We shall see.

BLANDINE. And all the other knights. They can't always stay in one place. They get bored and think up silly games to pass the time. Gawain was taking to drink.

ARTHUR. He's young and full of fun. One glass makes him tipsy. Blandine, I want to ask you something.

BLANDINE. What, Father?

ARTHUR. Do you miss Segramor?

BLANDINE. Of course I do.

ARTHUR. And . . . Launcelot?

BLANDINE. All of them.

ARTHUR. Do you love Launcelot?

BLANDINE. Naturally. Why do you ask me in such a strange tone of voice?

ARTHUR. And does Launcelot love you. . . . Has he ever told you so?

BLANDINE. Why, yes.

ARTHUR. Has he told you so . . . often? Whom do you think he loves most, you or Segramor? At times I've thought he preferred Segramor. Have you noticed any preference?

BLANDINE. Good Heavens no.

ARTHUR, *taking Blandine by the shoulders and looking into her eyes.* Has he ever told you that he preferred you to Segramor? That you were his little girl? That he loved you better than Segramor? Has he ever told you that he loves you more than me?

BLANDINE, *frightened.* Father.

ARTHUR. Let me see your eyes. Yes, your eyes are like mine. Everyone finds that we have the same eyes, don't they? And Segramor. . . . He has my gestures. . . . Don't you find that he has my gestures and my walk? That he walks like me? Let me see your eyes.

BLANDINE, *crying out.* Father! Father! Let me go. You're frightening me.

The door opens. The King lets go of Blandine.

GUINEVERE. Arthur! Have you gone out of your mind?

BLANDINE, *running to her mother for protection.* Mother!

GUINEVERE. There, there. There's nothing to be frightened of. I'm going to sleep in your room.

BLANDINE. Really and truly?

GUINEVERE. We're both going to sleep there. Run along. I'll come in a moment. Your father is going to sleep in this room, and I in yours.

Exit Blandine.

ARTHUR. You've done what I told you?

GUINEVERE, *icily.* I've put your ridiculous letter in its place, but I forbid you to frighten Blandine. She's in a nervous enough state as it is because of Gawain. Good night. I've given in to your wishes and you may do whatever you think right, but I won't have you troubling a little girl with the phantoms of your imagination.

Exit Guinevere.

The King stands for a moment listening at the door. He covers his face with his hands and moves slowly across the room to the window. He presses one cheek against the window and looks out. Silence. Then suddenly, we hear what the King hears in his mind, a whispered dialogue between the Queen and Launcelot.

VOICE OF GUINEVERE. Take care, darling. He's returning from the hunt. He might see you.

VOICE OF LAUNCELOT. Let me hold your hand. Look at me. I love you.

VOICE OF GUINEVERE. I love you.

The King gives a sigh of rage and suffering. He leaves the window and looks at the loom, touches the wool. He stands staring at the unfinished tapestry.

VOICE OF GUINEVERE. My darling. Help me. Hold out your hands. No, no, let go. I don't want you to hold my hands, I want you to hold the wool for me.

VOICE OF LAUNCELOT. I love you.

VOICE OF GUINEVERE. Clumsy.

VOICE OF LAUNCELOT. Put your work down. Take me in your arms.

VOICE OF GUINEVERE. My dearest.

ARTHUR. Ha! The whole place is poisoned. The air is poisoned by words. I shall never hear anything else again. *You*, disloyal! *You*, a scoundrel! *You*, the friend of friends. Launcelot of the Lake! *My* Launcelot!

He crosses the room toward the bed and touches it.

Guinevere. My wife, my Guinevere. It's impossible . . . impossible. I can't. I won't. I won't listen. I won't hear.

He presses his fingers to his ears.

VOICE OF GUINEVERE. Hurry, darling, come here quickly.

VOICE OF LAUNCELOT. How pale you look against the pillow.

VOICE OF GUINEVERE. Warm me.

VOICE OF LAUNCELOT. Your body. Your little body which calls to mine. My darling.

VOICE OF GUINEVERE. My darling. My darling.

ARTHUR. No. No. Have pity. My heart is in my mouth. It's choking me. It's breaking. I can't go on living and hearing them everywhere. This torture can't go on. Where is the Grail? Animals are looked after, but who looks after men? No one. They remain alone, alone, alone.

He staggers downstage right, and sits facing the audience as if before an imaginary fireplace.

VOICE OF LAUNCELOT. The firelight dances on your face, on your hair, on your dress.

VOICE OF GUINEVERE. It's so good to be alone with you in my room.

VOICE OF LAUNCELOT. It's snowing outside. Arthur has gone hunting.

VOICE OF GUINEVERE. The firelight dances on your coat of mail. It's quite warm.

VOICE OF LAUNCELOT. You have put up your hair.

VOICE OF GUINEVERE. Don't undo it. My face is burning. My heart is burning.

VOICE OF LAUNCELOT. My darling.

The King stands stunned and motionless for a moment. Then he rises abruptly and turns his back to the audience.

ARTHUR. Lord, give me strength. Grant, Lord, that I may find strength. Lord, do not forsake me.

He advances toward a prie-dieu *and kneels, his face in his hands.*

VOICE OF GUINEVERE. Almighty God,

ARTHUR. Almighty God, calm my anger. I ask in the name . . .

VOICE OF GUINEVERE. Almighty God, protect Launcelot, protect our love —

ARTHUR. I ask . . . in the name . . . I ask . . . Almighty God.

VOICE OF FALSE GAWAIN. Auntie dear, Auntie dear. Excuse me for disturbing you at your prayers. Get up quickly. My uncle is out of the house. I persuaded him to go for a walk. Launcelot is waiting for you in his room.

VOICE OF GUINEVERE. Thank you. Oh, Gawain, I'm so happy. Thank you.

The King jumps up.

ARTHUR. No. No. Not him, not you, not Gawain. I refuse. Liars, filthy liars. I shall learn everything. No more weakness; it's no use trying to behave decently. I'll beat her. I'll drag her along the floor. I'll make her talk. Bitch!

He rushes to the door.

Why is life so cruel? I've been cut in two like a wasp and still go on living.

VOICE OF GUINEVERE. We must watch out. Let me see first if the coast is clear,

VOICE OF LAUNCELOT. Why must there always be this hiding and slinking around corners.

VOICE OF GUINEVERE. To protect you, to protect our love, I would stoop to any baseness. Don't be a fool.

VOICE OF LAUNCELOT. My little foolish one.

VOICE OF GUINEVERE. My darling.

VOICE OF LAUNCELOT. My darling.

As if he saw red, the King rushes to the door, opens it, and listens.

ARTHUR. I was right.

He closes the door again softly, hurries to the alcove, goes inside, and draws the curtains. Silence. Then Launcelot slowly opens the door, enters, closes it carefully, and walks on tiptoe toward the bed. He is wearing neither helmet, shield, nor armor, just a simple tunic with a dagger at the waist.

LAUNCELOT. Guinevere, darling. Guinevere, darling.

The third time close to the curtain.

Guinevere, darling.

VOICE OF ARTHUR, *imitating the Queen.* Yes...

Launcelot inspects the room, then slips between the curtains of the alcove. He is heard saying, "Guinevere, how did you know?" Then the fight begins.

VOICE OF ARTHUR. Take that. It is I. It's Arthur who strikes you. Take that and that and that, you thief. Here's another.

VOICE OF LAUNCELOT. You. My King and my friend.

VOICE OF ARTHUR. A loyal sort of friend you were.

VOICE OF LAUNCELOT. Forgive me. . . . As I forgive you.

Pause. The curtains part and Arthur appears. He looks at his right hand and takes one or two steps forward into the room.

ARTHUR. My King and my friend. Take that and that, you thief. Here's another.

He falls on his knees.

I've killed him. Everything is so still.

He calls.

Launcelot!

Louder.

Launcelot! It's a dream, a horrible dream.

He rises.

Sometimes I dream I'm dreaming. I must have got my hand wet and am dreaming that it's blood. Blood. Real blood. There's blood all over me, on my clothes, on my face. . . .

Crying out.

Launcelot! Launcelot!

He rushes to the door.

Murder! Help! Help! Arrest me! Arrest the murderer! Hang me! My head swims. Have pity. Guinevere! Guinevere! Quick! Quick!

The Queen appears in a long nightgown, with her hair down.

GUINEVERE. Arthur, what's the matter? Blandine had fallen asleep at last when I thought I heard a terrible cry. Are you ill?

Arthur stands motionless.

Blood. Ah!

The King points to the alcove, which she enters. Arthur sobs. After a moment, the Queen draws back the curtains and stands there petrified.

ARTHUR. Forgive me.

GUINEVERE. Don't ask for my forgiveness, Arthur. You have acted as you had to act. You have done the only thing that could be done.

ARTHUR. He cried: Forgive me as I forgive you. I lost my head. Everywhere I kept hearing you both. Jealousy is a terrifying weapon. My hand found his dagger. It was my hand which struck him. It wasn't me. He loved you. You loved each other. What was wrong in that? What was wrong, I say.

GUINEVERE. I'm not angry with you. You can see I'm perfectly calm. I had no idea he would return. I pinned up that letter without the slightest anxiety, I swear. It was fate which made you foresee this visit. It was fate which made you set this trap. It was fate which made you kill him.

ARTHUR. Kill me.

GUINEVERE. We were living a lie. Launcelot wanted to tell you everything. It was I who prevented him and insisted on your being kept in the dark. Everything was messy and impossible. Something like this had to happen. If you had exiled Launcelot, my duty would have been to make an effort to live with you. You have killed Launcelot. Now I must die with him.

ARTHUR. Guinevere. I forbid you. I'll save you by force. Who knows where suicide leads to or what doors it opens? Don't imagine that you can rejoin Launcelot that way.

GUINEVERE. I'm not going to kill myself, Arthur. I'm going to prove to you that marriages exist which are more legitimate than those on earth.

LAUNCELOT. Guinevere . . . is that you?

ARTHUR. He's still alive. Thank God. Quick! Quick! We must save him.

LAUNCELOT. Guinevere, everything's gone dark. Where are you?

GUINEVERE. I'm coming.

ARTHUR. What binds my limbs? Who is holding me back?

He can be seen struggling against a spell which holds him motionless.

GUINEVERE. The Elves.

VOICES OF THE ELVES. Launcelot of the Lake, Launcelot of the Lake, the Queen is yours. Take the Queen with you, Launcelot of the Lake.

ARTHUR. Don't leave me alone.

GUINEVERE. Where Launcelot is taking me we shall surround you with a friendship more cunning than any lie. Do you think I want to abandon Blandine and Segramor? Stay where you are, Arthur. Obey and be witness to a miracle.

ARTHUR. The Grail was false and love has forsaken me.

LAUNCELOT. Britain, I die.

He falls back dead.

VOICES OF THE ELVES. Launcelot of the Lake! Launcelot of the Lake.

GUINEVERE. I must die, Arthur, in order that the Grail may return.

Music.

It's easy. I shall lie down beside my beloved. At the bottom of the Lake I see the knight. The water distorts his form. Seen through the reflections and the ripples, it looks as if he moved. My new body is floating on the surface. It is sinking, gently, gently. And now Launcelot seems to be rising to meet me. I pass through luminous layers. Shadows escort me and prevent me from sinking too quickly. Don't mourn for me. If you only knew with what sweetness the Lake is drawing me in. Now I can hardly see you up there. He is rising, rising.

The King sobs.

He is becoming distinct. His eyes are open and look into mine. His floating arms wave a greeting to me, like the plants which surround his resting place. My ears hear nothing. My limbs are laid beside his. Good-by, dear, dear Arthur. Launcelot. Launcelot. Here I am.

VOICES OF THE ELVES. Launcelot of the Lake, the Queen is your Queen, marry the Queen, the Queen is yours, the Queen is your Queen, Launcelot of the Lake.

The curtains of the alcove close.

ARTHUR, *as he is released from the spell.* Free! My children, my children, my friend, my wife, I will set you free, I will unite you, I will give you my blessing.

He comes out of the alcove.

Too late. It's all over.

He collapses.

Over.

There is a knock at the door. The King jumps.

Who dares?

The door opens. Enter Segramor and Blandine.

BLANDINE, *pushing her brother into the room.* Segramor!

The whole scene should be played in a tumult of youth and high spirits round the motionless figure of the King.

ARTHUR. Segramor! What are you doing here?

SEGRAMOR. Father, haven't you heard?

BLANDINE. The most extraordinary things have happened.

SEGRAMOR. I thought Launcelot would have told you. Where's Mother?

BLANDINE. I woke with a start. I went to look for Mother and I found Segramor. Imagine my surprise!

SEGRAMOR. Launcelot must have gone to scout out the ground in advance. When he didn't return to the hunting lodge I said to Gawain —

ARTHUR. To Gawain?

BLANDINE, *laughing.* It's my turn. You tell the story so badly. Yes, Father, Gawain. The real Gawain. The only one.

SEGRAMOR. Can you imagine! Gawain wasn't Gawain but a sorcerer's apprentice who had assumed his form. The real one, our one, Blandine's fiancé —

BLANDINE. Was dying of hunger in a dungeon of the Dark Tower.

SEGRAMOR. The Dark Tower belonged to the sorcerer Merlin. Your Merlin, the master of the false Gawain who fooled us all under your very nose and made us ascribe his black magic to the Grail.

BLANDINE. Father. Father. Wasn't I right to suspect your minister? He was ruining Britain and our castle, and making use of the Grail to set us all against each other.

SEGRAMOR. Poor Mother is going to have a good laugh when she hears that she was the second incarnation of the sorcerer's apprentice. Sir Launcelot thought she was possessed by a devil.

BLANDINE. Poor Father. The story is crazy enough in itself and here we are telling it all higgledy-piggledy.

SEGRAMOR. And that's not all. Thanks to the talking flower, we've made a magic journey. Poor Gawain is half dead with embarrassment. At the moment he's trying to explain what happened to farm hands and kennelboys who can't understand a single word he says. He doesn't dare show his face inside the castle.

Blandine and Segramor burst out laughing.

BLANDINE. Father, why don't you laugh? Are you angry?

SEGRAMOR. Why don't you share in our joy? Gawain is safe, the forgers have been exposed, you are free, and Galahad will reveal the Grail to us all. Mother is going to be so happy.

BLANDINE. You're crying.

ARTHUR. My children. Your story is so violent and extraordinary that it is bound to be a shock, and will take a little time to get accustomed to. I would ask you for the details now, except that I have news for you which is more serious than anything you can tell me.

SEGRAMOR. Is it bad news?

ARTHUR. Listen to me carefully. You are my grown-up son, and you are my grown-up daughter. I need your help. You are the only friends I have and I expect from you both, however violent the shock I may give you, complete obedience.

BLANDINE. Segramor!

She presses close to Segramor.

ARTHUR. What I have to tell you is usually hidden from children, and the world would disapprove of my conduct. But I have just put myself beyond the judgment of men. I stand alone, face to face with my deeds. Segramor, Blandine, your mother and Launcelot were in love. Their real life was with each other. I stole it from them and I have just given it back to them. Look!

He leads them before the curtains and discloses the bier.

BLANDINE, *throwing herself on her knees.* Oh!

SEGRAMOR. Mother!

He also kneels and lays his cheek against his mother's hands.

ARTHUR. Pray. Try to understand. Forgive. I shall close the curtains and leave you undisturbed. It is my order that this day be a feast day. All are to worship at the bier of the new bride and groom.

In exaltation he opens the door violently. The False Galahad, who was listening at the door, pokes his head into the room. Arthur starts back, stupified.

ARTHUR. Sir.

FALSE GALAHAD. Your Majesty. Excuse me. My mistake (mistyke). I must have lost my balance.

ARTHUR. What were you doing there?

FALSE GALAHAD. I was listening ... I mean ... er, I ...

ARTHUR. Are you in the habit of listening at keyholes?

FALSE GALAHAD. Not exactly. Not exactly. You see, Unky-Wunky ...

He catches himself.

... Your Majesty ... where was I?

Mysteriously.

I was listening, in fact, I was trying to make (myke) out from the outside whether, on the inside, the place (plyce) was free.

ARTHUR. Free?

FALSE GALAHAD. Er, yes, whether you were alone. However, as I heard you talking and as it is the Queen's room, well, naturally, I, you understand. . . .

ARTHUR. I understand less and less.

FALSE GALAHAD. Sir Launcelot was most persuasive. He promised me the earth. To cut a long story short, by the time I realized that I was conspiring against your royal person and that the Queen was in the conspiracy with us, it was too late.

ARTHUR. My mind is giving way.

He kneels at the prie-dieu.

Lord, protect me from the devil. Make me deaf to all deceitful wiles. Keep me faithful to penitence and justice.

He hides his head in his hands.

FALSE GALAHAD, *shouting at Arthur's back.* Listen to me, will you? I have to tell you that I deceived you, that I plead guilty, that I was in the plot with Launcelot and that Launcelot was afraid of the loyalty, insight, and sincerity of your minister Merlin and that the whole thing was a sham, the chair, the Grail, the Quest, everything, and that Launcelot prompted all I said and did, and that I was involved in a conspiracy against my will.

He realizes that Arthur is not listening.

Mercy me, I don't think he's even listening. Do you hear, King Arthur? One might as well be haranguing a statue.

What's the use. If he shuts his ears, I'm just wasting my spittle.

The trumpets of Galahad sound offstage. The False Galahad pricks up his ears.

The trumpets. This is the end. Each man for himself.

He rushes out. The clash of armor is heard. The door, which was left half-open, admits Galahad, who is looking back.

ARTHUR, *getting up in a rage.* Whoever you are, whatever has happened, this goes beyond all limits of decency and respect. I will *not* put up with this uproar. I exile you.

GALAHAD. Arthur, Arthur.

ARTHUR. I exile you. There are two dead people in this room; this room belongs to the Queen. I won't stand it.

GALAHAD. Listen, Arthur, you must listen to me. You have been the victim of an absurd magic. I'm not the same person who left this room. I have just run head-on into myself, armor against armor. At first I thought I had smashed a mirror. To further his schemes, your Merlin would transform his young servant, Ginifer, into one or another of us in turn. The Galahad whom you quite rightly sent packing and whom I banged up against behind the door must be Ginifer's supreme incarnation, and I doubt whether in future Merlin will risk giving him the faces of his victims again. In giving him the face of a Knight of the Grail, he has gone beyond all bounds.

ARTHUR. The Grail. . . . What am I to believe? Who am I to listen to? The Grail has brought nothing to this place but disaster. Is it really true that you are not the wretch who confessed his imposture to me and accused Launcelot?

GALAHAD. I can imagine the sort of comedy which that scamp must have played for your benefit. No, Arthur. I am Galahad, the son of Launcelot and Melusine.

ARTHUR. I have killed Launcelot.

GALAHAD. The Grail will forgive you as I forgive you. Launcelot is not dead. The Queen is not dead. You have been living under a fatal spell. Where you were, nothing real could exist. Now everything is alive, everything can bleed. Nothing will act as a cushion or a drug to make life easy. Reality is beginning. Reality is harsh. Waking up will hurt.

ARTHUR. I was living upon illusions.

GALAHAD. Their charm is difficult to resist. In the place of the young charmer you lose, Blandine will get back her fiancé. You must be fair. The Grail and the elves are at work. They have so engrossed Blandine and Segramor that both have become deaf to all that is going on in this room and perhaps the elves are occupied with funeral rites, for they hate tombs and sometimes perform the work of gravediggers.

ARTHUR. And I, Sir Galahad. What will become of me?

GALAHAD. You? You will efface yourself, you will endure everything, you will pay. For one must always pay, pay, pay. The old life is dead, long live the new. Expel Merlin and his servant from Britain. Give orders that this day of mourning be celebrated as a wedding day. Be brave.

ARTHUR. Galahad . . . Shall I ever see the Grail?

GALAHAD. That depends on you.

ARTHUR. Tell me, Sir Knight, tell me . . . in order to see it . . . does one have to die?

GALAHAD. That would be too simple. No, Arthur, one has to live. The whole error of the world lies in thinking otherwise.

Gawain and Merlin enter.

GAWAIN. Your Majesty, I demand justice.

ARTHUR. There, there.

GAWAIN. This scoundrel has imprisoned me, chained me up, starved me, and made me a public laughingstock. My indignation is met with giggles and obscene little hints. I daren't present myself to Blandine. I'm too ashamed. Your Majesty, Uncle, if you have any love for Blandine and any respect for me, I beg you to punish this criminal and his valet, to make a public example of them.

MERLIN. Sir Gawain refuses to believe me. I would like him, Your Majesty, to hear from your own lips that his place was not so badly occupied and that, if he did have a double at the castle, this double had the good fortune not to displease Your Majesty.

ARTHUR. I'm taking my advice neither from you, nephew, nor from this fellow.

GAWAIN. He insulted the Queen. He dared —

ARTHUR. It seems to me, Gawain, that the Queen's honor and the honor of my house are my business. In any case, kindly keep your temper. That is something we all need to do here. This man will leave the castle and Britain with his valet, Ginifer. I exile them.

Merlin bows.

GAWAIN. Your Majesty —

ARTHUR, *to Merlin.* Go. Leave the country.

MERLIN. Your Majesty is showing great courage in the face of reality. Apart from the little matter of a certain letter, my only policy has been to clothe reality with flowers.

ARTHUR. I wish life to return to Camelot.

MERLIN. Life, Your Majesty, seems to have made a good start in that alcove.

ARTHUR. I would rather have real deaths than a false life.

MERLIN. Bravo! The enchantment shall cease. All that remains is for me to hope that your realm will not find the disenchantment too severe.

He bows, then turns to Galahad who is standing motionless in front of the alcove.

Ginifer!

Silence.

Ginifer, come here. The joke is over.

GALAHAD. You have made a mistake, Merlin. It is the real Galahad who is talking to you. There is a time for you to make fools of others and a time for others to make a fool of you.

MERLIN. I give in.

GAWAIN. Uncle, I'll go with him to make sure that your orders are obeyed.

Exeunt Merlin and Gawain.

ARTHUR. My poor little monkey. Was he really a demon?

GALAHAD. The spirit world swarms with tightrope dancers like him who keep your nose in the air while the master picks your pocket. You must make this sacrifice.

ARTHUR. But if I do, Sir Knight, will the Grail reward me? Will it show me any signs of its coming?

GALAHAD. Since the deliverance of the castle, it has never stopped manifesting itself.

ARTHUR. Sir Knight, could I be allowed to see one of these signs with my own eyes?

GALAHAD. I shall show you one now. Release your children from the spell which has made them deaf and dumb. Call them from the alcove but don't, on any account, show surprise when you see them. For, I warn you, you may be startled.

ARTHUR. What do you mean?

GALAHAD. Call them and see.

ARTHUR. Blandine! Segramor! Blandine.

He goes up to the alcove.

Come here.

BLANDINE. What, Father?

ARTHUR. Come out of the alcove.

SEGRAMOR. We're coming, Father.

He draws back the curtains and appears first. He has become Launcelot and Blandine has become the Queen. Except for their clothes and hair, which are as before, they are the actors who played the roles of Launcelot and the Queen who have been substituted for those who played the roles of Segramor and Blandine.

ARTHUR, *aside to Galahad.* The likeness is incredible. Why did it never strike me before?

GALAHAD. All your illusions are beginning to vanish. The dead have passed into them.

The children throw themselves at their father's feet and kiss his hands.

ARTHUR. Now, children, I insist that you dry your eyes. Today is a feast day.

Enter Gawain.

GAWAIN. Well, that's that. They're gone, and good riddance.

ARTHUR. Gawain. Your fiancée is here. You haven't looked at her.

GAWAIN. Oh, Blandine, I'm sorry. I felt so ashamed I didn't dare show my face in your presence. Heavens! Being away does make things look different. From a distance, I thought you were the Queen.

BLANDINE. Poor Mother.

GAWAIN, *to the King.* Uncle, please forgive me for the clumsy way I barged in on you just now, shouting and swearing when I should have been showing my sympathy. But I've only just heard.

ARTHUR. Let me repeat to you what I've been saying to your cousins. No one is to look sad or talk of mourning. That is an order. Blandine, Gawain. . . . You two must have a lot of secrets to tell each other.

Blandine and Gawain go into the embrasure of the window.

GALAHAD, *to the King.* Would you like to see another sign? Tell your son to touch his wound.

ARTHUR. Segramor, touch your wound.

SEGRAMOR, *baring his chest.* No — it can't be — I'm cured. The skin is healthy. The wound has closed. It doesn't bleed any more.

BLANDINE. You're no longer pale! Your eyes are bright! Look, Gawain, isn't he a fine figure of a knight? He might easily be taken for Sir Launcelot.

ARTHUR, *to Galahad.* She too.

GALAHAD. Gawain has been living in the shadows. It is a fresh way of looking at things. Everyone sees now what before was concealed by habit.

ARTHUR. Gawain saw Segramor yesterday.

GALAHAD. I know, but it is here, in the castle, that the enchantment has ceased and reality is beginning. Wonders will follow wonders, or rather what men call wonders, which only means, what they didn't see before. The Grail is announcing its coming.

ARTHUR. If only your quest could reach its goal at Camelot, and this glory be reserved for my house.

GALAHAD. The quest of the Grail is another matter, Your Majesty. I must look for Carbonek, but the Grail manifests itself wherever it chooses, and now this castle is free of all that prevented its coming.

SEGRAMOR. Father

BLANDINE. Father, Father, Galahad!

GAWAIN. Come here, all of you. Look! Look!

ARTHUR. What have they seen now?

GAWAIN. There!... on the road.... Merlin is leaving. There's a sort of ragamuffin skipping and hopping along beside him. Behind them, the fields are becoming green again, the trees covered with leaves; the grass grows, the mist rolls away, and you can see blue sky, clouds, sunshine.

ARTHUR. Life.

GALAHAD, *mysteriously*.... is at hand.

At this, the light increases and slowly it floods the room. The birds start singing.

ARTHUR. Sir Galahad ... it seems to me ... I would say ... No, I daren't.

GALAHAD. You're going to see it now.

ALL. The Grail! The Grail! The Grail! I see it. Do you see it? There it is!

GALAHAD. Do you see it, Arthur?

ARTHUR, *in ecstasy*. I see it.

GALAHAD. What shape is it?

ARTHUR. No particular shape. I couldn't describe it.

GALAHAD. Do you see it, Blandine?

BLANDINE. I see it.

GALAHAD. What color is it?

BLANDINE. All colors. I couldn't paint it.

GALAHAD. Segramor, Gawain, do you see it?

SEGRAMOR AND GAWAIN. I see it.

GALAHAD. What does it smell like? Where is it?

GAWAIN. Lovely!

SEGRAMOR. It blazes. It is nowhere. It is everywhere. It moves.

GALAHAD. It is within you. Each of you sees it as soon as he is in harmony with himself. Now you have all seen it, my task is done.

ARTHUR. Galahad, why do you ask us to describe the Grail? Surely, you should be telling us about it.

GALAHAD. I cannot see it.

ARTHUR. You!

GALAHAD. I shall never see it. I am the one who makes it visible to others.

Sunlight fills the room. Galahad draws back the curtains of the alcove.

GALAHAD. And now I shall draw back the curtains of the alcove. Look.

ARTHUR. Why. The bed is empty.

GALAHAD. That is the elves' doing. They hate death and manufacture invisibility as bees distill honey. Knights of the Round Table, the time has come for me to say good-by.

ARTHUR. Don't go, become one of us, stay here.

GALAHAD. Merlin moves quickly. He is already doing his damage somewhere else. I never stay long in one place. As you know, Arthur, I seek the High Adventure. Everyone must always pay, pay in his person and in his actions.

ARTHUR. King of Knights, our love goes with you.

GALAHAD. I am neither a knight nor a king. I am only a poet. . . .

SEGRAMOR, *kneeling before Galahad and kissing his tunic.* Poet!

GALAHAD. Like you, Segramor.

SEGRAMOR. Alas, I thought so once. The *Siege Perilous* has taught me to be less ambitious.

GALAHAD. On the contrary, you should congratulate yourself. The time may come when you will miss your blemish, for it is by some such blemish or other that men are kept in touch with the earth. My arms are without blemish and I can keep in touch with no one.

SEGRAMOR. If you must go, at least put off your departure for a little. We love you.

ALL. We all love you.

GALAHAD. I am snatched away from all whom I love.

Already he is outside and has shut the door. The children try to follow him but the King holds them back.

ARTHUR. Let him go.

The singing of the birds becomes louder.

BLANDINE. The birds. I never thought I should hear them again. What a row they're making!

ARTHUR. It's enough to drive one mad. Was it like this in the old days?

GAWAIN. I remember how they used to sound before my imprisonment. They sang just the same songs and kicked up the same sort of racket.

BLANDINE. The sunlight is so dazzling.

GAWAIN. We got into the habit of living in shadows and silence. Now the Grail has restored everything to order. Let us worship it.

ARTHUR. At my age, it is difficult to come to life again. My poor eyes! My poor ears!

He puts his arms around his son and daughter.

Blandine, Segramor, that reminds me, you understand the language of the birds. Won't you tell us what they're saying? Why shouldn't they add their word to the whole story?

SEGRAMOR. It's such a long time since I tried. I'm quite out of practice.

ALL. Try, Segramor, do, please do.... Please try.

SEGRAMOR. Wait a moment.

He shuts his eyes and listens. The birds·redouble their cries...

They're saying ... Yes, I've got it now. They're saying: Pay, pay, pay, pay, pay, pay, pay. You must pay, you must pay, you must pay. Pay, pay, pay, pay. pay, pay, pay. You must pay, you must pay, you must pay. Pay, pay, pay....

CURTAIN

BACCHUS

translated by

MARY HOECK

PREFACE

Bacchus is a play concerning hard kindness, which I oppose to soft kindness. This was the misunderstood theme of the *Letter to Maritain*. Rendering to God the intelligence attributed to the devil, which was more particularly attributed to him in the sixteenth century when the devil had the leading role.

Hans is kind. The Duke is kind. The Cardinal is kind. Lothar is kind. Christine is kind. That's what seems to me fresh in this play, as we usually look for strength in a background of evil.

A high-minded Roman Cardinal has the insight to perceive the high-mindedness of a young heretic. He tries to save him even after his death. He does save him from an ignominious death, by means of a "pious lie" and so permits of his burial in holy ground.

The play is not vowed to a cause. It shows nothing but the terrible loneliness of youth which has no allegiances outside itself and will not accept the tenets of any kind of policy.

The custom around which action turns is an old Byzantine one. But in Byzantium when the chosen one was elected, he accepted his own doom. He was sacrificed on the seventh day. I am not sure whether a Dionysus was involved. The rather attenuated form of the custom survived in Switzerland until recently, at Vevey, I think at the time of the wine harvest. Ramuz told me about it and spoke of it as disastrous because the young men elected lost their heads over it and refused to go back to their former dull way of life. Naturally I envisaged the custom carried to its nth degree, when the whole show went beyond the limits of a masquerade.

The deep confusion of minds in the sixteenth century, which was dominated by the wisdom of Erasmus, does not allow my characters to use very clear arguments. They can only throw intuitive but often contradictory gleams of light on the scene and feel their way blindfold through darkness full of snares and flashes of lightning.

The ideas expressed in *Bacchus* are not those of the author, they belong to his characters. This is what the stage demands, as it is a place which belongs to objectivity and action.

NOTE WRITTEN AFTER THE FIRST NIGHT

Bacchus shows the plight of youth seeking to find itself but not knowing which way to turn among the dogmas opposing it. This is what happens to Hans.

In reply to Catholic comments, it is necessary to appreciate that the Pater Noster is said as by a child, that any seemingly subversive sentences are said by a "village idiot," by a young heretic, or by a vulgar provost. It would be childish to impute them to me or to blame me for them.

JEAN COCTEAU
1951

Bacchus was first performed at the Théâtre Marigny on December 20, 1951, by the Madeleine Renaud — Jean-Louis Barrault Company.

CHARACTERS

HANS, *Bacchus*
THE DUKE
LOTHAR, *The Duke's Son*
CHRISTINE, *The Duke's Daughter*
CARDINAL ZAMPI, *Envoy Extraordinary of the Holy See*
THE BISHOP
THE PROVOST MARSHAL, *Head of the Garrison Town*
THE SYNDIC, *Head of the Merchants' Companies*
KARL, *Captain of the Archers*
FIFTEEN ARCHERS

DÉCOR

Action takes place in a German town near the Swiss borders in the year 1523 in an audience chamber in the Duke's castle. The hall is plain, in the English baronial style of the period. At the back of the stage there is a large doorway leading to a flight of steps. Center stage, left, a window looks onto the Cathedral Square and a concealed balcony. Center stage, right, a low door gives access to the other rooms and floors of the building. By the side of this door there is a huge fireplace surmounted by a mirror which slopes slightly forward.

In the middle of the hall to the left, there is a long table, surrounded by upright chairs and chairs with arms. The table is covered with sheets of parchment, writing sets and goose quills. To the right of the door at the back of the stage, there is a large chest.

The window and the small door are opposite each other, and are both surrounded by light architectural structures in the shape of beams such as those seen in Holbein's *Thomas More and Family* at Basle.

For décor and costumes I have taken inspiration from the paintings of Holbein and Dürer, and from the Naples tapestries.

As the curtain rises, the audience chamber is empty, except for Lothar, who picks up some red material and a crown of vine leaves from the table. He puts on the crown and drapes the material around him, then he goes over to the sloping mirror above the mantelpiece, and in front of it he arranges the folds of material and the angle of the headdress. Christine comes in through the doorway at the back of the stage, pretending not to see her brother. She goes toward the little door on the right. As she opens the little door, Lothar springs back toward the table. Christine comes forward.

CHRISTINE. Did I startle you?

LOTHAR. I didn't see you come in.

CHRISTINE. Too busy with your little self.

LOTHAR. No. But my little self needed a lot of room to show off its costume. How do you like it? Of course it's not finished yet.

No reply.

Well?

CHRISTINE. I suppose it would be more civilized to finish it off.

LOTHAR. You're too witty for me.

CHRISTINE. As for you . . . you're too blind.

LOTHAR. Blind?

CHRISTINE. Look here, Lothar, where did you find that costume?

LOTHAR. In Ulrich's cupboard.

CHRISTINE. Aren't you ashamed of rummaging around in Ulrich's room, stealing his costume and strutting about in it like a peacock?

LOTHAR. I must. I need it. The wine festival begins tomorrow, and you're not going to buy me the stuff I need.

CHRISTINE. Neither I nor your father.

LOTHAR. Very well, then.

CHRISTINE. Lothar, don't you understand — your brother is dead, and you're wearing all that's left of his costume.

LOTHAR. Ulrich would be glad to see me in it.

CHRISTINE. Don't you understand that this costume killed him?

LOTHAR, *flinging off the crown*. What?

CHRISTINE. The only thing to be said for you is that you were too young to be told the truth.

LOTHAR. What truth?

CHRISTINE. Ulrich killed himself because of this disgusting festival. Now perhaps you see what it would mean to Father if you put your name forward and wore your brother's old costume.

LOTHAR, *slowly taking off the finery*. Ulrich killed himself. . . .

CHRISTINE. Yes, Lothar, and this is how it happened. Take warning. He wanted to be Bacchus. You know what that means every five years to the people here.

LOTHAR. To be a god and a king for seven whole days. Who wouldn't like to give it a try?

CHRISTINE. Then they burn the costume in the Square, and Bacchus goes back to what he was. That's what Ulrich couldn't stand. The heartless set we belong to played out the comedy for him right to the bitter end. They made an idol of him. But as soon as the festival was over, they took it out of him for his perversities by making a public fool of him, until they made his life impossible. First he went into a temper, then he became silent like a wild thing, finally worn out by their damnable jokes he drowned himself. Mother died of it... that's what our family has to thank the wine harvest for.

LOTHAR. I didn't know.

CHRISTINE. And now that you do, surely you'll take off that costume and put it away where you found it — where Ulrich himself hid it.

LOTHAR. No, Christine. That's not my idea at all!

CHRISTINE. Don't be a fool!

LOTHAR. No! I'll avenge Ulrich by entering the competition and winning. That'll do for them! And when I've got the power, I'll use my week to rub their noses in the dust.

CHRISTINE. But they're not the same people.

LOTHAR. Today's lot are no better.

CHRISTINE. For one thing, you've neither the looks nor the money for the jury to choose you.

LOTHAR. I'll take my chances.

CHRISTINE. You can do more than that for Ulrich.

LOTHAR. How?

CHRISTINE. The Church refused to give him last rites and burial in consecrated ground. The Church refused them, and so I have declared war on the Church, and on our so-called friends, who are its slaves.

LOTHAR. Christine, don't talk so loud.

CHRISTINE, *in a low voice.* I'd never have opened my mouth if I hadn't known that you're in the underground movement too.

LOTHAR. You're mad!

CHRISTINE. Listen to me, Lothar. You're only sixteen and I'm twenty. I have to be a mother to you, and you must listen to me. Anyone can be burned here for saying "yes" or "no."

LOTHAR. But — !

CHRISTINE. Now, listen. Your life and mine are at stake. Don't forget you're in the public eye; if they follow you, they'll get me. And my motives are not yours — they're serious. You mustn't expose me to danger. No one even suspects me.

LOTHAR, *bringing her forward to the front of the stage.* Now, Christine, as you've been frank with me, I'll tell you something you'll hardly believe.

CHRISTINE. Be quick. Father will soon be back.

LOTHAR. I went to a meeting yesterday, Christine.

CHRISTINE. I knew and that's why I wasn't there.

LOTHAR. It was held in a cellar in the Upper Town — it was all in the dark. Suddenly, the door began to open and I saw — can you guess?

CHRISTINE. Get on with it. . . .

LOTHAR. I saw Father come and go like a ghost — he must have seen me.

CHRISTINE. It was only your imagination.

LOTHAR. It wasn't. I'll swear it on the Bible.

CHRISTINE. Father . . .

LOTHAR. Father. I didn't ask any questions. One can't at these meetings.

CHRISTINE. I'd have known — if it was so. . . .

LOTHAR. No, Christine. They arrange it so that we don't meet him. I should not have been there yesterday, but for a mistake.

CHRISTINE. If he does know about us, he doesn't want to, and he wants us to pretend we don't know about him. Until he speaks about it, we must pretend it was a dream. But it was no dream — I knew.

LOTHAR. What did you know?

CHRISTINE. I was trying to mislead you a moment ago. But now I must be really frank with you. I knew Father took part in these meetings in secret, but we weren't supposed to know.

LOTHAR. Do you think he goes there for the same reasons as you do?

CHRISTINE. Yes.

LOTHAR. But, Christine, he's too powerful to be nothing but a follower. There must be something more behind it. Now, I'll tell you something else — he knows where Martin Luther is hidden away, and last year he went to see him in his mountain hide-out.

CHRISTINE. Does he really know Martin Luther?

LOTHAR. He went to Thuringia, to Wartburg. The Elector of Saxony keeps him hidden there — I'm right, I know it. And now Father's been to see him in his new hiding place in the hills. I remember heaps of things which show I'm right.

CHRISTINE. If he's in communication with Brother Martin, he's in terrible danger. The Emperor spares Luther, the little pope of Wittenberg as they call him, in the mean-

time, but he doesn't spare his followers. The Archbishop
of Trèves grabbed all his goods. Let's give up the movement. That's what our friends would advise us to do if
they dared to mention the subject.

LOTHAR. Now I know why they ask me to so few meetings.

CHRISTINE. You are a booby. It's not only that. They're
afraid you might give them away.

LOTHAR. I'll be on the lookout. Perhaps some day Father will take you into his confidence, Christine. If he does,
tell him I do have some sense, that I admire Luther and
that I could wish for nothing better in all my life than to
see him and hear him.

CHRISTINE. That won't be for some time. Since he burned
the Papal Bull of Excommunication, the powers that be
are after him in every country. He can't do a thing in public now.

LOTHAR. He's a brave man.

CHRISTINE. Truth, as he sees it, is dearer to him than
life. But if he wants to convince others of that truth, he'll
have to look after his life.

LOTHAR. Why are people now against him and his work?

CHRISTINE. Because of false prophets like Carlstadt, Mün-
zer, Sorch, and Zwingli, who want his fame for themselves.
They run him down and destroy his work while he's away.

LOTHAR. Then, isn't it true that he hates the peasants?

CHRISTINE. Of course not! People tack the crimes of the
upper classes onto him. He's always been on the side of
the underdogs; that's why he joined this cause; if Luther
hated them, Father would soon give up his party. He'd hate
it. People spread these rumors to discredit a man who is
working solely for the country people and against all that
is crushing them.

LOTHAR. What about his marriage?

CHRISTINE. Turn a deaf ear to all these rumors — do. They're only old wives' tales.

LOTHAR. He's free to marry if he wants to.

CHRISTINE. If he wants to, he will. But it's all no business of yours. And now that we know that we're both on the same side, take off that costume and put it back where you found it.

LOTHAR. I don't want to.

CHRISTINE. We all have to sacrifice ourselves in one way or another.

She kisses him.

By the way, it's here, in this room, that the Bishop has arranged to hold the meeting which will choose this year's Bacchus. All the bigwigs will be arriving soon. Don't be seen about the place for the rest of today — and avoid being conspicuous in dangerous places. Promise me!

LOTHAR. I promise.

CHRISTINE. Walk about in the open where they're making ready for the Fête. Speak to everyone. Be a credit to the family!

She takes the crown and the lengths of material and throws them into a chest which she then closes.

LOTHAR. I'll be seen by everyone, everywhere!

The Duke enters at the back.

DUKE. Going out?

LOTHAR. I am going to watch them putting up the bunting on the stands.

CHRISTINE. Have a nice time!

Lothar goes out at the back of the stage.

DUKE. Good morning, Christine.

He kisses her.

CHRISTINE. Good morning, Father.

DUKE. How is your protégé getting along?

CHRISTINE. The kitchen staff are gaping at him with wonder.

DUKE. May I join the wondering throng?

CHRISTINE. No! I want you to see him with the others. I want him to be a complete surprise.

DUKE. Aren't you taking the risk that he may shock them by doing something foolish?

CHRISTINE. There's nothing to fear. He's extremely gentle, and follows me about like a dog. I think I am the only person who has ever succeeded in getting him to follow them.

DUKE. How much does he understand?

CHRISTINE. Nothing. He accepts everything. It amuses him. He does not live in the world we live in.

DUKE. What world does he live in?

CHRISTINE. The world of childhood and of animals. Sometimes what he says is so funny that everyone bursts out laughing.

DUKE. I am very much afraid that he may upset the Princes of the Church.

CHRISTINE. Frenchmen elect a pope of fools, and the Princes of the Church accept him.

DUKE. Their church is not ours. We are not in France.

CHRISTINE. Better to elect a fool as Bacchus than a sane young man who finishes up as a fool.

DUKE. Don't ever refer to Ulrich! Is Lothar still set on competing?

CHRISTINE. I told him the truth.

DUKE. Christine!

CHRISTINE. He's old enough to understand, and besides he might have heard it from others.

DUKE. And . . . has he given up the idea?

CHRISTINE. Yes! He has been very understanding about it.

DUKE. You work miracles!

CHRISTINE. I told him to go out because of your council meeting. I don't want him putting his finger in our pie.

DUKE. He talks too much.

CHRISTINE. Don't misjudge him. He's a much more sensitive boy than he appears to be.

DUKE. Too sensitive. I am afraid for him on many scores.

CHRISTINE. Such as?

DUKE. I dislike his associates. He's seen in places he ought to avoid.

CHRISTINE. He's young.

DUKE. One has to be careful of associates. There are too many idle people in this town who do nothing but watch other people and make mischief. The times encourage slander.

CHRISTINE. Is that meant for me?

DUKE. For you, for Lothar, and myself. One should keep indoors all the time. Now you, for instance, since your mother's death, your place is at home, looking after Lothar.

CHRISTINE. I go out very little.

DUKE. Do so as little as possible. The peasants' revolt is becoming more serious. I was anxious when I knew you were in the village streets. Theft and massacre are going on all the time.

CHRISTINE. The peasants have nothing against me.

DUKE. It is no longer a personal question, neither of being liked nor disliked. There's an element abroad which is out to kill.

CHRISTINE. The story of my protégé is enough to show that. When nobles organize a manhunt and set a pack of hounds on peasants, they need not be surprised if the peasants retaliate.

DUKE. The atrocities perpetrated by the peasants put ours in the shade. They must be stopped, stopped at all costs.

CHRISTINE. What can you mean?

DUKE. If we let them do as they like, they will ruin both our privileges and their own. Mr. Everyman will take charge. We shall be governed by the common herd.

CHRISTINE. So you, even you, approve of the way the life of the people is drained out of them. You approve of the tithes condemned in the Bible. Do you, even you, approve of peasants being treated as the property of the nobles, of their game and their firewood being stolen, of their feudal obligations being multiplied, of injustice, of the widow and orphan being despoiled by the law of succession, of the herdsman being slaughtered more surely than his herd. Did not Saint Paul teach that there should be neither masters nor slaves?

DUKE. If the revolt succeeded, both secular authority and the Word of God would perish equally. They want to share the goods of others and to keep their own. A ruler who upheld them would be failing in his duty and would be responsible for the crimes of the rabble. If only peasants knew the troubles of their rulers. They have only to pay their tithes and other dues. Is that not just? The land they till is ours. Unfortunately only the crossbow teaches these brutes what their duty is.

CHRISTINE. I can't believe that it is you who are speaking. What has changed you so? You who are so kind and charitable, how can you say such things?

DUKE. Just as I would hang evildoers.

CHRISTINE. But what has made such a complete change in you?

DUKE. A voice.

CHRISTINE. What voice?

DUKE. I can't tell you. It pains me very much, Christine. But my last journey into the hills helped to open my eyes.

CHRISTINE. What did you see in the hills?

DUKE. Things and people who opened my eyes.

CHRISTINE. I respect what you say without understanding it.

DUKE. That is as it should be. But let us speak of more pleasant subjects, such as your protégé.

CHRISTINE. Hans is a peasant.

DUKE. A village idiot. That is not the same.

CHRISTINE. He is a peasant.

DUKE. Rashness never helps the cause we serve. Your protégé might act as a screen to certain causes.

CHRISTINE. Am I to understand that you, of all people, would use a simpleton so as to make out that you are opposed to massacring others like him? You would stroke with one hand and slaughter with the other. That's frightful!

DUKE. Christine, Christine, do not try to understand.

CHRISTINE. I am sure of one thing only and that is that if things turn out as you say, I know how we'll both react. Neither of us will be party to such a crime.

DUKE. We're living in tragic times in which kindness may become foolishness. Unthinking kindness does not appeal to me.

CHRISTINE. Your kindness would never be blind . . . to betray betrayors is not betrayal.

DUKE. To betray, Christine, is to betray.

CHRISTINE. There is no betrayal in going back on our leaders if they take the wrong road.

DUKE. If they are our leaders, then their way is right and we must follow it. But let's not talk of such things; they should never be spoken about within these four walls. Especially as I am expecting visitors who are now on their way. How old is your Bacchus?

CHRISTINE. Twenty-nine.

DUKE. That's the upper age limit for competitors.

CHRISTINE. Names are accepted up to thirty.

DUKE. Heaven grant he may succeed! I am at the end of my tether!

CHRISTINE. I shall do my best because I love you. May heaven inspire your worthies and the Princes of the Church to consider our suggestions and to approve of them!

DUKE. I doubt very much if they will.

CHRISTINE. I shall leave you and go back to work on my masterpiece, but I shall no longer do so joyfully.

DUKE. A masterpiece does not give joy to those who shape it alone. Try to make your Bacchus irresistible!

CHRISTINE. Poor dear! He little knows what we've got in store for him.

DUKE. They'll rag him.

CHRISTINE. He's used to that. Good luck! At the first sign from you I'll bring him in.

DUKE. How does his mother feel about the way we've kidnapped her son?

CHRISTINE. The mother of Hans is a peasant, my dear Father, and the peasants love me because I love them. Remember that!

She goes out by the little door on the right.

The Duke opens the door at the back of the stage to admit the Cardinal, the Bishop, the Provost Marshal, and the Syndic.

DUKE. Forgive me, gentlemen, for being porter at my own door. I did not wish the ears of strangers to find their way among us. There is no one else on this floor.

BISHOP. My lord Duke, we have the honor of receiving a visit from His Eminence, the Cardinal Zampi, envoy extraordinary of the Holy See.

DUKE, *bowing.* Your Eminence.

CARDINAL, *bowing.* My lord Duke.

BISHOP. His Holiness has sent His Eminence to inspect these provinces and to acquaint himself more fully concerning the nature of the poison which is spreading here. As he is spending a few days in our diocese, I spoke to him of our council meeting and he wished to be present at it.

DUKE. Forgive us, Your Eminence, for imposing on you deliberations relating to a masquerade.

CARDINAL. On the contrary, my lord Duke; where I come from at the Court of Rome, everyone watches his own step and his neighbor's, the Holy Father alone being free to speak as he wishes; except for a few diverting strangers, such as the Abbé du Bellay, we have little chance of entertainment. I am therefore glad of the opportunity you are offering me.

BISHOP. A council meeting is about to discuss means of giving back to a masquerade its real character. It has regrettably lost it several times in the past, in rather sad circumstances.

CARDINAL. What do you mean by that?

DUKE. Has Your Eminence been fully informed on the subject of the masquerade?

BISHOP. Ecclesiastical business has prevented me from acquainting His Eminence with the details of the matter.

CARDINAL. Unless I am mistaken, it concerns a Bacchus who is elected at the time of the wine harvest.

SYNDIC. A very old custom, half Swiss and half German.

CARDINAL. Does it affect your town in particular, or does it take place in all German towns at the time of the wine harvest?

PROVOST MARSHAL. It's a thoroughly bad custom, and a Byzantine one into the bargain. Our fellow citizens are bursting with pride over it, because they don't know where it comes from and think that it is theirs. Before the peasants' revolt, it drew people from the four corners of the Reich. But no one feels safe on the roads now. Besides it's unbelievable that the Church should give its blessing to a pagan feast and indeed it would do us a good turn if the whole thing were blown sky high.

BISHOP. You might moderate your expressions in front of the Cardinal. The Church is a hierarchical institution which directs the conscience of men. It is not for you, Provost, to criticize what it does.

DUKE. Gentlemen, Gentlemen. . . .

PROVOST MARSHAL. I thought the point of our council meeting was to consider ways and means of breaking this custom which is shocking in a Christian country.

BISHOP. That's enough!

CARDINAL, *thoroughly enjoying it all.* Don't worry, Provost Marshal, I shall repeat your words to the Holy Father and I am sure he will take careful note of them.

PROVOST MARSHAL, *in a shrill voice.* Thank you very much, very much indeed!

BISHOP. Provost, Provost!

PROVOST MARSHAL. I don't want to find myself in the stew!

CARDINAL. To what stew are you referring?

PROVOST MARSHAL. I mean —

DUKE. Now, now, Gentlemen. We are not here for internecine disputes. I apologize to Your Eminence. The Provost has always been a little lively in his speech.

PROVOST MARSHAL. Lively I am and alive I want to remain. I don't care for being burned alive by the Holy See. Everyone knows how such things begin, but no one knows how they will end.

SYNDIC, *sniggering.* Everyone does know!

BISHOP. I hope you don't doubt the clear vision of the Ecclesiastical Tribunals?

PROVOST MARSHAL. Heaven forbid! The gods are dead, long live the gods.

BISHOP. Provost, you are incorrigible! Believe me, we are no more tolerant of Greek than of Hebrew writings. I am not unaware of the recent discoveries of a language called Greek and that a book called the New Testament written in that language begets heresy and that nothing can be got out of it but thorns and vipers. The same may be said about the book called the Old Testament, as those who can read Hebrew become Jews. Besides, the Archbishop of Mainz told us last year at the Diet of Augsburg, that the Bible was written contrary to our faith and our sacerdotal power. I am sure that His Eminence will approve.

The Cardinal gestures vaguely.

Having said this, I think it is useless to continue the discussion, and it is now necessary to enlighten Cardinal Zampi on the reasons for this conference.

CARDINAL. Well said!

The Cardinal sits down at the center of the table, facing the audience. To his right the Bishop, left the Duke. The Provost Marshal and Syndic at the end of the table to the right of the Bishop.

BISHOP. Your Eminence, our host has been the cruel victim of this masquerade. May I speak of your sad loss, my lord?

DUKE, *bowing.* Please do so.

BISHOP. Five years ago, our host's son, then nineteen years of age, was chosen as Bacchus. Every five years someone is elected for this role; it gives absolute authority for one week to the person chosen. This week of fame turned the boy's head, and on the seventh day the youths who surrounded him — I'm sorry to say we were with them — made fun of him and his pride, which was quite excusable at his age. This affected him much more deeply than we imagined. His fits of temper roused his companions. Then, to make a long story short, he killed himself.

Silence.

The Duchess died of grief.

Silence.

You will understand, Your Eminence, why we feel it so
deeply incumbent on us to avoid any repetition of such a
tragedy if at all possible.

SYNDIC. And that's not the whole story.

PROVOST MARSHAL. Just a minute! His Eminence should
be told first, how five years before that the festival brought
about another disaster. The young Wilhelm de Haage,
when he was elected Bacchus, indulged in such excesses
that I should be ashamed to give you a list of them. The
people wanted to stone him and we only saved his skin by
sending him into exile.

CARDINAL. Does this election give the chosen person
complete freedom to act as he will?

DUKE. Complete.

CARDINAL. Our Italian carnivals take a less dramatic
form. Allow me, my lord Duke, to express my profound
grief for you, and let you go on with your story.

DUKE. These are the considerations which led us to seek
a way out such as the Provost Marshal spoke of with so
much gusto. We had come to think of it as desirable that a
custom which had caused so much mourning and scandal
should be abolished.

CARDINAL. But these are surely exceptional cases.

PROVOST MARSHAL. I can tell you of others. Young Sig-
fried Wolf considered the paragraph which gives the right
of life and death to be valid. To condemn to death is one
thing: the condemned person can always be reprieved at
the right moment. To kill is another story.

CARDINAL. Did he commit murder?

DUKE. That is, alas, so, Your Eminence, and the man he
killed was a personal enemy against whom he had not
dared to take action until safeguarded by his position.

CARDINAL. The devil!

BISHOP. That's it! It seems as if the devil literally has a hand in it.

CARDINAL. It is much too late for me to take any categorical measures to refer the matter to higher authority. Is your festival not tomorrow? The town is full of stands and banners.

PROVOST MARSHAL. The Church can do what it wishes to do.

CARDINAL. I have no special powers. However, the Holy Father who knows nothing of your fears, is highly in favor of the masquerades of Rome, Florence, Bergamos, and Venice. Masquerades prevent the populace from thinking when they are idle. A man who thinks is our enemy. That is the opinion of the Holy See.

SYNDIC. It is our duty, dear Provost Marshal, to remind His Lordship the Duke and our Bishop that the Emperor is not amused by these amusements. He will look with ill-favor on anyone who takes advantage of his Italian cam-campaign in order to restrict a custom of which the pageantry should be respected.

BISHOP. I might add that the peasants' revolt does not conduce him to alienate the populace any further by robbing it of one of its long treasured diversions.

SYNDIC. It would be a grave danger. During this week the people spend their savings. It is a decent way of letting money come back to us and relieving the budget.

BISHOP. Let that pass . . . Let that pass. . . .

CARDINAL. I thought that in His great wisdom the Holy Father had eased the burden of the clergy by the sale of indulgences.

PROVOST MARSHAL, *dragging out his words and looking heavenward.* Well! You see . . .

CARDINAL. Speak out, speak out!

PROVOST MARSHAL. The sale of indulgences is not very popular with us. The people feel that Rome is bleeding us and that we are her milch cows. They speak disrespectfully of the Church as the "lady with the box."

BISHOP. Provost Marshal, you are losing control of your tongue!

CARDINAL. Let him go on, let him go on. It is essential for me to know the position.

BISHOP. The fault does not rest with the Church. Certain nobles traffic in relics and indulgences, and the feeling against them is laid at the door of the Church.

SYNDIC. You are no doubt aware, Your Eminence, that the various merchant companies which I represent have their own chapels in the Cathedral and stalls at which they sell their goods. Feast days lead to a lot of spending. People buy, they get rid of their money. It gives a very good yield to faith.

CARDINAL. I understand. The Emperor Charles the Fifth is right, customs are not abolished in a minute. They are derived from faith. That is what reassures me about the progress of the reformation . . . They'll repent at leisure.

BISHOP. The gangrene goes deep, Your Eminence. Even in Switzerland, Zwingli is at work.

CARDINAL. Zwingli is not to be feared. He is a poet. Besides the Anabaptists will look after him. Let them deal with him. They'll baptize him in their own way, headfirst into some lake. The Church is one Church and the wolves will devour each other.

PROVOST MARSHAL. They call Rome the she-wolf.

CARDINAL. We are aware of these things and of the support given to the heretics by Prince Philip. The Holy Father laughs at these insults. His life is spent on a higher level. But if events should take a serious turn, His Holiness wishes me to look for a remedy for them. This is why he has sent me.

PROVOST MARSHAL. I am sorry to say things are looking very bad, although they have eased since Brother Martin has found shelter with the nobles who fear the breaking up of their estates and who hide him away in the hills. The Elector Frederick is suspected of having spirited him away to Thuringia.

BISHOP. Your Eminence probably knows as much of these events as we do. To resume: the Antichrist (who speaks of the Pope as Antichrist) only believes in the devil and teaches that the Evangelists never speak of Christ as the Son of God. He hates the common people because they begin to follow those of his disciples who no longer agree with his teachings. He regards the peasants as ranters and thinks they ought to be throttled. Now all this is in our favor and the moment seems ripe for drawing the people back to our side, by allowing them all reasonable distractions, and for stiffening our policy against the feudal potentates who protect a rebel monk and tear him from the grip of justice.

CARDINAL. Luther drinks and has fits. He is a drunkard and an epileptic. He will not trouble us for long. And besides, if he marries (and he will, if only to give an example to others), marriage will deprive him of the mystery which is necessary to those who wield power. We shall have more worries in Flanders and Sweden or with the Rotterdam philosopher, Erasmus.

PROVOST MARSHAL. They tell me that in France there is some Abbé called Cauvin or Calvus or Calvin, who is getting busy on his own account.

CARDINAL. The King of France bears with him. He is amused by him. His is the reign of pleasure but he is highly intelligent and encourages the arts. If ever the Abbé goes too far, he will act. But then the French are always somewhat heretical.

BISHOP. I am very much afraid of moderate heretics.

CARDINAL. I agree with you. We can only leave them to stew in their own juice.

DUKE. Gentlemen, may I be allowed to remind you that we are here to make decisions and that time presses?

CARDINAL. How many competitors are there?

DUKE. About twenty.

CARDINAL. Who are the jury?

DUKE. Ourselves with a few prominent men who will vote with us.

CARDINAL. It is too late to make a clean cut. But perhaps there is still some way round, some compromise.

DUKE. That is what I wish to speak to the council about. It is an idea of my daughter Christine's. She has been distressed because her young brother wished to compete.

BISHOP, *to Cardinal.* The Duke's daughter is a splendid person. Rather lively, but a splendid person.

CARDINAL. By all means, let us —

DUKE. The idea may seem fantastic. I admit that it gave me a shock at first, but in the end I thought it would be workable. Here it is: in the nearest village to the town, there is an idiot.

CARDINAL, *looking toward the Bishop.* There are many, even in towns.

BISHOP. I know the individual. Unless I am much mistaken, the person in question is one of those simpletons who is often venerated in his own village.

DUKE. That is correct. Many of our village folk culti-
vate the presence of such creatures. Forgive us this superstition, Your Eminence.

CARDINAL. Italy is not free of such notions. They are
divided there between regard for village idiots and fear of
the evil eye.

DUKE. My daughter tells me that this village idiot has
a handsome face and fine carriage. He is called Hans and
he is the only son of a peasant woman.

BISHOP. I was right, but this Hans was not an idiot
from birth. He became one as the result of a most unfortunate incident.

CARDINAL. What was that?

BISHOP. The Provost Marshal should tell us about it.

PROVOST MARSHAL. It was during a hunt — a band of
young noblemen amused themselves by setting their pack
on him, and chasing him like an animal.

CARDINAL. Is that possible?

DUKE. Only too true, I'm afraid.

PROVOST MARSHAL. Yes! That's the sort of thing that our
fashionable youth get up to. Their worst and latest craze
is flirting with the Reformation.

Interrogatory gesture of Cardinal to Bishop.

BISHOP. Why, yes! Some out of spirit of contradiction to
their families and others because a whole family is secretly converted.

CARDINAL. What is it that draws families into heresy?

PROVOST MARSHAL. Their pockets. They are afraid of the
New World's gold passing them by and reducing their circumstances, and that Fugger's Bank in Augsburg would
only favor the feudal lords. They would be robbed of their
privileges and condemned to retrench their spending.

CARDINAL. And what do the heads of families expect from the reformers?

PROVOST MARSHAL. The people were on the march and they wished to please the people. Now the people are in revolt and Brother Martin is strangling them.

CARDINAL. Is Brother Martin a turncoat?

BISHOP. He has no choice. Truth prevails in the end. Imposture needs quick results. It takes money to get them.

DUKE. Gentlemen, gentlemen! We are wandering from our point and that is typical of the times we live in. No one speaks of anything but the Reformation, which is too great an honor to pay it. Thank God, there are other subjects of conversation, as for instance the one which has brought us together and to which I must recall your attention.

SYNDIC. I am so sorry, my lord Duke. The Reformation plays its part in our business. There is a danger that secret societies here may take a hand in it. They may foist on us a Bacchus who thinks like themselves and who might use the masquerade to work on the masses.

BISHOP. My dear Syndic, one must be wary of masks. There are so many of them here. But this danger does not come into the picture. We are four out of twelve. Two other votes are on our side and so one more would give us a majority. I should be surprised if the fortuitous and holy presence of the Cardinal does not put some fear in the hearts of even our most brazen councilors who may now be chary of coming into the open. The game would not be worth the candle. The result is therefore a foregone conclusion.

Turning to the Duke.

My lord Duke . . .

DUKE. I know that the events which made an idiot of this young man were disastrous, but they may be turned to our account. It might be sound policy to play into the people's hands by breaking with our habit of choosing one of our own class in favor of the election of one of theirs.

CARDINAL. You're not afraid of a scandal? And of making those who turn in bitterness to heresy more bitter still?

DUKE. I don't think so. Everyone will at least pretend to approve of your great wisdom.

CARDINAL. Does this mean that you are offering me the direction of your jury?

DUKE. To be its honorary president, which commits you to nothing and which covers us.

CARDINAL. It is difficult for me to refuse to be of this service to you.

PROVOST MARSHAL. Before the manhunt, was our young man not the pupil of a priest whom we burned?

CARDINAL. A priest! What was his name?

BISHOP. The vicar of our village. The Abbé Knopf.

CARDINAL. I think I know that name. Knopf . . . Knopf . . . Did he have anything to do with occult sciences?

PROVOST MARSHAL. He was a madman. A necromancer. An astrologer. An intellectual. In a word, a heretic. He was condemned in Rome and burned alive on the spot.

DUKE. If my proposals do not offend you, it would be advisable to act with prudence. I should be grateful if it could be arranged so that the whole weight of responsibility did not rest on my house alone.

CARDINAL. Might I question your daughter?

DUKE. I was going to propose this to Your Eminence. I shall fetch her.

CARDINAL. We shall wait until she comes.

The Duke goes out by the small door.

CARDINAL. What do you think of this young girl?

BISHOP. She is a little spirited — But I think well of her.

PROVOST MARSHAL. Tut, tut, tut.

CARDINAL. What do you mean, Provost Marshal?

PROVOST MARSHAL. That she is rather too modern for my taste.

CARDINAL. But what else?

PROVOST MARSHAL. Rather too modern.

CARDINAL. Do you mean that she is on the side of modern ideas?

PROVOST MARSHAL. Heaven forbid that I should make a charge of that kind! But I find her rather too modern, too free.

BISHOP. Make yourself a little clearer.

PROVOST MARSHAL. She has too many friends.

CARDINAL. That is no crime.

PROVOST MARSHAL. Oh! No, not at all. But in my young days the aristocracy did not have friends, they only had relations.

CARDINAL. I must challenge you there, Provost Marshal! It is necessary to move with the times so long as propriety is observed. Your old families must be living under restrictions which youth cannot endure and which it is dying to reform.

PROVOST MARSHAL. Now those are the last words which I expected to hear from Your Eminence!

BISHOP, *tapping the table.* Come! Come!

CARDINAL. Never mind, my dear Bishop. He is right. It is so easy to say things that are dangerous, without being aware that they are so. It must be the devil who whispers them to us.

Enter Duke and Christine.

CHRISTINE, *curtsying.* Your Eminence! My Lord! Gentlemen! ...

CARDINAL. Your father has been telling us of a rather unusual suggestion that I understand comes from you. Is that the case?

CHRISTINE. It is.

CARDINAL. Under what circumstances did you meet your candidate?

CHRISTINE. May I begin by saying that I do not always share the opinions of those in our walk in life.

PROVOST MARSHAL, *bending toward Cardinal.* Here we go!

CHRISTINE. To my shame I was a member of a hunting party which resulted in Hans losing his reason.

CARDINAL. And you tried in vain to stop this unworthy sport?

CHRISTINE. That is what happened, Your Eminence. I came home sick at heart, disgusted with my friends. I decided to go back to the village and as far as possible to undo the damage done. It was then that I learned that this unfortunate peasant had become what they call a demented person.

CARDINAL. Demented?

CHRISTINE. Yes, Your Eminence. It may come from the French word "demeuré," someone who has stayed childish. He had no one but his mother. I helped them from time to time. Last year, the men responsible for the tragedy again did something dreadful.

CARDINAL. Do not be afraid to tell us.

CHRISTINE. They forced him to witness five of his comrades being tortured.

CARDINAL. Did he understand what was happening?

CHRISTINE. Not at first. He laughed. But then he started to scream and writhe. Everyone thought he was dying of epilepsy. Later on he calmed down, but he spoke like a fool.

CARDINAL. Can he speak?

CHRISTINE. Like us, Eminence, but what he says does not make sense, and his words are often quaint like a child's. The village people like to hear him talk, for he makes them laugh.

CARDINAL. May we see him?

CHRISTINE. That would be best, Your Eminence. I thought that if my idea appealed to you, I might prove to you that it was not unreasonable and that the appearance of my protégé would not spoil the tone of the festivities.

CARDINAL. They say that he is handsome.

CHRISTINE. His good looks are not of our class. He has been washed, scrubbed, brushed, and dressed up. At present he is in the kitchen quarters in the required costume and the servants are admiring him open-mouthed.

CARDINAL. Well! It's now our turn to do so. Let us see this rare bird.

CHRISTINE. Tame him if you will, Your Eminence. He knows nothing of the pomp of Rome. He is a shy animal.

CARDINAL. We shall not eat him.

To the Duke.

I authorize your daughter to present her discovery to us.

DUKE. Fetch him, Christine.

Exit Christine.

CARDINAL. The Vatican is crammed full of statues of antique gods. I shall be glad to see one made of flesh and blood.

PROVOST MARSHAL. It's unbelievable that the Church should permit a masquerade celebrating a pagan god.

BISHOP, *throwing up his arms in despair.* Now he's off again!

CARDINAL. A pagan god is a puppet, Provost Marshal. The Church is not disturbed by such things and indeed can join in the healthy enjoyment of the people. Bacchus is the God of wine. Our Lord Jesus Christ changed water into wine and this still forms part of the Mass.

PROVOST MARSHAL. These heretical swine want to do without the wine of the Mass.

CARDINAL, *drily.* Do not let us speak of them. I shall be doing so in due season and in the right quarters.

Enter Christine by the small door, pushing Hans before her, dressed as Bacchus.

There is a prolonged silence. Christine leads Hans to the Cardinal who looks at him closely. Hans is looking into space. During the whole scene, he wanders about the hall, obliging members of the council to turn around and to follow him with their eyes wherever he goes. Everyone shouts at him, drawing out their syllables as if speaking to a deaf person.

BISHOP. Do you know the Lord's prayer?

CHRISTINE. He knows it very well.

BISHOP. Say it.

Silence.

I'll help you. Say it with me. . . . "Our Father which art in Heaven . . . "

Silence.

Have they cut out your tongue?

HANS, *drawing back in horror.* Oh, no! Not mine! Not mine!

CHRISTINE. Some of his comrades had theirs cut out. Your Worship has frightened him.

BISHOP. Now, now, Hans! Pull yourself together and say the Lord's Prayer: I'm listening. "Our Father . . . "

HANS. Back home, the priest hides behind a little grating. He thinks I don't see him, but I do. I see his eyes.

CHRISTINE. Perhaps you make him feel shy. Sometimes he answers questions he has not been asked.

CARDINAL. Let us be very gentle with him.

To Hans.

Do not be afraid. Sit down.

HANS. Not me! Sometimes the devil changes into a chair and you only notice it because the chair has a game leg.

CARDINAL. Not so silly . . .

BISHOP. Do you know the devil?

HANS. Oh, yes!

BISHOP. Have you seen him?

HANS. Oh, yes! Often.

Everyone looks at everyone else.

BISHOP, *with some fear.* What does he look like?

HANS. He flies around the sun.

CARDINAL. That sounds like the Abbé Copernicus. He told one Tribunal that the earth goes around the sun. It was not difficult to show he was wrong. We said to him: "If the earth goes around the sun, then Joshua would have had to stop the earth. And everyone knows that it was the sun he stopped."

BISHOP. That puts it in a nutshell. The Abbé Copernicus is mad.

CARDINAL. We regard him as such. That's what saves him. He's as obstinate as a mule.

DUKE. May I put a question to him?

CARDINAL. Of course.

DUKE. Can you read?

HANS. Oh, yes! I can read up to five.

BISHOP. Do you remember your teacher, the Abbé Knopf?

HANS. Oh, yes! He could read up to ten.

BISHOP. It seems to me that he could read a little too well. It did not help him much. Did you know they burned him for a heretic?

CHRISTINE. Your Lordship, he can't understand. That's too difficult for him, it muddles his poor head.

BISHOP. He is following me perfectly well. Hans, did you know that they burned your master the Abbé Knopf?

He makes signs.

Fire! Fire!

HANS, *edging back.* Oh, no! Brother Knopf lives with us. He has become a cat and he likes drinking boiling water.

BISHOP. Boiling water?

HANS. Yes! The other day I left him alone by the fire in the kitchen. There was a pot on the fire. When I came back into the room there was smoke everywhere but no water in the pot. He'd drunk it.

PROVOST MARSHAL. He's making fools of us.

CARDINAL, *thoughtfully.* I wonder.

CHRISTINE. That is the very kind of story which amuses the village folk. I knew this one about the cat.

DUKE. One could not doubt his simplicity.

PROVOST MARSHAL. That remains to be seen. Some of our fine fellows play the fool to get exemption from service.

To the Cardinal, in a low voice.

Would Your Eminence allow me to try an experiment?

CARDINAL. Do as you please.

PROVOST MARSHAL, *in a low voice.* Speak to him, keep his attention occupied.

During what follows, the Provost Marshal gets up and comes forward slowly behind Hans.

CARDINAL. Question him, my dear Bishop, question him.

BISHOP, *abruptly.* Do you know Martin Luther?

Silence.

CHRISTINE. How could he know him, Your Worship? He does not leave the farm.

The Provost Marshal is now immediately behind Hans. He seizes him by the shoulder.

PROVOST MARSHAL, *in a thundering voice.* I arrest you!

Hans turns around to the Provost Marshal and smiles at him.

CARDINAL. His conscience seems to be clear enough.

CHRISTINE. Look at his smile. He's like a child.

PROVOST MARSHAL. There are some children about the place who are possessed by the devil. Here, they call them *"Kil Kropfs."*

CARDINAL. And with us *"Suppositi."* Let him be, Provost Marshal. He is either a simpleton or extremely clever.

PROVOST MARSHAL. I can't make anything out of him.

BISHOP, *pushing the Provost Marshal to one side and going up to Hans.* Hans, do you know a rebel monk called Martin Luther?

DUKE. Poor lad! Don't you think, my dear Bishop, that that is a senseless question?

BISHOP. It is an important question to me, and he understands some things very well. I'll repeat it.

Separating every syllable.

Do you know a re-bel monk called Mar-tin Lu-ther?

HANS. Oh, yes! He's the devil!

CARDINAL. Well answered!

BISHOP. And His Holiness the Pope? Do you know about him?

HANS. Oh, yes!

BISHOP. What does he mean to you?

HANS. He's the devil.

PROVOST MARSHAL. Not so well answered.

CHRISTINE. Hans!

SYNDIC. He's a cretin!

CARDINAL. No, an idiot. That's not the same thing, Syndic. A cretin is a thinking idiot.

BISHOP, *to Hans.* The Pope is your Father.

HANS. Oh, no! My father is dead. He bought a good place in Heaven. My mother gave all our savings for it.

PROVOST MARSHAL. Fiddlesticks!

CARDINAL. But if his mother bought indulgences, she's a good Christian. I congratulate him for having such a good mother.

HANS, *slowly pointing to the Bishop with his finger.* Who is that beautiful lady?

DUKE. That is not a lady; it is your Bishop.

HANS. She has a beautiful dress.

He touches the Bishop's robe and the Bishop recoils.

CHRISTINE. Hans, you are being stupid. These gentlemen are questioning you. Answer these gentlemen.

HANS, *still looking thoughtfully at the Bishop.* She has a beautiful ring. I had a beautiful ring. He took it.

CARDINAL. Who took it?

HANS. All of them. They were singing the Vespers. He wanted to take my horse.

CHRISTINE. There is a horse at the farm and he rides it beautifully.

CARDINAL. Do you like riding a horse?

HANS. My horse took me for a cart, and it dragged me to town. . . . No! No! It was a cart that took me for a horse and I had to drag it up to the village. . . . It was full of people who screamed and screamed. . .

Hans lies down on the floor.

CHRISTINE. He's tired. He'll talk nothing but nonsense now.

CARDINAL. I have nothing more to ask him. I have come to my own conclusions.

PROVOST MARSHAL. I should like to question him too. In spite of my respect for Your Eminence, I am not so sure about this man.

CARDINAL. Question him then.

PROVOST MARSHAL. Listen to me, Hans.

HANS. I want to go to sleep . . .

DUKE. My dear Provost Marshal, he's dog-tired.

PROVOST MARSHAL. One minute, my lord Duke. Listen to me carefully, Hans. Do you know what money is?

He brings a coin out of his pocket.

Mo-ney?

HANS. Oh, yes! It's the devil. My mother showed me his picture on a gold piece.

PROVOST MARSHAL. Has no one offered you money? For anything, offered you mo-ney?

CHRISTINE. He knows nothing about money.

PROVOST MARSHAL. I hope not. Sometimes the Reformers pay their spies a lot.

CHRISTINE. Poor Hans! He's remote from your plots.

BISHOP, *to Hans.* Do you believe in miracles?

HANS. Oh, yes! The first time I went into the water I was afraid of melting. I did not melt. I asked the Holy Wafer before Mass if it was a miracle. It said, "No, it was no miracle, the miracle was melting in the mouth."

BISHOP, *bending toward the Cardinal, and whispering behind his hand.* Very evil spirit!

CARDINAL, *laughing.* What spirits are you talking about? These are only country stories.

BISHOP, *to Hans.* Do you pray to God?

HANS. Oh, yes! He gave me the ring they stole from me.

DUKE. You won't get another sensible remark out of him.

BISHOP. That's what we might have expected. One last question. Ask him, Christine, if he does his religious exercises.

CHRISTINE. I am very willing to do so, but he won't understand.

She picks up Hans.

Hans, His Lordship the Bishop would like to know whether you do your religious exercises.

BISHOP, *shouting.* If you go to Mass.

HANS. He always goes to Mass.

BISHOP. Who do you mean by "he"?

CHRISTINE. He means himself. He often speaks of himself in the third person.

PROVOST MARSHAL. I should prefer a dumb idiot.

CARDINAL. They are preferable but very rare.

HANS. I am very sleepy.

BISHOP. You shall sleep. Well! Before going to sleep will you, like a good child, say the Lord's Prayer?

CHRISTINE. I am afraid he can no longer follow you.

CARDINAL. We might let him off saying the Lord's Prayer.

BISHOP. Let's try all the same.

DUKE. It won't add anything to our findings.

BISHOP, *putting his hands together and closing his eyes.* "Our Father which art in Heaven, hallowed be Thy Name. Thy Kingdom come . . ."

HANS. . . . Kingdom come . . .

BISHOP. Now he's getting on. "Thy will be done. On earth as it is in Heaven."

Silence.

"Give us this day our daily bread."

HANS. . . . Daily bread . . .

BISHOP. "Forgive us our trespasses, as we forgive them that trespass against us . . ."

PROVOST MARSHAL. That's the most difficult thing in our beastly times.

DUKE. Really, Provost Marshal —

BISHOP. "Lead us not into temptation, and deliver us from evil. Amen."

HANS. Amen.

BISHOP, *after making the sign of the Cross.* He seems to remember the Lord's Prayer.

CARDINAL. Very little. And if he remembered the Lord's Prayer he might remember much else. It is better that he should remember as little as possible what his master probably taught him.

DUKE. Take him away, Christine, and let him sleep.

CHRISTINE. May he compete with the others?

CARDINAL. We shall discuss that in a moment.

BISHOP, *with a flabby wave of the hand.* Good night, young man.

HANS. Good night, Madame.

PROVOST MARSHAL, *laughing.* He keeps to his point!

BISHOP. Provost Marshal, I do not find this lack of respect funny!

CARDINAL. My dear Bishop, it is not lack of respect, it is lack of sleep.

CHRISTINE. He is asleep on his feet. Forgive him, Your Worship. I am taking him away. Come along, Hans, you are being stupid.

She pushes him toward the lower door. They disappear.

DUKE. To what conclusion have you come, Your Eminence?

CARDINAL. He entertaincd me.

BISHOP. Not me.

CARDINAL. And as regards his physical appearance, he merits our full support.

PROVOST MARSHAL. Your Eminence is too kind. I admit he looks quite handsome, but these Greek gods disgust me. The whole lot of them are on the devil's side.

CARDINAL. They are no longer anything but images.

PROVOST MARSHAL. I should like to destroy them as Luther does our holy images.

CARDINAL. Luther does not mind his own image. They tell me that his own portrait painter, Cranach, is always with him.

DUKE. What is our decision?

BISHOP. That rests with His Eminence Cardinal Zampi.

CARDINAL. I am a visitor. I should prefer that the Duke who is better qualified than I —

DUKE. Not at all, Your Eminence. It rests with you.

CARDINAL. What does your Bishop think?

BISHOP. I am neither for nor against.

PROVOST MARSHAL. Tomorrow all candidates march around the square and the jury votes for one of them. Before you make your decision, gentlemen, think carefully of one thing. For many months past the young noblemen have been doing all they could to vie with each other in the magnificence of their attire. Our decision will cause annoyance.

SYNDIC. Annoyance to whom? That's what counts.

PROVOST MARSHAL. The rabble naturally hates the lords. But luxury inspires respect, even enthusiasm. It's a funny thing but it's true.

CARDINAL. Let us run the risk ... I am not against it. Indeed it may prove illuminating. Try out the fool.

PROVOST MARSHAL. Nothing easier, it's a secret ballot. It will be a last-minute surprise.

BISHOP. Forgive me for being frank, my lord Duke. Is Christine not solely prompted by the fact that she wants to avenge a fine-looking young man of whom others have made fun?

DUKE. That is possible. Christine keeps her motives well hidden.

CARDINAL. That alters nothing. Put young Hans on the list, I make myself responsible.

PROVOST MARSHAL. All right, Your Eminence, I give in. But perhaps before you consent to this nomination, you should be aware of the terms of the dangerous, the very dangerous liberties allowed by the wine harvest celebrations.

CARDINAL. Is that necessary?

PROVOST MARSHAL. I insist, Your Eminence, that our Bishop should let you know what is involved. I have underlined the most tricky conditions.

CARDINAL. Very well, my dear Bishop, read this document to us.

The Provost Marshal passes the papers to the Bishop.

BISHOP. *Article XI.* Bacchus shall hold these privileges from noon of one Sunday to noon of the following Sunday.

Article XII. On the second Sunday, an effigy of Bacchus shall be publicly burned; the effigy shall be clad in the costume worn by him in the festivities.

PROVOST MARSHAL. That's the only difference compared with the Byzantine custom. There Bacchus himself was the burnt offering.

BISHOP, *continuing to read. Article XIII.* Bacchus shall choose his home as he will. It shall be given up to him entirely for the seven days of his reign, whatever may be the rank of its owner.

CARDINAL. What! The Bishop's Palace?

BISHOP. The Bishop's Palace if he wishes.

CARDINAL. Good gracious! Go on!

BISHOP, *as he reads, the Cardinal now follows with lips and gestures. Article XVI.* Every family in the city, rich or poor, must give him presents (clothes, materials, jewels, carriages). Each person must give up whatever he holds most dear and whatever costs him most to give up.

Article XIX. Bacchus shall have a guard of honor, consisting of fifteen archers and a captain, who will escort him wherever he goes and watch over him. The bodyguard will be entirely under his orders and no one else's. They shall be chosen by the Provost Marshal from among the best soldiers of the garrison.

PROVOST MARSHAL. So be it.

BISHOP. *Article XXIII.* Everyone, without distinction of rank or title, shall bow before him and call him "my lord." His parents shall serve him on their bended knees.

Article XXVIII. Bacchus shall have the right of life and death over his fellow citizens.

Article XXX. Bacchus shall have the right to enter churches on horseback, even during Divine service.

Article XXXV. Bacchus shall have the right...

CURTAIN

PROVOST MARSHAL. Hôw did it all happen? Since yesterday, I can get nothing but contradictory accounts or stories
repeated parrot-fashion.

DUKE, *to Lothar.* Tell the Provost everything as you told
it to me.

LOTHAR. I shall tell you everything in detail, but I wish
I couldn't.

PROVOST MARSHAL. Why?

LOTHAR. I mean I'm sorry I was with that poisonous
crew.

PROVOST MARSHAL. How many were there?

LOTHAR. About twenty of us and we all had a lot to
drink. Nearly all of them were competitors who had been
turned down. You can imagine the state of mind they were
in. They had made Hans drunk and were treating him
with mock deference, insulting him with honor. They es-
corted him back to his home according to custom. As his
home is a wretched farmstead there were a hundred op-
portunities for making him more ridiculous. When they were
nearly there, they threw him into the pond.

PROVOST MARSHAL. Was he still in his costume?

LOTHAR. Yes, but it was in tatters. . . . He swam about.
He came out of the water and when the Count's son threatened to throw him in again, Hans got hold of him and

threw him in instead. You know the boy, there's not much of him. He had drunk and eaten like a pig. We saw him struggle, go down, come up again, go under once more, and by the time we got him out, it was too late.

DUKE. It was not murder then. It was only a case of self-defense and it was more or less a game to Hans.

LOTHAR. No, it was no game to him, but it was not murder.

PROVOST MARSHAL. That is not the story our noble families make of it.

DUKE. It will be easy to establish the facts.

PROVOST MARSHAL. Hmm, no ... Your friends have concocted a story which is very different from yours.

LOTHAR. There were peasants there who witnessed it.

PROVOST MARSHAL. Their evidence won't count for much. But go on with your story.

LOTHAR. The whole crowd wanted to get Hans. But courage is not their strong point and they were afraid of attacking a person who was under the protection of your protocol. The body was taken to the farm. And there we were struck dumb by surprise.

PROVOST MARSHAL. What did you find there?

LOTHAR. Hans' mother, the peasants who expected him, and the rest of our crowd. They were trying to bring the corpse back to life. Then Hans stood up and shouted in a terrible voice, "Let this be a lesson to you."

DUKE. Did his mother suspect anything?

LOTHAR. Certainly not. She fell on her knees, thinking that it was a miracle.

PROVOST MARSHAL, *jerkily*. And did you guess at once that he was no idiot, that he had only been pretending to

be one? Or did you think that what happened by the river
had acted as a shock, had brought him back to his senses
which he had lost just like that ten years ago?

LOTHAR. We knew at once that he had been pretending
and he soon made it all clear. He said: "My reason returned when you tortured my friends, but I knew I could
only be safe if you thought me an idiot and so I decided
to seem one. I watched you and studied you in silence.
Now luck has given me a role in which I can speak and act
and I shall take advantage of it. Be warned." When he
spoke those words there was something regal about him.

PROVOST MARSHAL. It's unbelievable.

LOTHAR. Our warriors were quaking with fear. They took
away the victim and left the farm like whipped curs, grov-
eling.

PROVOST MARSHAL. That's not what they say.

DUKE. What do they say?

PROVOST MARSHAL. That the fool was an impostor, playing a game which was part of a plot in which I'm sorry to
say they implicate your daughter Christine and your family.

DUKE. What an extremely unpleasant state of affairs.

LOTHAR. And the same charming collection did not stop
there, but on the next day, following the old customs, they
brought Hans, accompanied by the fifteen archers, with
great ceremony here, as this is the place he had chosen for
his home.

PROVOST MARSHAL. Pity he chose your house!

LOTHAR. He knows no other.

PROVOST MARSHAL. And to crown all he lets you stay
here! Pity he didn't show you the door; then you could have
defended yourself better.

DUKE. Defend myself? Has it come to that?

PROVOST MARSHAL. My lord Duke, you know this town. It is full of intrigues. When you declared yourself in favor of an unusual choice for Bacchus, you overthrew an old and honored custom. The young people are working up their families against you and, in short, public opinion is not in your favor.

DUKE. They know for what painful reasons I accepted Christine's suggestion. Maybe I came to this decision too quickly and too lightly.

PROVOST MARSHAL. They know ... They ... They know what touches them, not others. And the first thing your Bacchus has done doesn't help at all.

DUKE. Is that so?

PROVOST MARSHAL. Is that so? In front of my very eyes he ordered them to open the prison doors. All the beauties I was keeping there are at large.

DUKE. Is it true that he harangues the crowd?

LOTHAR. He does harangue them and he does it very well. He pleads for kindness and the crowd acclaims him. Nothing subversive as far as I know.

PROVOST MARSHAL. You don't consider it subversive to open the prison doors?

LOTHAR. To be frank, Provost Marshal, I like the fellow, and his ways of conducting himself interest me.

DUKE. Lothar!

LOTHAR. What would you like me to do about it? The rest of us would not have dared to do what he does.

DUKE. Heaven grant that he does not commit any more outrages.

LOTHAR. Don't count on that. He seems to me to know quite well how to make the most of his rights.

PROVOST MARSHAL. Since you approve of the actions of a lunatic, it is my duty to warn you that it looks far from well for you to follow him in his antics and that everyone is amazed at it.

DUKE. It's youth, Provost Marshal, it's youth! Youth enjoys a masquerade. They like to see a few conventions upset.

PROVOST MARSHAL. A few conventions upset! Killing a son of one of our noblest families!

DUKE. A terrible accident, but just an accident. There is no question of murder.

PROVOST MARSHAL. You be careful, my lord Duke. If you have any sympathy with this creature, don't make it public. That's my advice to you.

Enter the Cardinal, the Bishop, and the Syndic.

BISHOP. My lord Duke, here's news for you!

DUKE. What has happened?

BISHOP. Your Bacchus has ridden into church on horseback.

LOTHAR. You gave him permission, my lord.

BISHOP. Not supposing that he would dare to take it.

The Duke signs to Lothar to leave.

SYNDIC. And that's not all of it. He tore off his belt and used it to drive out the stallkeepers who sell their wares in the sacred precincts.

BISHOP. The stallkeepers have been granted proper licenses. The various guilds over which our Syndic presides have the right to sell their goods there.

SYNDIC. No one ever dreamed of complaining about it.

BISHOP. I demand justice.

CARDINAL. Play the game, my dear Bishop. This is a masquerade. We signed the protocol.

BISHOP. Your Eminence, your indulgence astounds me.

CARDINAL. We signed. I deplore this young man's excesses, but he is not under our jurisdiction. The Holy Father would find it both comical and a little too naive if I were shocked by his doings.

BISHOP. A scandal like this!

CARDINAL, *repeating the words used by the Bishop in Act One.* "The Church is a hierarchical institution which directs the conscience of men." It is not for you to criticize my actions. May I point out that this young man has only followed a high example before which we must bow. He has chased moneychangers from the Temple.

BISHOP. Heaven forbid that I should criticize Your Eminence. But Our Lord Jesus Christ is Our Lord Jesus Christ.

CARDINAL. What would have been our attitude of mind had we been dignitaries of the Church in the Synagogue of Jerusalem?

BISHOP. I find it difficult, very difficult to follow you.

SYNDIC. The guilds don't look at things that way at all.

CARDINAL. I have dropped in among you at the time of an unusual but recognized festival of which you are now experiencing the full implications. I might add that this masquerade enlightens us on many aspects of a question which I might otherwise never have noticed.

BISHOP, *bitterly.* I bow before your august wisdom.

SYNDIC. The fact remains that complaints are complaints and disorder's disorder.

CARDINAL. Do not make a tragedy out of events which result from a farce. A little disorder may well have its place, Provost Marshal. It can even show up errors which habit concealed.

PROVOST MARSHAL. I am responsible for the maintenance of order, Your Eminence.

CARDINAL. So am I, Provost Marshal, yet I find myself in the midst of priests and peasants in revolt.

PROVOST MARSHAL. And what of this dead man?

CARDINAL. There are many dead men in this revolt.

Enter Hans at the back of the stage.

Hans is dressed as a nobleman. As he opens the door his bodyguard, consisting of fifteen archers, is seen standing on the steps. He closes the door behind him.

HANS. Low Masses don't appeal to me.

CARDINAL. It is our duty to say Masses both high and low.

HANS. I have come to inform you, Sir Syndic, that I have forbidden the paying of petty tithes.

SYNDIC. Petty tithes?

HANS. Petty tithes. And if you look at me like that I shall forbid all tithes.

SYNDIC. Sir!

HANS. Call me "my lord." That is my title, please use it.

SYNDIC. I will not put up with your insolence another minute.

He rushes to the door.

Guards!

CARDINAL. Gentlemen! Gentlemen! Calm yourselves! The guard whom you are calling belongs to Bacchus. I want to speak to him. Leave us alone!

SYNDIC. This is going beyond all limits.

CARDINAL. That is what I said to your Bishop. We have passed beyond all limits. You admitted that.

Turning to the Duke.

My lord Duke, forgive me for using your house as if it were my own.

DUKE. But I am no longer in my house. Your Eminence is in the house of the person to whom he wishes to speak.

CARDINAL. Where's my head?

BISHOP. Anyone might lose his head . . .

CARDINAL. Come, come . . . my dear Bishop, don't lose yours. I prize it and will probably be in great need of it.

The Bishop, the Duke, and the Syndic go toward the door. The Duke opens it and makes way for the Bishop to pass.

BISHOP. After you, my lord.

He moves back to make way.

DUKE. I beg of you, I am your host.

BISHOP. Where was *my* head?

DUKE. Where we all keep them.

He turns to Hans.

I thought I was at home. Force of habit.

The Duke, the Bishop, and the Syndic go out. The door shuts.

CARDINAL. And what about your head?

HANS. I wonder.

CARDINAL. Does all this amuse you?

HANS. It fills me with horror.

CARDINAL. Yet you are committing yourself, act after act, to very dangerous innovations for a man who covets popularity.

HANS. Popularity comes from the people alone.

CARDINAL. And what do the people say?

HANS. They listen to me. . . .

CARDINAL. What do you tell them?

HANS. I shall tell them that they are the victims of strong underground forces that fight over them and of which they are the dupes.

CARDINAL. The Reformation? The feudal system? The banks? . . . The Church?

HANS. Exactly.

CARDINAL. You will drive them to revolution.

HANS. Christ was a revolutionary. He was killed as a revolutionary and a heretic. "He stirred the people." So the crowd shrieked out to Pilate, according to Saint Luke. Jesus was a revolutionary and an anticlerical.

CARDINAL. You are not Christ.

HANS. I am his very humble disciple.

CARDINAL. I see. . . . You are one of those who hold up Christ's example to Christ's Church.

HANS. I am one of those who disagree with Martin Luther who treats the peasants like swine, saying they have no soul. The proof of that, says he, lies in the fact that a dead pig and a dead peasant are dead once and for all. I am one of those who disagree with Rome for bleeding us to pay for wars against Turks and to build basilicas. I refuse to bind myself to either of these frightful organizations. I try to stay pure.

CARDINAL. And what does purity mean to you?

HANS. Purity is expressed neither by actions nor by words. It proceeds from no law. It is the substance in which the soul has being. The devil is pure because he acts according to his being; he can only do evil.

CARDINAL. You are only a poor peasant. From whom does your wisdom come?

HANS. From my master whom you burned because of his wisdom.

CARDINAL. And what did your master teach you?

HANS, *almost breathlessly.* That human beings should be glad to be free of all dogmas. That the Kingdom of Heaven is not around us but within us. That miracles are what we do not yet understand. That nothing begins nor ends. That our limitations prevent us from admitting Eternity. That God could neither have been begotten nor have created. That time is not, but is only perspective. That every minute is eternal. That that of which nothing can be spoken broke into crumbs and that one of these crumbs is the earth which begot parasites — that's us!

CARDINAL. With teachings of that kind, your Abbé Knopf must have burned like dry wood. But tell me, if something broke into crumbs, does this not imply time?

HANS. No, Your Eminence. Eternity is made up of contradictions which dovetail and are wedded together in such a way that it seems as if they followed each other one after another and that they either could be or not be. Christ said so.

CARDINAL. Said so?

HANS. In two tiny sentences he gave humanity, even apart from the supreme gift of His Presence, two other gifts beyond price.

CARDINAL. I should like to hear these sentences from your lips.

HANS. Here is the first: "Father, all things are possible unto Thee, take away this cup from me." Which means: "Can you help me to avoid the inevitable?" After that who could not seek forgiveness for any moment of weakness?

CARDINAL. And the other?

HANS. The other was spoken on the Cross. "Father, why hast Thou forsaken me?" Which means: "Have you changed toward me?" After that who would not have an excuse for any doubt?

Enter the Captain of Archers at the back of the stage.

HANS. Karl! Do not disturb me.

CAPTAIN. My lord, the Syndic told me to find you at once.

HANS. Why?

CAPTAIN. One of the thieves whom you set free from prison has stolen a bolt of cloth from a stall in one of the chapels. The stallkeeper asks for justice and the Syndic wants to know what he's to do.

CARDINAL. Not easy. . . .

HANS. Who is the real thief? The man who steals from the merchant, or the man who steals from his customers, and in a Church to boot? The merchant is the real thief. Tell the Syndic to ordain in my name, that the thief should keep the cloth and the merchant sell the goods at half price.

CAPTAIN. But —

HANS. There are no buts. And see to it that my orders are carried out.

Exit Captain.

CARDINAL. And by that action you have eliminated two of your supporters. The one will curse you and the other think you a fool. The thief will advise the other thieves to steal. The merchant will arouse the merchants' corporations. The Syndic and the Provost Marshal will set the story to music. . . .

HANS. I don't care.

CARDINAL. It's hard to be hard. But, alas, earth is a hard place.

HANS. It is for man to make it sweet.

CARDINAL. It was so, but no longer is, through his sin.

HANS. What sin?

CARDINAL. Original sin.

HANS. If man had committed a fault, a sin, it would have been God's. He is responsible for our actions.

CARDINAL. And what of free will?

HANS. Free will is God's alibi.

CARDINAL. Do you dare to say that God only pretends to give us freedom?

HANS. If God, who lives outside time and yet encompasses it, has created man for His damnation and ours, He must be a monster.

CARDINAL. Upon my word! So you even revile God!

HANS. I should only be following in the footsteps of the prophets, if I did so. Luther says, "What prophet has not reviled God?"

CARDINAL. That's because, oddly enough, he thinks himself a prophet. But you do not go so far, do you?

HANS. No, Your Eminence. Although a mind which is slightly unhinged may at times prophesy without being aware of it.

CARDINAL. You admit yourself that God's ideas and ours cannot be the same. His ways are inscrutable.

HANS. If they are inscrutable, it is possible that he may punish what you call good and reward what you call evil.

Pause.

CARDINAL. Are you not slightly drunk?

HANS. Bacchus is a god whom drunkards made in their own image. Does your Eminence know Dionysus? Do you know the Greek gods?

CARDINAL. I get them rather confused; there are so many!

HANS. There were many Greek gods, Your Eminence, and never an unbeliever. There is now one God and many unbelievers.

CARDINAL. And if I am not mistaken, you are one.

HANS. Me, my lord! My fellow countrymen fear the devil more than they believe in God. My crime is to believe in God more than in the devil. It's very unfashionable.

CARDINAL. God leaves us free to choose.

HANS. Free? What do you say to the horrors the priests hold up, high and low, right and left, to frighten us? Man walks amidst trials, rewards, and punishments. Man has made of God a judge, because he himself judges and condemns. But make no mistake. Brother Martin says that God is foolish but he would not say it of the devil. He would be afraid. The best people believe that wickedness shows intelligence and that goodness comes from foolishness. That is the tragedy.

CARDINAL. You say that "man has made of God a judge." Your forget that God made man in His own image.

HANS. And man returned the compliment. If they had less fear of a cruel God, people would gain self-confidence, they would regain their dignity and responsibility as human beings. They would stop being trembling beasts. They would become "man." They would put to God's account those things which they now put to the devil's and so justify Him. Heaven would be triumphant and Hell would lose its sway.

Let us imagine together an age in which neither good nor evil, neither beauty nor ugliness exists nor are they separated one from the other, being nothing but a pure whole, a perfect marriage without divorce one from the other, a kernel from which choice and therefore heresy are excluded. The whole is broken and man begins. God demands love for Himself and He therefore chooses beauty, beauty which is invisibility. Visible beauty becomes the devil, prince of this world, dowered with fabulous riches and splendors. Let the creatures of the earth choose. The devil is bedecked in jewels, God chooses the shadow. He will know henceforth who loves him and who lets himself be taken in. Do I shock you?

CARDINAL. Your version of Genesis interests me. It is most original.

HANS. Then comes Christ, King of hidden beauty. He makes the unseen seen. But the seen remains unseen for those who cannot see, and that is for the multitude. Then comes the Church. What does it do? It shows a fierce God, a God who condemns, who burns and who wreaks vengeance. This was the only way to give him back his power to put the devil's beauty in check.

CARDINAL. God is good.

HANS. Let him prove it.

CARDINAL. You have just said that God must be loved without waiting for Him to give proof of His love. Didn't you say that?

HANS. I said, that is to say . . .

CARDINAL. You don't know what you say. You talk completely at random. What is more, like all freethinkers of your type, you are a pedant — Have you shown me the essence of your doctrine?

HANS. If I had a doctrine, I would not be talking at random. Jesus Christ contradicted himself. He said: "He who is not against you is for you." But He said further: "He who is not with me is against me." Passion and struggle lead to self-contradiction.

CARDINAL. Your doctrine, which is not one, is scarcely adapted for simple souls, although it is to them that you wish to speak.

HANS. The soul is that unique liquid which flows in all of us. It changes shape and color according to the bottle which holds it. Simple souls easily feel what touches them. They do so better than educated people who wish all bottles to be of their own shape and color.

CARDINAL. Do you presume to include the doctors of the Law in that category?

Violently.

Your impertinence always harks back to a point at which you turn the words of Christ against those who teach them.

HANS. Must I say nothing?

CARDINAL. Forgive me for being hasty. Our Italian masquerades are lighter in tone and in a masquerade each must play his own role. I was departing from mine. I confess I am not used to such conversation, although the affair of the navels in Rome gave me a slight foretaste of it.

HANS. The affair of the navels?

CARDINAL. Our painters intended to stop painting any trace of the umbilical cord on the abdomens of Adam and Eve, saying that they were not born of woman. That was the start of this little quarrel.

HANS. The quarrel is not without foundation.

CARDINAL. It is rather in your style. That is why I am telling you about it.

HANS. What was the end of it?

CARDINAL. The Holy Father cut it short.

HANS. What did he say?

CARDINAL. He countermanded the order. The effect was immediate.

HANS. They had to live.

CARDINAL. They had to live, and so have you. The Court of Rome shall know nothing of your extravagances. This is a confession. Take advantage of your position. You need not fear me, little brother, but the walls of this town have ears.

HANS. What is worse the ears of this town have walls.

CARDINAL. Mine have none and they are open wide. What is your program?

HANS. To awaken the sleeping strength of love. To abolish fear. To be kind as others are unkind. To love as men kill. Kill hatred. Not look to any end.

CARDINAL. A magnificent program. But you are left with five days. It took seven days to create the world and it would take much longer to reform it. For seven years the Reformers have been busy.

Showing his outspread hand.

You are left with five days.

HANS. Unless people intend otherwise.

CARDINAL. You mean, unless they rise up and make a reality out of this farce.

HANS. Reality comes true in the end, even if it seems to fail. It took a long time for the straw of the manger to become the gold of your miters.

CARDINAL. And the blood of Christ to become our purple. I know these hackneyed phrases. Come, tell me. How would the humble treasure left to us by the poverty of our Lord Jesus Christ, how would it have been proved to the world, if its direct heirs had not shown its wealth?

HANS. This wealth comes from no one's pocket. It belongs to the soul.

CARDINAL. Alas, men only believe what they see. It is necessary to make wealth visible in order to spread invisible wealth abroad. The people only respect pomp and that is costly. It has to be the root of our sacerdotal power. They must pay for being foolish and blind, pay for the painful necessity which they impose on us of sanctifying a trick and of using it. In this we only copy nature. Plants attract insects by their color and scent.

HANS. You know what prince it is who wears the jewels of the Father. Their rightful place is neither on your crosses nor your chasubles. Do not be astonished that they should give you His name.

CARDINAL. That Martin Luther should give us that name.

HANS. You lead him on.

CARDINAL. Your Luther is a peasant by birth, but now he has become a small tradesman and he wants a cheap Church. I repeat the people respect pomp and ceremony. Make no mistake. You owe your success to pomp and ceremonial costume.

HANS. You do not know our people.

CARDINAL. The people are the people. They will follow your bacchanalia. They will rejoice in the suspension of tithes and the lowering of prices. They will be amused by your subversive speeches. But wait until they wake up to find themselves with taxes doubled, higher prices, and with their donkey's ears sticking between the shafts of a cart.

HANS. We shall see.

CARDINAL. Your caprices are intriguing and astonishing but they do not convince. The course you are steering is not straight enough.

HANS. I have no respect for those who steer a straight course.

CARDINAL. It will be your own fault when they carry banners through the town which say: "Down with Popery." "Down with Tithes." "Down with the Nobles." "Down with Luther." Always "down with, down." And what do you propose in their place? You want to dissolve sects and parties, in favor of your own. And what is your party? It is a fair question I am asking you. You don't even know the answer.

HANS. If I knew, I should be a party to a Party. And this is what I am against.

CARDINAL. One solitary man can only impose his will on others through secret societies, through the police, or by means of the banks. This means a regime of cunning and terror altogether repugnant to you. You could not lend yourself to it. Fear of God or fear of piercing arrows. Without this man would think himself free to follow your example of freedom. Disorder would rule the day.

HANS. Through disorder we find ourselves. The minute someone else interferes, we never find anything again.

CARDINAL, *after a moment's silence.* Brother, little brother . . . If only you were willing to put yourself in order, back into order.

HANS. Into orders?

CARDINAL. Perhaps. Could you but discipline your soul, free it from its wild strain, repair the rents in your intelligence, you would become a remarkable theologian, a monk such as we lack.

HANS. I do not care for monks' bellies.

CARDINAL. There are lean ones.

HANS. I care neither for gluttons nor ascetics.

Silence.

CARDINAL, *getting up.* You care for no one but yourself.

Hans slumps down into a chair with his face in his hands. Now, the Cardinal walks up and down. He comes up to Hans and takes him by the shoulders.

CARDINAL. Come, come. I am not an ogre.

HANS, *violently.* Leave me alone. I hate judges who bend lovingly over the accused.

CARDINAL. This is neither the Diet, nor the Sacred College, nor the Court of Rome. I do not accuse you. I am only watching you and examining the contradictions in your dialectic. It is far from being foolish, but it is childish. And to tell you the truth, I have my suspicions about this heresy of yours.

He stands stock still.

Shall I speak to you as man to man?

HANS. I thought that was what we had been doing.

CARDINAL. You know enough to think me ridiculous, but not enough to convince me.

Pause.

Who employs you?

HANS. I don't understand.

CARDINAL. This is what I mean: no one batters his head against a stone wall. I want to know who pays you. Is that clear?

HANS, *getting up.* This is damnable. So the Reformers are perhaps right after all. Are you one of the ogres who fill the papal tills with first fruits, tithes, confession certificates, and other scandals which drain Germany of its blood.

CARDINAL, *as if he had not heard.* I should like to know what strange end those who employ you have in view.

HANS. What cowardly insults. I am alone and a free man.

CARDINAL. Prove it.

HANS. If I belonged to a party, I should betray my freedom of soul through this party or this party through my freedom of soul. Besides my master warned me against the moral comfort which encourages laziness. To join a party is to seek comfort, as a party encloses its members and protects them from the anguish of choosing between hundreds of shades, by offering them a plain party color.

CARDINAL. Have you ever considered that heroism may lie not so much in liberty as in the acceptance of orders which revolt our spirit or repel our intelligence?

HANS. I can obey nothing but my conscience.

CARDINAL. The mind of man never ceases to disobey his conscience.

HANS. That is what I am fighting against in myself.

CARDINAL. What drove you to falsehood?

HANS. Falsehood?

CARDINAL. Yes! Well! To play the village idiot.

HANS. A manhunt made me lose my reason. Seeing what they did to my companions gave me my reason back. I played the part I played because it was my only safeguard. Out in the country they hound us down. But traditions are strong there. An idiot is respected. He is left untouched. No one could foresee the circumstances which led me to become Bacchus. The rest I worked out for myself. Even my mother did not know the truth. Responsibility for my actions should fall on no one but me.

CARDINAL. I rather thought the Duke and his daughter might be mixed up in some strange undertaking which you conceal. But I like them and hope I am wrong.

HANS. You are wrong. I swear it on the Bible.

CARDINAL, *rising, moving a few steps back, and looking at Hans for a long time. Per Baccho,* little brother. Is it possible that you are truly an innocent man?

HANS. If you mean the contrary to being guilty, then I am. I admit my innocence. Is that a crime?

CARDINAL. I would rather see you plead guilty. I would rather that you were a Turk. Then I should know what I am facing.

HANS. Am I to understand that you would prefer me to be guilty?

CARDINAL. Perhaps. An innocent person may be dangerous, a guilty one gives himself away. An innocent one escapes our nets. He is guilty of strength alone. If a criminal expresses himself he is judged by an act. If an innocent man acts he begets nothing but anarchy.

HANS. I am sorry for you.

CARDINAL. And I am sorry for you. You are a strange goodhearted creature. And I should hate any harm to come to you through us.

HANS. You burned my master at the stake. Burn me.

CARDINAL. Heaven forbid!

HANS. Are you afraid of martyrs?

CARDINAL, *haughtily*. We have our own.

HANS. You are no doubt right, my lord, to burn us alive. All things devour themselves and fire is a savage thing which devours itself. I cannot think that a stop can be put to such a slaughter which is the very stuff of life. Maybe it will take on the look of a night festival, of a bonfire. I should be an awkward, an unbearable martyr. Because I should like them to dance around my stake in honor, not of my defeat, but of my victory.

CARDINAL. What victory?

HANS. My defeat. No real victory is possible without defeat. Those who win battles sink under the weight of victory, and the losers are victorious because everyone cares for them and looks after them. Christ knew that.

CARDINAL. What, again! Do not interpret the Word of Christ nor add your own to it. The human word tends to become miraculously flesh and to spring into action. Those who speak words hardly recognize them later when they are converted into actions. Sometimes these actions recoil upon those who spoke the words.

HANS. There are words which are never spoken and which might save the world.

CARDINAL. Tell me of one, other than the words of Christ.

HANS. I shall tell you a story from ancient Hindu mythology. I got it from my master and there is none more beautiful. Would you have the patience to hear it?

CARDINAL. I love being educated.

HANS. It's not a long story; here it is. A great prince was about to die. An archangel appeared to him.

CARDINAL. Do Hindus have archangels?

HANS. All religions have them.

CARDINAL. Go on with your story!

HANS. The archangel appeared and said: "You have been a great prince and you will dwell among us. But first you must go through an ordeal. You must go down into Hell; I will be your guide." He led him there. In Hell the prince saw fearful torments. Among others he saw this one. Out of the mud there protruded the head of a man, split open, and through the opening, boiling lead was being poured onto his brain. "What did he do?" asked the prince. "I cannot tell you" said the archangel, "it was too terrible." The prince continued. "Is this suffering eternal?" "Eternal." "And — can nothing be done for this man?" "Nothing." And the prince insisted: "Can nothing be done to save this man?" Said the archangel: "Well! Someone might take his place." Then the prince said: "I shall take his place." Then Hell split open. Now there is no Hell.

Long silence.

CARDINAL. Your prince must have been a very, very silent man. You speak too much to say one memorable word. I am afraid we should never understand each other. I belong to the right and you to the left.

HANS. All Christ's followers belonged to the right and none to the left. They betrayed Him and denied Him and followed Him to His agony. Who stood up for Him?

CARDINAL. A man from the right. A man responsible for order, the Procurator of Judea.

HANS. It is not enough to wash one's hands. I am afraid you are right, it would be impossible for us to understand each other, Your Eminence.

CARDINAL. Your presumption is appalling. You are running into the flame like a moth. I must leave you.

He goes to the door and turns back.

But before I leave you, you must hear in so many words what shows through every slightest thing you say, all your blasphemies, the contradictions in which you seek in vain to find yourself. It is a terrible fact and your only tragedy — you do not believe in God.

Christine comes in quickly by the low door and stops.

CHRISTINE. Forgive me, Your Eminence. I was on the way out and did not know you were here.

CARDINAL. Come in, come in. I was going out myself. Stay a moment with this restive creature. Perhaps a woman's hand would be firmer and kinder than mine.

He opens the door.

HANS, *bowing.* Your Lordship!

CARDINAL, *bowing back to Hans.* Your Lordship!

Exit Cardinal.

CHRISTINE, *shrugging her shoulders mockingly.* Your Lordship! Are you still inviting ridicule?

HANS. As long as possible.

CHRISTINE. Fortunately, time draws to a close while your joke goes on and on in our house.

HANS. Forgive me. But by special decree of your father, your house is mine. I allow you to stay here purely out of kindness.

CHRISTINE. I thought you were a village idiot, but not that you were a lunatic.

HANS. You think I am a lunatic because I am no longer a village idiot. There is a difference.

CHRISTINE. What difference?

HANS. That you cannot bear having been the victim of a lunatic and that you liked being the benefactress of an idiot.

CHRISTINE. Dupe, not victim.

HANS. Now we're off!

CHRISTINE. You are not merely ridiculous, you make me ridiculous. Some think me a silly fool and some suspect me. I congratulate you on your work.

HANS. You would be quite happy under suspicion. It is a part full of mystery which you would not dislike. But a woman never forgives having been taken in, and if, into the bargain, she is treated as a silly fool, the measure of her misery runs over. You can't be very fond of me.

CHRISTINE. What are you talking about? I ignore you.

HANS. If you ignore me why are you here?

CHRISTINE. It was pure accident. I thought the room was empty. I thought you were in the act of addressing a crowd of donkeys.

HANS. These donkeys might well upset your apple cart.

CHRISTINE. My apple cart is safe enough. I have nothing to do with donkeys.

HANS. I know, I know . . . You only have to do with horses which gallop about with charming boys who set their hounds on human beings.

CHRISTINE. Those boys may have had something to do with the pity I felt for you. They have nothing to do with my scorn for you.

HANS. Your scorn looks oddly like anger.

CHRISTINE. You know nothing about my anger and I hope you never will.

HANS. I am not afraid of it. I know all about the bacchantes.

CHRISTINE. Stay with your bacchantes and leave me out of it. I am going.

She goes to the door, but Hans prevents her from going out.

HANS. Not until you show me your temper.

CHRISTINE. You dare . . .

HANS. You are behaving like a vain young lady. You are worth more than that. I should like to see the woman in you.

CHRISTINE. What are you trying to do? Leave me alone and go back as quickly as possible to those who direct you and pay you.

HANS. What! You too!

CHRISTINE. It does not interest me whether others see it or not. My faith is all that matters to me. It only remains for me to convince others by my attitude as a vain young lady that I am not the tool of an intrigue about which I know nothing and care less. I am going.

HANS. You are not going.

CHRISTINE. Of all the —

HANS. What matters to me is that you should understand that I do not belong to any sect or party.

CHRISTINE. What matters to me is that I should go. If you are free, let me be free.

HANS. I might have joined the Reformers. Everything drew me to them. But Martin Luther is considering a match which is not a love match. That is the only kind I acknowledge.

CHRISTINE. You amuse me. What does a peasant know of Martin Luther and his marriage?

HANS. A peasant knows that Luther is organizing the extermination of his brethren.

CHRISTINE, *crying out.* You're inventing that.

HANS. Ha! So Luther interests you, does he?

CHRISTINE. Not in the least. It only makes me indignant that a peasant should talk of things he knows nothing about and that he goes about boasting.

HANS. A peasant! Well! Well! It would be curious if facts showed you up as harboring one of the peasants whom you pretended to be fond of and whose downfall you were secretly planning.

CHRISTINE. What are you daring to say?

HANS. I wonder if the idiot Hans was not used as a screen to cover long-term policies which those who engineer them take good care not to shout about from the house tops.

CHRISTINE. So you even malign my father. Let me tell you, he's far above all your politics and the questions which split Germany. He does nothing which could not be done in broad daylight, and Lothar is only a nitwit. If you are a spy, you'll learn nothing here.

HANS. A spy would remain silent, and I speak. I speak, as Cardinal Zampi says, at random. That upsets everyone in a cautious town.

CHRISTINE. You are upsetting me. That's what concerns me. I command you to let me out.

HANS. Command? It is for me to command.

CHRISTINE. What?

HANS. You will leave only if I wish it. Your temper is rising, Christine.

CHRISTINE. I forbid you to call me Christine.

HANS. Your anger is rising — it has reached your thighs.

CHRISTINE. My anger is rising — I shall spit in your face if you don't let me out.

HANS. Do so. That's a woman's trick. Your eyes are flaming and you are ugly now. It's magnificent. Your anger is rising. It has reached the tips of your breasts.

CHRISTINE. You're a low beast.

HANS. Your eyes are brimming over. Your anger is there.

CHRISTINE. Are you going to let me pass? Yes or no?

HANS. No!

CHRISTINE. Your impunity is only make-believe. You will be stoned, flayed, burned alive.

HANS. Fire cannot be burned.

CHRISTINE. You think you are fire.

HANS. I am fire and you are ice. It's fine when they meet and smoke and rage and ravage, and when the red-hot iron penetrates the ice it spits in fury like a thousand cats.

CHRISTINE. Must I call for help?

HANS. My archers won't stir.

CHRISTINE. Your archers are only men-at-arms. They only play at obeying you.

HANS. They obey *me*.

CHRISTINE. They can't be afraid of a puppet.

HANS. A puppet is a man to be feared.

CHRISTINE. I am not afraid of you. If you touch me I shall strike you.

HANS. That is what I want. Jesus Christ gave us love's greatest invention: we eat Him and we drink Him from afar. I want to eat and drink you. To eat and drink you — I want your lips on my lips, your skin against my skin.

CHRISTINE. You disgust me. Your jaw is set like a dog's, looking at a piece of meat.

HANS. A dog's, that's right. He's just like me.

CHRISTINE. The joke's too long-drawn out. You should keep your jokes for politics.

HANS. I have no politics but love.

CHRISTINE. Are you taken in by this masquerade?

HANS. Life is a masquerade, and everyone is taken in by it. I like you.

CHRISTINE. I don't like you.

HANS. That doesn't matter. Great things always begin badly. A couple consists of two human beings having a fight.

CHRISTINE. Don't come near me.

HANS. I shall come near you. I am going to tear falsehood out of you.

CHRISTINE. It's wonderful to hear you speak of falsehood.

HANS. You chose me. You washed me, you took my filth from me, you stripped me under pretext of making me presentable. I no longer breathed. I shut my eyes. I tried to make your hands stay in my dirty knots of hair, on my dirty shoulders, on my dirty knees. I became your masterpiece. My lie was a lovely one.

CHRISTINE. Are you not ashamed of yourself?

HANS. I am ashamed of your falsehood, of the lies you tell yourself out of pride and nothing else.

CHRISTINE. Do you imagine I am lying when I say I despise you and order you to let me out?

HANS. You are lying when you say that you despise me and order me to let you out.

CHRISTINE. You are incredible.

HANS. Exactly, no one gives me credit.

CHRISTINE. For the last time, let me out.

HANS. Where will you go?

CHRISTINE. That's the climax!

HANS. You will be going out into a world which hates you because your name is linked with mine.

CHRISTINE. Do they hate you then?

HANS. Your world is not my world, and your people are not my people.

CHRISTINE. They are the people who are in power.

HANS. They will not always be in power.

CHRISTINE. No doubt you wish to persuade your people to seize our property by force.

HANS. What we desire we must take by force.

CHRISTINE. If I am not mistaken, you wish to take me by force.

HANS. You are very intelligent. Everything in this house is mine.

CHRISTINE. You are mad.

HANS. Be mad, too!

CHRISTINE. I am going mad with anger.

HANS. That is not enough. Your anger must turn to madness.

He takes her in his arms while she struggles to get free.

CHRISTINE. I am going to scream.

HANS. It's not a case of "going to scream." . . . Scream!

She screams as she fights for freedom.

Scream. Scream! The ice is smoking and blood is rushing through your veins. Your nails tear. At last something's happening to you.

CHRISTINE. I shall raise the town against you.

HANS. Raise it. The people like nothing better than trouble.

CHRISTINE. If they like trouble, let it be yours; let them burn you.

HANS, *laughing.* That's happened. I am burning . . . I am burning. . . .

CHRISTINE. Take your mouth away. I shall bite off your tongue.

HANS. What a woman! . . . or nearly . . .

CHRISTINE, *with fists pounding his chest.* You beast!

HANS. So she bites and scratches and spits. Bang away! Struggle! Shriek! Wake up the sleeping town.

The door at the back opens, and the Archers appear, alarmed by the noise.

Stop!

He pushes Christine toward the Archers who close the door and bar her way.

Enough of this game. My men must think I am being murdered.

To the Archers.

It is true, gentlemen. I am being murdered. Here is my murderer but don't hurt her.

The Archers surround Christine.

She is so weak. A weak, a very weak, young girl. Take her to my room. Keep close watch over her. Don't let her call from the window for help. Weak people are uncommonly strong. Here's proof of it, on my face and on my hands.

Enter Lothar from the back of the stage. He walks through the group of Archers.

LOTHAR, *to Christine.* Christine, what is happening?

CHRISTINE. That creature has now made me a prisoner, after insulting me and preventing me from going out. I suppose you won't lift a finger to protect me.

LOTHAR. He is master here.

CHRISTINE. That's what I thought. Your presence is as hateful as his. Let's go upstairs, gentlemen. Lock me up out of sight of these two despicable creatures.

The Archers lead Christine to the low door and open it.

HANS. You won't be long alone.

CHRISTINE, *quietly.* I hate you.

She goes out, framed by the Archers. The door closes behind them.

LOTHAR. What's been going on with Christine?

HANS. Nothing. I love her. Greek gods don't waste time.

LOTHAR. Hans! It's not possible . . .

HANS. She is safer in my arms than in a town where they might look on her as an accomplice in a murder for which I am not even responsible.

LOTHAR. Are you serious? You love Christine?

HANS. Since the day I saw her on horseback, red with shame because her friends were mocking me. It was probably that instant more than the manhunt which made me lose my wits. When she came to fetch me at the farm, I nearly gave myself away, forgetting my role, I nearly made an idiot of myself . . . for good. I am going up to her . . . there'll be a fight . . .

LOTHAR. I am warning you; Christine is like Ulrich. She is capable of anything.

HANS. That's what I'm counting on.

LOTHAR. I think that's my father coming back. I shall tell him everything.

HANS. You are quite free. Everybody's free. Everybody.

He goes out by the low door. Lothar runs after him, but changes his mind, as he hears the Duke coming in by the big door.

DUKE. Lothar, where is your sister? Call her. I have something to say to her.

LOTHAR. Christine has gone out.

DUKE. Gone out? Where has she gone?

LOTHAR. She must have gone somewhere where she was not in danger of meeting Hans whom she detests because he got the better of her. She is wrong in hating him, as he is the only person who can protect her against the town. They are looking at her *and* at us in a very ugly way.

DUKE. I am very anxious indeed. Christine is in danger, I am sure of it. Something tells me so. Where is Hans?

LOTHAR. Hans? In the barrack square; I believe he is arranging an archery tournament. I hope to win a medal. I am a very good shot.

DUKE. There's a curse on this masquerade. It is all being spoiled. Your Hans amuses the mob and that is what causes misunderstanding. The street is not the town. The towns-folk seem to think Christine responsible for street disor-ders. The Syndic and the Provost have spread the rumor that she knew the truth about the young man and that some intrigue is afoot. I should not have lent myself to a young girl's folly.

LOTHAR. Do you dislike Hans?

DUKE. I neither like nor dislike him. He is my guest.

LOTHAR. You're wrong. He is your host. What's more, they take you for his accomplice. You should have given the place over to him from the very first: left the house to him. In other words, you should have done things strictly according to the rules of the game. But I love and admire you because you always do what is not done.

DUKE. You are wrong, Lothar. I live behind a mask. Liv-ing in society makes it necessary for us to do so.

LOTHAR. It is not necessary to wear a mask. That is what Hans has taught me. He is like you. He always does what is not done, but he wears no mask. His face is bare. It is beautiful.

DUKE. If you think we are alike in our clumsy ways, you are probably right, yet you are nevertheless wrong. I can-not drop the mask and leave my face bare.

LOTHAR. I should like this adventure with Hans to force you to drop your mask.

DUKE. That is, alas, impossible.

LOTHAR. It would be possible if things got so bad that we had to leave everything. Now, I've got that out.

DUKE. You are dreaming.

LOTHAR. Yes! I am dreaming of a wilderness where no masks would be worn, a refuge from this city of masks. Where, for instance . . . Christine would be married to Hans.

DUKE. Are you going out of your mind?

LOTHAR. Christine cannot marry one of the human monsters who surround us here.

DUKE. Do you realize where this young man comes from.

LOTHAR. Never mind. He is noble.

DUKE. I do not deny it. In his own way he is. But he has become a scandal and it is almost our fault; Lothar, understand that they are trying to incriminate your sister in such dangerous actions that I cannot be sure of the places she depends on for shelter.

Listening.

Did you not hear something?

LOTHAR. No.

DUKE. I thought I heard screaming in the house.

LOTHAR. Your nerves are on edge. If you wish we can go and look for Christine.

DUKE. She wanted to be of some use to me. It is not her fault, she is like your poor brother, not responsible for the ideas which come into her head. The responsibility is mine.

He leads Lothar to the door at the back of the stage.

LOTHAR, *on the step.* You remember the law of the sea.

"The Captain is not held responsible for acts of God."

As he goes out, the Duke stops and raises his head.

DUKE. This time I am sure I heard something.

LOTHAR. There are archers in the hall where Hans has his rooms and they are drinking. I am astonished that one does not hear more of them.

DUKE. Listen — someone screamed.

LOTHAR. It's in the street.

They go out.

CURTAIN

ACT THREE

The Cardinal, the Bishop, the Duke, the Provost Marshal, and the Syndic are in council.

Long silence. The Provost Marshal walks up and down, then comes to a stop in front of the Duke.

PROVOST MARSHAL. Well, my lord Duke, if everyone insists on treating this bad joke as a miniature reign, then surely the temporary king's greatest mistake was when he disbanded the funeral procession of his own victim. We can pass over all his other blunders. At last the people understand that as the immediate result of the relief which he proclaimed, we were obliged to double the taxes to make up for the deficit and restore the balance. So, from one Sunday to the next our Bacchus has made himself hated by all, even by those who were willing to believe in him.

Silence.

CARDINAL. Can you see any way in which we can prevent this masquerade from ending in tragedy?

PROVOST MARSHAL. If the Cardinal were not in this house, it would be taken by storm and I should be helpless. That is where we have got to — a state of siege.

DUKE. What I cannot understand is that the Square should be empty and everything so silent.

PROVOST MARSHAL. Silent! It's more than silence, my lord Duke. Listen to it. It's the deuce of a queer silence, like a hunt ready to spring on its quarry.

BISHOP. How many men have they?

PROVOST MARSHAL. All the young people, middle-class and noble, and quite a lot of armed volunteers from the lower orders. They've got hold of the arms we give out to defend the town from the peasant.

DUKE, *at the window.* There is no one to be seen.

PROVOST MARSHAL. Once again: it is only respect for His Eminence and for the Cathedral precincts that pulls the wool over our eyes. They do not show themselves. This makes matters worse. They are all in the nearby streets. In their homes, families are sitting silently looking at the hands of the clock. They are waiting.

CARDINAL. Waiting for that exquisite moment when vengeance can be taken without risk.

SYNDIC. Man is like that, Your Eminence. What can *we* do about it?

CARDINAL. And the garrison?

PROVOST MARSHAL. It is powerless against a state of siege. Powerless first of all because in this dirty business they have gone soft. They don't like people making a fool of me.

DUKE, *to Syndic.* Have you spoken to your colleagues?

SYNDIC. What do you want me to say to them? They would shout me down. The liquidation of this charming incident has to be reckoned in cut losses and bad jokes.

DUKE. It is terrible.

PROVOST MARSHAL. Yes, it is terrible. In that empty Square there is a stake which has not built itself. Men worked at it all night. Even the meanest men run to it with pieces of wood they have hoarded for their winter fires.

DUKE. But the stake is part of the masquerade. An effigy of Bacchus is to be burned there.

PROVOST MARSHAL. Just try to stop them burning the man himself!

CARDINAL. Do you think they might even do that?

BISHOP. It would be against all our laws. Only the Ecclesiastical Tribunal can assume so grave a responsibility.

PROVOST MARSHAL. You make me laugh. How can you prevent such things from being done without the jurisdiction of the Ecclesiastical Tribunal? You can threaten. You can excommunicate. It won't stop anything.

DUKE. You said yourself that the presence of Cardinal Zampi kept the rising in check.

PROVOST MARSHAL. Until the hands of the clock meet at twelve, his presence may protect you. After that I can answer for nothing and I even advise your Eminence not to expose yourself to the insults of the mob. It might end with worse; we might find ourselves saddled with a sorry mess.

DUKE. If what you say is true, Provost, it's out of the question to let this young man be burned without doing everything we can to save him.

PROVOST MARSHAL. Of course; I'm all for it. I represent law and order, and to burn disorder is not to restore order; quite the contrary, in fact. But what can I do against a whole town with nerves strung up to breaking point.

CARDINAL. Supposing I were to address —

PROVOST MARSHAL. They would think that Your Eminence was protecting a man who belongs to the Church.

CARDINAL. That is not the case. His tragedy is that he belongs to no one.

PROVOST MARSHAL. Then he's a fool. The mob will get rid of him in its own way, which is not ours but which has always been theirs. What do you think I could do?

DUKE. Could he escape?

PROVOST MARSHAL. Try it! They hold all roads. There is not a chink left to let him out.

CARDINAL. What about the Cathedral? It gives the right of sanctuary.

BISHOP. They have thought of that too. The guilds are in it. The Cathedral porch may look empty, but only in front, not behind.

CARDINAL. My dear Bishop, our tribunals have not condemned this man and the rules of this masquerade do not allow them to proceed against him. Our humanity alone can speak. Since we do not condemn, we must save. A solution must be found at once.

PROVOST MARSHAL. Find it. I can find none.

CARDINAL. Are you acting in good faith, Provost Marshal?

PROVOST MARSHAL, *screaming*. Me!

DUKE. Cardinal Zampi means that you are not exactly fond of this Bacchus and that perhaps it would not distress you if you saw things go wrong.

PROVOST MARSHAL. Well! Of all the . . .

SYNDIC. As for me, I have attempted what proved impossible. But I wash my hands of my failure in front of my colleagues. Let the crowd burn your young man, it's all the same to me.

DUKE, *to Provost Marshal.* Can't you be frank too?

PROVOST MARSHAL. I am not in the same position. I can see why this clash puts the Syndic neither up nor down. But I am responsible for law and order, and if things go wrong I have to answer for what happens. I don't like it at all.

CARDINAL. That being so . . .

PROVOST MARSHAL. That being so, if Your Eminence has some idea, will you tell me about it, and I shall do as you say.

CARDINAL. I shall give it thought, but, alas, there is now but little time. I must talk it over with the Duke and the Bishop. I wonder, gentlemen, whether you would go into the town and try to make one last effort.

PROVOST MARSHAL. If I tried any such thing at the moment, I should be finished off and then I should be of no further use to anybody.

SYNDIC. I shall go to the Cathedral and have a word with the merchants.

PROVOST MARSHAL. Be careful; as soon as they get themselves up in arms and armor, they are worse than my soldiers.

SYNDIC. I know . . . I know . . .

PROVOST MARSHAL, *bowing.* I shall leave you, gentlemen.

To Syndic.

Come. We shall return in order to defend Your Eminence as soon as events dictate.

They go out.

BISHOP. How charming! . . .

CARDINAL. I was not at all anxious that these gentlemen should be present at our discussions. They do not greatly appeal to me.

DUKE. Nor to me.

BISHOP. They have one excuse. They have to defend their jobs.

CARDINAL. I have an idea . . .

DUKE. What is it, Your Eminence?

CARDINAL. Recantation . . .

BISHOP. Recantation of what? The young man does not belong to any religion.

CARDINAL. I beg your pardon, he is Catholic.

BISHOP. Surely a Catholic does not ride on horseback into a church. His sacrilegious heresy has disgusted the whole town.

CARDINAL. I shall be responsible. I am speaking of a denial, but the word recantation will strike home better. Nothing would be easier than to say that he was an agent of the Reformation and that he is returning to the bosom of the Church.

DUKE. My lord! That would be a lie. . . .

CARDINAL. My lord Duke, are you by any chance afraid of reprisals by the Reformers?

DUKE. Not in the least. But I dislike lies.

BISHOP. There are such things as pious lies.

DUKE. Couldn't you say to simplify things that he was a Catholic agent of the Church who had gone beyond the terms of his commission and that he now confesses as much?

CARDINAL. My lord Duke! To make His Holiness responsible for a lie —

DUKE. Did you not say that a lie? . . .

CARDINAL. Let us understand one another. We can have nothing to do with those who call the Papal Sovereign "The Scarlet Woman and Antichrist."

The Bishop makes the sign of the Cross.

DUKE. Quite so. But I dislike the method. One dislikes using weapons used by the enemy.

CARDINAL. Do you see another way out?

DUKE. Exorcism — He could be declared possessed of the devil and publicly exorcised.

CARDINAL. Only those who are possessed can be exorcised.

BISHOP. And isn't he?

CARDINAL. I do not think so. Neither God nor the devil commands his soul. I should be glad to give it back to God and for our little brother to make his peace with the Church.

DUKE. Wouldn't it be possible simply to accuse Hans of heresy and free him from the taint of recantation?

CARDINAL. Recantation does not preclude punishment and I should not care to encroach upon secular jurisdiction under which our young man does not come. All that I can do is to stretch my powers a little and call a denial a recantation. But I need a plea.

DUKE. I am afraid this ruse will deceive no one and that they will pursue him later wherever he goes.

CARDINAL. Naturally; that would be too simple. Things will not stop there. If I announce a recantation I must take advantage of the moment of surprise, of truce, to remove our young man to a monastery where we shall shut him up until people calm down and events resume a normal course.

DUKE. Do you mean him to take the cloth?

CARDINAL. I am speaking extempore. We shall protect him. Then we'll see what we can do.

DUKE. He will never agree to what you propose.

CARDINAL. People say that they want to be burned. They say so. But faced with actual flames they think differently.

DUKE. He will be obstinate.

CARDINAL. There is one person who might convince him.

DUKE. Who?

CARDINAL. Your daughter.

DUKE. Christine!

CARDINAL. This young madman has made a great impression on both your son and daughter. Has not your daughter's attitude quite changed from what it was on the day of the masquerade?

DUKE. That's true. I put it down to the horror Christine had of injustice. On the first day this false idiot hurt her feelings. She could not bear his success. She is drawn to those who are failures.

CARDINAL. Possibly. I cannot judge the reasons which changed her attitude. But certainly it has changed, and I think that your daughter alone could prove to Hans that his martyrdom would be useless.

DUKE. What do you suggest?

CARDINAL. The hands of the clock are moving on, my lord Duke. Fetch your daughter. We shall speak to her.

The Duke goes out by the little door.

BISHOP. Does Your Eminence think it seemly for us to concern ourselves with this affair?

CARDINAL. We shall concern ourselves with it if I say so.

BISHOP. Far be it from me to judge the conduct of Your Eminence, but —

CARDINAL. There are no buts. Burning a man alive is a right which our courts reserve for themselves. If we let the people burn a man, our courts thereby lose their rights. They no longer count.

BISHOP. No doubt . . . no doubt . . .

CARDINAL. Without any doubt. That is why, my dear Bishop, we must prepare our program. You will leave me alone with this young girl and you will walk across that empty square.

Bishop pulls a wry face.

Give the order that the Cathedral bell be rung as soon as this window is opened. That will be my signal. Then come back. It is important that at the critical moment we should all be together in this hall, if it be true that we have to face an armed attack.

BISHOP. An armed attack!

The Cardinal calms him with a gesture and pushes him out.

The Duke enters by the small door with Christine.

CARDINAL. My lord Duke, may I ask you to leave me alone with your daughter while you await me in your apartments? Have some writing material ready for me there.

Exit the Duke by the small door.

My lady, this is an evil hour. You no doubt know that a stake has been erected in the Square. And you know the use of stakes.

CHRISTINE. In the present instance, to burn an effigy.

CARDINAL. No, young lady. The official body has not been asked for the costume with which I understand it is customary to deck the effigy with great pomp and ceremony. In some crises, the crowd becomes an elemental force beyond our control. It will not burn an effigy of Bacchus. It will burn him in person. Neither the Provost Marshal nor the Syndic will come to his aid. You can expect nothing whatever from them.

CHRISTINE. The wretches.

CARDINAL. Nothing changes. Twenty-five years ago when we burned Savanarola, in Florence, his youthful bodyguard buried thorns in the planks leading to his place of execution, in order that he should hop about and make strange faces to amuse the *Signoria*. On the other hand, the role of a Prince of the Church is to practice charity and to prevent crime. The time is approaching when the mob will take the upper hand. We must act before them. I have a proposal to make and I should like you to collaborate with me.

CHRISTINE. What can I do faced with a mob which makes me part of this story and which hates me?

CARDINAL. Nothing, I grant you. But if you are willing to listen to me you will learn what I expect of you.

CHRISTINE. Forgive me, Your Eminence, for becoming excited.

CARDINAL. Here it is. I discovered without trying to understand nor even wishing to do so that your dislike of this young man had changed to kindness, understanding, and tacit approval of his subversive attitude of mind — of which you at first disapproved. Is that so?

CHRISTINE. That is so.

CARDINAL. Good. You had been taken in and we were both dupes. I felt not the slightest bitterness about it. A masquerade is a masquerade. You felt bitter. But later I noticed that you had changed round completely. I do not ask for your reasons. They belong to you. But I do ask for your help in convincing this young man whom the fire attracts, that fire burns and that even a phoenix will not be reborn from his ashes. The house is guarded, escape impossible. I propose other means.

CHRISTINE. I rely on your wisdom.

CARDINAL. Very good. I was afraid you might suspect me of some trick. I am incapable of such a thing. I wish to save this young man, that is all.

CHRISTINE. My lord, I am listening.

CARDINAL. All that is left us is recantation.

CHRISTINE. Recantation?

CARDINAL. Yes, yes! My only power lies there. Let him sign a document recognizing his errors and he will be free.

CHRISTINE. Free?

CARDINAL. Free . . . free . . . indefinitely. His recantation will astonish, will create a diversion, and will permit me to entrust him to the Bishop, who will entrust him to the priest, who will lead him to a place of refuge.

CHRISTINE. Do you mean to a monastery?

CARDINAL. It is the only place of refuge over which I have control. He will no longer be in danger there. He can wait there until hatred dies down and other crimes turn public attention from him. The people are quick-tempered, but their memory is short. The victim of one day becomes the hero of the next.

CHRISTINE. And . . . if Hans signs the paper . . . he would then go out of our house free?

CARDINAL. I shall soothe the mob. I shall say a Mass. I shall see to it that truth triumphs.

CHRISTINE. I don't know what to answer, Your Eminence. I ask nothing better than to take the horse to the water, but I cannot make him drink.

CARDINAL. He will. Women have irresistible arguments.

Silence.

CHRISTINE. I shall obey you.

CARDINAL. I hope so. I do not care to think of this window as a theater box, a box from which we might watch a hideous scene.

CHRISTINE. How vile!

CARDINAL. Yes, it would be vile. And it is in order to avoid this vile show that I am pleading with you and that you will promise me to play your part.

CHRISTINE. I have already promised Your Lordship that I will obey you.

CARDINAL. I want to make sure that you will.

CHRISTINE. If it is the only way of saving Hans —

CARDINAL. The only one.

CHRISTINE. If it is the only way of saving Hans, I shall work for it with my whole strength.

CARDINAL. Our hope lies in you.

Silence.

CHRISTINE. Does my father know of your plan?

CARDINAL. Do not let us speak of the Duke. He is a father. His heart makes him blind. It is for one of your spiritual Fathers to see in his place.

Christine curtsys.

I shall go upstairs to the Duke to draft the document. Our signatures will suffice. I shall send you this young Bacchus who gives us such a tangled skein to unravel.

He touches her on the forehead with his thumb.

Exit Cardinal through the small door. Christine goes to the window, lifts the curtain and looks at the square searchingly. Then she comes back to the table, lets herself sink into a chair, her elbows on its arms, and buries her face

*in her hands. Enter Hans, in peasant's costume. He goes
up to Christine and puts his hand on her shoulder. She
turns around, startled.*

CHRISTINE. Hans! Why are you wearing that costume?

HANS. It is the only suitable one now and it's the first
one you knew me in.

CHRISTINE. Hans . . . it's frightful . . .

HANS. What's frightful?

CHRISTINE. This town, this hate, this waiting.

HANS. It had to come.

CHRISTINE. I didn't think that it would come to this.

HANS. I told you that a free man couldn't stay free.

CHRISTINE. There is some difference between a prison . . .

She points to the window.

. . . and the stake.

HANS. They will not dare.

CHRISTINE. They will dare.

HANS. I'm sorry I dragged you into this tragedy.

CHRISTINE. Don't turn the tables on me. I brought this
tragedy on you. It is my fault. I loved you when I saw you
in the country and out of selfishness I brought you here.

HANS. You loved a poor harmless animal. As soon as he
showed his real nature, you fought him.

CHRISTINE. Very little. You soon made me see what a
fool I was.

HANS. I love you, Christine. Don't be afraid. There'll be
a miracle.

CHRISTINE. Miracles only happen to those who are worthy of them.

HANS. You are worthy of them.

CHRISTINE. You don't believe in them . . . but you are worthy of them. I'm not worthy of any miracle. Love has killed all my spirit. Now I am ashamed of being a weak woman. Where is the strength which made me use my whip on those who laughed at your innocence? Where is the strength which made me eager to avenge Ulrich? Where is the strength which made me drag you into town, clothe you, present you before the judges and convince them? Where is the strength which made me resist you, insult you, and fight with you?

Silence.

HANS. What did the Cardinal say to you?

CHRISTINE. He amazed me. I really think that except for Lothar and Father, he is the only human being in the town.

HANS. In Rome they are more broad-minded than here. Italians love love. Does he guess anything?

CHRISTINE. Yes, Hans. He let me know that he did.

HANS. And the Duke?

CHRISTINE. He suspects nothing. In spite of his justice and goodness, his real nature is so severe, so rigid, so stern —

HANS. So Protestant.

CHRISTINE. Be quiet, Hans. You must not even think such things.

HANS. It is because I protest against everything that they are going to burn me.

CHRISTINE. They will not burn you. The Provost Marshal and the Syndic are rotten to the core. They are all pretending to protect you from the crowd. The Bishop will close his eyes. But the Cardinal is sincere. He will save you.

HANS. How? What can robes do against armor?

CHRISTINE. He has devised a way.

HANS. Tell me.

CHRISTINE. Hans, it is the only way. The only one. Don't ride your high horse at the very mention of it. Don't shut your mind to it; welcome it, Hans.

HANS. Tell me about it first.

CHRISTINE. All that you need to do is to sign a paper.

HANS. A paper?

CHRISTINE. Yes, that's all. A document prepared by the Cardinal, in which you will declare that you have gone beyond the limits of the masquerade, that you have tried to stir up the people, and that you do not believe the sacriligeous things you said. In exchange you will be free.

HANS. And after this recantation? . . .

CHRISTINE. Only for form. The Cardinal knows quite well that a man does not change in a minute.

HANS. And after this recantation? . . .

CHRISTINE. You will be hidden in a monastery.

HANS. Retract . . . Hide . . . It's impossible.

CHRISTINE. If you love me, you'll be willing.

HANS. I was willing to play the fool to escape from being tortured, but I refuse to play a part which would make me unworthy to live in order to avoid torture. I should be tortured then from within.

CHRISTINE. Our love must come before everything.

HANS. My poor Christine, would you love a man who was exiled, jeered at, a laughingstock?

CHRISTINE. You'll escape from the monastery. I shall join you and you'll be able to do things once more. Luther is in hiding and I shall hide you. I shall interest powerful people who will help you and I shall uphold you in your work.

HANS. What work? My only work was love and I have reaped nothing but hatred.

CHRISTINE. One would think that my love meant nothing to you.

HANS. It does, Christine. But because I love you, I will not let you share my failure. If I am burned, I win. If I escape, I lose.

CHRISTINE. What do you win?

HANS. From free man to free man, from burning stake to burning stake, God will in the end conquer the devil who disguises himself as a hermit.

CHRISTINE. Don't be so foolishly obstinate. We love each other and must live together somehow or other. But now there is only one way out. Accept it for love of me.

HANS, *after a moment's silence.* Listen to me carefully, Christine. The Abbé Knopf buried some gold. It came from the Reformers. It was a matter of implicating a very high-up person who is against them. They intended to make him imagine that they could make gold which he's short of and then to compromise him in a trial for witchcraft. The Church learned about this. This gold was the real reason for arresting Knopf. He denied all knowledge of it even at the stake. The Reformers dare not try to find the gold. But I know where it is. You will get it and as soon as I can leave my hiding place I shall join you. Then we shall cross over to Switzerland and from there to France.

CHRISTINE, *clinging to him.* Hans!

HANS. I cannot let you go.

CHRISTINE. If you had refused, I would have shouted the truth to everyone and we would have burned together.

HANS. With this gold we shall be able to get away to a country where love counts more than politics.

CHRISTINE. Don't tell anyone about this gold. I love you.

HANS. I loathe myself.

CHRISTINE. If you loathe yourself for signing, then refuse. I shall declare before all that I am your mistress. You know quite well the consequences of such an admission even if my lover had not been you.

HANS. You would do it, I know, that's why I give in.

CHRISTINE. Hans, that's not what I am asking you to do. I only wanted to be sure of your love.

Enter Lothar by the low door.

CHRISTINE. Quick, Lothar. The Cardinal offers Hans a purely formal recantation. It is the only way to save him.

LOTHAR. And does Hans cheerfully intend to do something as low as that?

CHRISTINE. I do not see anything low in it.

LOTHAR. Naturally, you are a woman, and in order to keep your man you would persuade him to do anything.

CHRISTINE. You don't think of his mother. He has one.

LOTHAR. How good, how very good of you to think of her for him. Women who live at home are astonishing. They think of everything.

CHRISTINE. As for you, *you* think of nothing. You would like to see him being burned.

LOTHAR. Hans and I have a pact.

CHRISTINE. What pact?

HANS. Forget about it, Lothar. It is only a piece of child-ishness, Christine.

CHRISTINE. I want to know about this pact.

LOTHAR. It concerns no one but ourselves. It's a secret between us.

CHRISTINE. Hans cannot have a secret from me.

LOTHAR. So you're jealous of his friends. Is that the latest?

CHRISTINE. I'm not jealous, but I hate your incurable flippancy. You are always playing some theatrical part. But this time it is no play and you are driving Hans to his death.

LOTHAR. Hans is old enough to decide for himself.

CHRISTINE. He will sign.

HANS. Lothar is right, Christine, I will not sign.

CHRISTINE. So you are refusing to sign because this young cub is stopping you from doing so and you have a pact with him.

HANS. I refuse to sign because I cannot betray a cause.

CHRISTINE. What cause?

LOTHAR. His cause.

CHRISTINE. You make me laugh. Did he go on with his preachings?

LOTHAR. You distracted him from them.

CHRISTINE. Nothing turns a man away from his faith, if he has one.

HANS. That's enough, Lothar. Mind your own business.

CHRISTINE. He only minds other people's business.

LOTHAR. Hans' ideas are my business.

CHRISTINE. Hans' ideas! You make me laugh. If Hans had any ideas he would have followers, and he has no one but me. I am his only follower.

LOTHAR. And I!

CHRISTINE. Let him find some others.

LOTHAR. Then, if Hans has no ideas, what interests you in him?

CHRISTINE. Lothar!

LOTHAR, *shouting,* I know, I know what interests her. I know and I'll tell you.

HANS. Be quiet, I tell you.

LOTHAR. She loved you better as an idiot, when you followed her about like a dog.

HANS. Will you be quiet?

He grabs Lothar and throws him into a chair

LOTHAR. I'm saying nothing. You both make me sick.

Lothar slumps down and puts his arms and his head on the table.

HANS. Come on, Lothar . . . Come on . . . Be a man.

CHRISTINE. Don't ask him to be a man. Let him cry like a girl. His weakness disgusts me with my own. Let's fight without him, Hans. I demand that you sign this paper. I demand it.

HANS. No, Christine, no.

CHRISTINE. You're unreliable creatures. Both of you. And as you are both unreliable creatures —

HANS, *catching hold of her arm.* Be quiet, they are coming down.

Enter the Cardinal and the Duke through the low door. The Cardinal is holding a document.

CARDINAL. You only have to sign there.

HANS. May I read it?

CARDINAL. Please do. Do not be surprised at some of the elaborate phrases. The formula is always the same. I have to use these words.

Hans reads.

DUKE. We have a quarter of an hour left. Don't be too long.

HANS. I should like to know what my signature will involve.

CARDINAL. What do you mean?

HANS. I want to know whether once I sign it I shall be free.

CARDINAL. Free . . . But let us be frank. You will have to disappear into a monastery and obey its rules.

HANS. And then?

CARDINAL. Come, Hans, be reasonable. A monastery is not a fortress. Our monks will welcome you without asking who you are. You would have to keep your own council and obey.

HANS. And . . . to take the habit.

CARDINAL. Not all at once. You would be a novice. It would only be if you felt that the cloisters suited you, and if you, or rather, your superiors, decided that you were worthy of taking vows.

HANS. And if they don't think me worthy?

CARDINAL. You would go to another monastery and other Reverend Fathers would take your instruction in hand.

HANS, *after a moment's silence.* A remarkable theologian ... A monk such as we lack ...

CHRISTINE. Your Eminence will no doubt forgive me for saying that I did not know that Hans would have to take orders.

CARDINAL. That was understood. We cannot hide a man. We can only welcome him into the bosom of our family.

CHRISTINE. Hans cannot take orders.

CARDINAL. And why not?

CHRISTINE. He has no vocation and you know it. He would bring nothing but trouble to the monks.

CARDINAL. Trouble? He would have no time. The rule is too strict for that.

CHRISTINE. That's what I wanted to know. Hans will not sign.

CARDINAL. You promised me to persuade him.

CHRISTINE. I did not know that this meant a complete break with everything.

CARDINAL. What do you mean by "with everything"?

CHRISTINE. By "everything" I mean that freedom which he has made *his* rule.

CARDINAL. Should you not rather say that you consider that he is no longer free.

CHRISTINE. Your Eminence!

CARDINAL. You forget that he has no choice and that our institution is the only one which will save him from a dreadful end.

DUKE. You have no right to influence him, Christine. You are already answerable for his present dilemma. Duty demands that you should even try what seems impossible to get him out of it.

LOTHAR. Christine has her reasons and I have mine. But her attitude is the right one. We are not influencing Hans. If he refuses to sign, no one in the world will make him change his mind.

CARDINAL. I know neither your reasons nor your sister's. But I can guess that your sister's are of a kind which may well give her pause when a frightful death closes in upon a man who is offered a way of escape.

CHRISTINE. Your way out leads to another kind of death. Hans would be dead.

CARDINAL, *in a low, terrible voice*. To you!

HANS. Your Eminence, I would be most grateful if you would put an end to this discussion. It is painful to me and it implicates people whom I love and admire and who have nothing to do with my refusal.

DUKE. My boy. My dear boy! The Cardinal is offering to save your life.

HANS. Let the Cardinal remember: did I not say to Your Eminence that my true victory lay in failure?

CARDINAL. Those were paradoxes.

HANS. They were not mere paradoxes. Just as in my eyes this masquerade is no masquerade. And because it has never been a mere masquerade it must rise to the level of tragedy and not fall short of it. Should I become a monk, my lord, that would indeed be a masquerade in which I should change from one fancy dress to another.

LOTHAR. That is why I love him!

DUKE. When one loves anyone, Lothar, surely one saves him.

LOTHAR. Not always.

He goes to the window, separating himself from the others, and looks out.

CARDINAL, *to Hans.* You definitely refuse to sign this?

HANS. Yes, Your Eminence.

CARDINAL. A pity. My only consolation is that the Church offered to help you and will not be guilty of your death.

HANS. Did you not say that our mind often refused to obey the dictates of our conscience. And did I not answer that I tried to overcome this bad habit. I should like to obey you, Your Eminence. But an order is an order and my conscience tells me to disobey.

LOTHAR, *looking out of the window and without turning his head.* You've still got fifteen archers and a captain.

CARDINAL. What can fifteen archers and a captain do to quell a riot?

DUKE. Lothar's right. Fifteen archers can keep the mob in check just long enough for a man to skirt the walls and cross the woods and so get over the frontier. Once in Switzerland he would be safe.

CARDINAL, *to Hans.* Are you sure of your men?

HANS. Sure

CARDINAL. You *were* sure. Let us try an experiment.

HANS. What experiment?

CARDINAL. Tell them to arrest me.

DUKE. Arrest Your Eminence?

CARDINAL. It is an experiment to which I am willing to lend myself and you will all play your parts.

HANS, *opening the door at the back of the stage.* Karl!

Karl appears.

Call six of my men.

Six men enter. To the Cardinal.

Your Eminence, I am sorry that my safety obliges me to refrain from showing you the respect due to you.

To Karl.

Arrest this Priest.

No one moves.

CARDINAL. Arrest me, gentlemen.

HANS. Arrest this Priest. That is an order.

No one moves.

A conclusive experiment . . . You are dismissed, or rather you will be in a few minutes' time. Fall in outside the door.

The archers go out. The door closes.

CARDINAL. The king is dead, long live the king. Only one force could now arrest me. It is the force of inertia very understandable in the case of men who see time shortening between the joy of being hangmen and the fear of being hanged.

Enter the Bishop, Provost Marshal and Syndic by door at back of stage.

DUKE. Well, gentlemen, and what is your news?

BISHOP. The Cathedral is occupied by sixty men-at-arms.

PROVOST MARSHAL. Not mine.

To Syndic.

They must be yours.

SYNDIC. I wanted to sober them down. But no one listens to me any longer. They all look at me askance.

DUKE. Is flight out of the question?

PROVOST MARSHAL. More than a hundred and fifty young men are stationed in the streets leading to the open roads. And I could not have failed to call the garrison without rousing suspicion.

HANS. Admit, Provost Marshal, that you did not try very hard.

PROVOST MARSHAL. You are incredible! Look out of the window for yourself. I have placed a picket between the stake and the Cathedral and yet the Square is no longer empty. It seems as if they are coming silently up through holes in the ground. You'd think that they are afraid that if they utter a word they will not hear the clocks or that they will stop the jack o' the clock from striking. Even a child is dragging a branch bigger than itself to add to the pile. And a one-legged man might throw on his crutch.

HANS, *by the window.* It's vile!

He turns around violently.

It's filthy. Even the manhunt was not so bad. There was a commotion, splashing about, screaming, and barking. I was swimming like a beast. I became a beast. There was something so mad about it that fear changed to madness and was no longer fear but a monstrous music of wild trumpetings and laughter and pounding hearts, and singing ears and horses and water frothing and foaming. There were water weeds clinging to my legs and wet leaves stuck over my eyes. I clung to roots. Hatred sounded a fanfare. But here it is the silence of dull hatred. They are lying in wait for the chance to let go their secret blood lust. They are going back to what they were. They are cowardly, that's why they are silent. They are saving themselves up for the kill. Even the little wooden men who wait with their bronze hammers to strike the hour are more human than they are. I shall not reach my funeral pyre alive. They will beat me and strangle me and drag me along — but what they throw into the flame will be my carcass.

Crying out.

There must be something to do. You must find something. I won't have such a filthy death. I won't have it.

CARDINAL. A little ink would save a lot of blood.

CHRISTINE, *dragging Hans forward.* Hans, I must have been mad. Sign. You must sign. I beg you to sign.

HANS. They are watching us. Don't give them the pleasure of a scene.

DUKE. There are only a few minutes left, Hans, I solemnly beg of you to reconsider.

CARDINAL, *putting his hand into his robes.* A little ink . . .

LOTHAR. Hans, don't listen to them!

He leaves the window, goes straight through the groups of people, and goes out of the door at the back of the stage, banging it to.

Christine takes Lothar's place at the window.

CHRISTINE. The grizzly beasts!

PROVOST MARSHAL. They're coming from all sides. The square is swarming.

SYNDIC. Look, my lord Duke. All faces are turned to your balcony.

He makes a gesture as if he would open the window.

BISHOP. Toward us!

DUKE. Do not open the window.

HANS. It is for me to open it. I still belong to myself; I am still in my own house. I shall speak to the people.

PROVOST MARSHAL. You make me think of one of our heretics. On the top of the stake, he cried out, "My people," and the executioner said to him, "You'll have a chance to speak when it's over."

HANS. I shall cry out to this town what it deserves to hear.

SYNDIC. Be careful that he does not throw himself from the balcony.

PROVOST MARSHAL. I don't advise you to throw yourself from the balcony. It is not very high and hatred would receive you with open arms.

HANS. I will speak.

DUKE. You have already spoken too much.

PROVOST MARSHAL. My captains have excellent counter-weapons for chatterboxes: drums.

He makes a sign at the window and the drums roll out. They go on rolling to the end of the act.

CARDINAL. A little ink and the bells will ring. They would ring above the drums.

HANS. I want to look at the stake, at my funeral pyre, to see it face to face.

He tries to open the window. Christine, the Provost Marshal, and the Syndic prevent him.

PROVOST MARSHAL. Keep still.

HANS. I order you to let me open the window.

PROVOST MARSHAL. All right, you win. Open it!

CHRISTINE. No, Hans!

HANS, *struggles and gets free, shouting out.* A condemned man has the right to do what he wants! I open it.

He flings open the window and disappears from view. He is heard to shout: Shoot and shoot straight.

General movement to the window. Then, all move back, as Hans comes back and leans on the window frame, his hand on his chest in which an arrow is sticking.

Free. . . .

Then he slips down and falls backward. Christine rushes forward, lifts him up, kneeling down and putting his head on her knees. The bells of the Cathedral begin to ring. The Syndic wants to draw out the arrow.

CHRISTINE. Don't draw out the arrow!

BISHOP. Close the window!

The Provost Marshal closes it. The sound of bells and of drums becomes fainter.

DUKE. Where is Lothar?

PROVOST MARSHAL. I am afraid he shot the arrow.

DUKE. Then they'll hack him to pieces.

PROVOST MARSHAL. No one in the Square seems to realize what has happened. He must have leaned forward and he must have been shot at from below.

CHRISTINE. Hans! Look at me! . . . Speak to me. . . .

The door at the back is opened. Lothar comes in, framed in the doorway by the six Archers and Karl. They take the bow which he is holding from him.

LOTHAR. He has escaped the lot of you.

PROVOST MARSHAL. I charge you with murder. I arrest you.

LOTHAR. I suppose you want your bonfire.

DUKE, *who has been kneeling by Christine to support her, gets up.* Since my children are bent on their own ruin . . .

CARDINAL, *putting his hand on the Duke's arm and speaking in a low voice.* Your children will need your testimony. Do not speak irrevocable words.

SYNDIC, *at the window.* The hour is about to strike. They'll burn him, burn him dead.

CARDINAL. They will not burn him dead, nor would they have burned him alive. Gentlemen, this young man had recanted his errors and was going to enter orders. He was safe.

LOTHAR. That's a lie.

DUKE. Lothar!

CARDINAL. I have his signed recantation in my pocket.

CHRISTINE. It is not true! Hans, Hans! Get up arise from the dead! Denounce them. Tell them that they lie.

BISHOP. We have convents where mad virgins are kept quiet.

LOTHAR. You wanted to steal Hans. You wanted to rob him of his martyrdom.

CARDINAL. You robbed him of it yourself.

In the voice of a ruler of men.

Once for all, will everyone be quiet. Bacchus shall be clothed in his costume. The stake shall become living light around him while he lies in state and the crowd shall file past his body. I shall say the Prayers for the Dead and bless this young man. Go down on your knees.

The Archers kneel down, forcing Lothar to do the same. The Provost Marshal and the Syndic remain standing. The Cardinal slowly turns around and looks steadily at them. They go down on their knees reluctantly. The Cardinal lifts up his hand to bless.

CURTAIN

The Speaker's Text of
OEDIPUS
REX

Libretto by Jean Cocteau

Music by Igor Stravinsky
translated by
E. E. CUMMINGS

This English translation of the Speaker's Text of *Oedipus Rex* was commissioned by the Juilliard Opera Theatre. The opera is sung in Latin, and only this text was written in French.

Vocal Score: Facing page 1*

You are about to hear a Latin version of King Oedipus.

This version is an opera-oratorio; based on the tragedy by Sophocles, but preserving only a certain monumental aspect of its various scenes. And so (wishing to spare your ears and your memories) I shall recall the story as we go along.

Oedipus, unknown to himself, contends with supernatural powers: those sleepless deities who are always watching us from a world beyond death. At the moment of his birth a snare was laid for him — and you will see the snare closing.

Now our drama begins.

Thebes is prostrate. After the Sphinx, a plague breaks out. The chorus implores Oedipus to save his city. Oedipus has vanquished the Sphinx; he promises.

Vocal Score: page 14

Creon, the brother-in-law of Oedipus, has returned from Delphi, where he consulted the oracle.

The oracle demands that Laius' murderer be punished. The assassin is hiding in Thebes; at whatever cost, he must be discovered.

Oedipus boasts of his skill in dealing with the powers of darkness. He will discover and drive out the assasin.

*In Boosey & Hawkes 1949 edition.

Vocal Score: page 26

Oedipus questions that fountain of truth: Tiresias, the seer.

Tiresias will not answer. He already realizes that Oedipus is a plaything of the heartless gods.

This silence angers Oedipus, who accuses Creon of desiring the throne for himself, and Tiresias of being his accomplice.

Revolted by the injustice of this attitude, Tiresias decides — the fountain speaks.

This is the oracle: the assassin of the King is a King.

Vocal Score: page 43

The disupte of the princes attracts Jocasta.

You will hear her calm them, shame them for raising their voices in a stricken city.

She proves that oracles lie. For example, an oracle predicted that Laius would perish by the hand of a son of hers; whereas Laius was murdered by thieves, at the crossing of three roads from Daulis and Delphi.

Three roads . . . crossroads — mark well those words. They horrify Oedipus. He remembers how, arriving from Corinth before encountering the Sphinx, he killed an old man where three roads meet. If Laius of Thebes were that man — what then? Oedipus cannot return to Corinth, having been threatened by the oracle with a double crime: killing his father and marrying his mother.

He is afraid.

Vocal Score: page 63

The witness of the murder steps from the shadows. A messenger, announcing that King Polybus of Corinth is dead, reveals to Oedipus that he is only an adopted son of the King.

Jocasta understands.

She tries to draw Oedipus back — in vain. She flees.

Oedipus supposes that she is ashamed of being the wife of an upstart.

O, this lofty all-discerning Oedipus: He is in the snare. He alone does not know it.

And then the truth strikes him.

He falls. He falls headlong.

Vocal Score: page 78

And now you will hear that famous monologue "The Divine Jocasta Is Dead," a monologue in which the messenger describes Jocasta's doom.

He can scarcely open his mouth. The chorus takes his part and helps him to tell how the Queen has hanged herself, and how Oedipus has pierced his eyeballs with her golden pin.

Then comes the epilogue.

The King is caught. He would show himself to all: as a filthy beast, an incestuous monster, a fatherkiller, a fool.

His people drive him (gently, very gently) away.

Farewell, farewell, poor Oedipus!

Farewell, Oedipus — we loved you.